KING OF THE HALF HOUR

The Television Series
Robert J. Thompson, *Series Editor*

Nat Hiken, 1947. *Courtesy of Ambur Hiken Starobin.*

DAVID EVERITT

KING OF THE HALF HOUR

NAT HIKEN AND THE GOLDEN AGE OF TV COMEDY

SYRACUSE UNIVERSITY PRESS

Permission to reprint the following material is kindly acknowledged: The Fred Allen Show scripts
(excerpts) by permission of the Trustees of the Boston Public Library.

The paper used in this publication meets the minimum requirements of American National Standard for
Information Sciences—Permanence of Paper for Printed Library Materials, ANSI Z39.48-1984.∞™

Library of Congress Cataloging-in-Publication Data
Everitt, David, 1952-
King of the half hour : Nat Hiken and the golden age of TV comedy / David Everitt.—
1st ed.
p. cm.—(The television series)
Includes bibliographical references and index.
ISBN 0-8156-0676-1 (alk. paper)
1. Hiken, Nat. 2. Television comedy writers—United States—Biography. 3. Television
producers and directors—United States—Biography. I. Title. II. Series.
PN1992.4.H55 E84 2000
812.54—dc21
[B]   00-030089

In memory of my father,
EDGAR ROGERS EVERITT

David Everitt is a free-lance writer. He is the author of such books as *Film Tricks: Special Effects in the Movies* and *For Reel* and has contributed to such publications as *Entertainment Weekly*, *Biography*, *Television Quarterly*, and *The New York Times*.

Contents

Acknowledgments

My thanks to:

Harold Miller, Ann Wilkens, and the rest of the staff at the State Historical Society of Wisconsin, for all their help in shepherding me through their Nat Hiken collection.

The archive department at the Museum of Television and Radio, for making it possible to view rare programs from their inventory of recently acquired material.

David S. Siegel, Alan Cooperman, Mohan Pai, Claude Cain, Jay Hickerson, Ron Hutchinson, David Parker, and Carol Burnett, for aiding me in my search for Nat Hiken shows on both radio and television.

Richard Pack and *Television Quarterly* magazine, for agreeing to publish my first article on Hiken in 1989, thus starting me on this journey.

Jeff Kisseloff, for steering me in the right direction when searching for hard-to-find interview subjects.

Nicole Catgenova, Robert Thompson, and Amy Farranto at Syracuse University Press, for their interest and guidance throughout this project.

All those people interviewed for this book who were gracious enough to share their memories of Hiken (and who are listed in the bibliography), and especially Hiken's immediate family—Ambur Hiken Starobin, Dana Hiken Buscaglia, and Mia Hiken—for all their cooperation.

My wife, Laurie, for providing encouragement and for serving as my invaluable, in-house editor, and to my two sons, Anthony and Gregory, for their patience throughout this long endeavor.

Huntington, New York   David Everitt
November 1999

Introduction

Fred Gwynne suffered from a bad case of the jitters as he entered the rehearsal hall at Broadway and 51st Street. Only a part-time actor at this point in his career, he spent most of his days as an advertising copywriter for J. Walter Thompson, and now here he was about to tackle a lead role in *You'll Never Get Rich*, the new Phil Silvers series from CBS. He came to a stop inside the hall and gazed at the bare floor and wide-open space. To his anxious frame of mind, the place seemed cavernous and dingy. Nearby stood a small group of actors. They clustered together, talking rapidly, vigorously, laughing loudly at the jokes they bounced off one another. They were obviously a tight clique, and Gwynne did not even consider intruding. The gangly, six-foot-five-inch actor stood in the middle of the room, unsure what to do next.

The challenge of his new role might have been enough in itself to put Gwynne on edge, but the suddenness of his casting had made matters even worse. He had acquired his role without an audition, he had not met anyone connected with the production, and he had no idea who his contact would be now that he was here. He continued to stand and fret, when along came a man of medium height with graying hair. He handed Gwynne a scrap of paper and, without a word, walked off.

Gwynne did not know what to make of it all. "I thought maybe I had dropped the paper and maybe he was the janitor giving it back to me," he remembered. "I was so unnerved by the whole situation. I really couldn't figure it out. Finally, I held it up and there were a few words scratched on it in pencil and it seemed to ring some sort of bell, it seemed to have something to do with my part. I got enough nerve to walk over to the troupe and said, 'Who was that man?' They looked at me and said something to the effect of, 'Schmuck, you don't know Nat Hiken?'"[1]

This was a reasonable response. Less than gracious perhaps, but reasonable. Anyone involved in New York television in 1955 was likely to know who Nat Hiken was, even someone like Fred Gwynne, who was still skirting the show business fringe.

Those familiar with the days before television knew Hiken as the head writer for the great radio comedian Fred Allen. Since then, his reputation had rested on his work for Milton Berle, Monty Woolley, Bert Lahr, and Bette Davis; most recently he had written and directed an acclaimed television variety series for Martha Raye. The man Gwynne had mistaken for a janitor was, in fact, one of television's most sought-after comedy creators. And his position in the industry was about to soar even higher.

You'll Never Get Rich, the program in which Gwynne was going to perform, would soon be renamed *The Phil Silvers Show* and would ultimately be best known as *Sergeant Bilko*. It would become a classic of TV's Golden Age and one of the most hilarious shows ever made. A few years later Hiken would mastermind *Car 54, Where Are You?*, the last memorable New York-based comedy series of its era and another favorite of both critics and the public.

Milton Berle would describe Hiken as "a genius." Phil Silvers would characterize him as "the most fertile TV comedy mind of the 1950s." From 1955 to 1962, Hiken won eight Emmy Awards, and in a 1956 poll of TV comedy writers conducted by *Time* magazine, he was selected as "the finest writer in TV today"—and this at a time when Hiken's contemporaries included such future luminaries as Mel Brooks, Larry Gelbart, Neil Simon, and Woody Allen.[2]

Hiken's reputation today, however, is another matter.

The question "Schmuck, you don't know Nat Hiken?" no longer applies. From the height of his profession in the 1950s, he has been reduced forty years later to little more than a footnote in many histories of television. Even though his greatest achievement, *Sergeant Bilko*, was adapted in recent years into a Steve Martin movie, Hiken remains a forgotten television pioneer.

This book began as an attempt to discover for myself who Nat Hiken was. Growing up in the 1950s and early 1960s, my two favorite TV comedies were *The Phil Silvers Show* and *Car 54, Where Are You?* Naturally, like any other child, I paid no attention to the behind-the-scenes credits. All I knew was that the shows were funny, enormously appealing, and somehow different from other comedies at the time. Years later, after college, I began to watch these shows again in reruns and finally noticed the connection between them—the credit for Nat Hiken as producer, director, and writer. The name meant nothing to me. I was puzzled. How could someone create two such out-standing comedies and remain so obscure? Standard broadcast-history references told me little. Eventually, I wrote an article about him to gather information about his largely undocumented career.

The more research I did, the bigger the story became. First, I learned of the extent of his reputation—the accolades, the awards, the admiration of his colleagues. Second, I came to appreciate the full scope of his ability. Hiken was one of television's first hyphenate talents. First, though, he was a writer. He brought a wonderfully skewed perspective to his scripts, conjured up uproarious characters and situations, and devised ingenious plots. His responsibilities as producer and director allowed him to preserve this distinctive farcical slant on screen, making him one of television's true comedic auteurs. For his particular ability to craft the sitcom episode, he was considered in his day the king of the half hour. Even if the general public does not remember, the most historically minded of today's TV comedy creators acknowledge his accomplishments. Jim Burrows, director of such series as *Cheers* and *Friends*, describes Hiken as "a founding father of the situation comedy."[3]

A third point that became increasingly clear during my research was the place Hiken's story held in a larger story: the rise and fall of television's Golden Age.

Consider the television scene in 1955. To be sure, the airwaves were filled with their share of pointless programming, but prime time was also highlighted by classic sitcoms, including not only *The Phil Silvers Show* but also *I Love Lucy, The George Burns and Gracie Allen Show,* and *The Honeymooners*. Comedy-variety programs featured the superb characterizations of Sid Caesar, the sublime timing of Jack Benny, and the inspired knockabout mania of Martin and Lewis. Live video dramas provided an outlet for such young writers as Paddy Chayefsky and Rod Serling. The common threads linking all of these shows were creativity, a sense of spontaneity, and a distinctive, often ethnic personality. Turn the clock ahead to 1962 and what do we find? Dominating the comedy scene were the likes of *Leave It to Beaver, Bachelor Father, The Donna Reed Show*—interchangeable sitcom families composed of cookie-cutter Middle Americans, and not especially funny Middle Americans at that. As for drama, live video plays were already a thing of the past. *The Defenders* may have been on hand to infuse the TV screen with some dynamic conflict, but viewers were more likely to find pat medical potboilers along the lines of *Doctor Kildare*.

In just seven years, television had declined from bracing dramas to predictable time killers, from exuberant comedies that delighted live audiences to assembly-line entertainment designed to inspire canned laughter. Television's Golden Age did not last long—little more than ten years—but it unraveled in even less time. Vibrant programming faded quickly, and so did some of its best talents.

As much as anyone, Nat Hiken rode the trajectory of the Golden Age, climbing high with its spectacular rise and dropping out of favor with its precipitous decline. In the early fifties, when the medium was attracting its first viewers, he established himself as a leading talent and became a fixture in the colorful social scene that surrounded the industry. He reached his peak some five years later when television entered its halcyon days of freewheeling creativity. Then, in the early 1960s, his position in the industry eroded as television lost its spark and became the bailiwick of corporate bean counters. He died just a few years later.

Nat Hiken's story mirrors a brief, exciting period when inspired producers and writers, based primarily in New York, enjoyed the opportunity of shaping a new medium. He embodied early television's finest qualities: independence and imagination, as well as a demand for the best and an appreciation of the melting-pot experience. These qualities also made it difficult, if not impossible, for him to adapt when the TV industry began to transform itself in the early 1960s: he remained independent at a time when networks sought control over their producers; he insisted on excellence and comic vision when mediocrity and homogeneous programming became the norm; and he was a compulsive, hands-on creator, attentive to his shows' every detail, at a time of increasing specialization.

Hiken's experience offers a personalized perspective on an extraordinary era in broadcasting. This book aims to convey that perspective, while also refocusing attention on a neglected comedic master. For all his accomplishments, and for all the laughter and good cheer he orchestrated, Nat Hiken deserves to be rediscovered.

KING OF THE HALF HOUR

Milwaukee Boy

Nat Hiken came from a family of storytellers. Memory of this oral tradition goes back to the early 1900s, when Hiken's grandfather held forth in a small Russian-Jewish community outside Bobruysk, somewhere between Minsk and Pinsk. So devoted was Hiken's grandfather to verbal exercise that he had little time for anything else. Some descendants remembered his name as Jacob. Others remembered him merely as the Old Man. One thing they all could agree upon was his livelihood. He had none.

The Old Man lived the ideal existence imagined by Sholom Aleichem's Tevye in *Fiddler on the Roof*. He spent nearly all his time discussing biblical parables in the village synagogue, or regaling friends and family with his wry anecdotes. Jacob's approach, however, was somewhat different from Tevye's. Aleichem's folksy hero dreamed he would live as a gentleman of leisure after he had become suddenly rich. Jacob did not bother waiting for a windfall. He pursued the idle life while still poor.[1]

The job of providing for the family was something he left to his wife. And it was no small job. In keeping with one of the Bible's mandates, Jacob applied himself to being fruitful and multiplying. He sired eight sons and one daughter. With so many mouths to feed, some fathers might have been defensive about lapsing into such a passive role. But not the Old Man. He made this very clear years later, after immigrating to America, when he gave some helpful pointers on his impending eulogy to the local rabbi. As family lore has it, Jacob said, "When I die, don't get up and give a big speech about my being a good provider and being generous in charity, because people will come up and

1

look at the casket to see if they came to the right funeral." When the time arrived for Jacob's memorial service, the rabbi repeated this story for the assembled mourners. They were greatly amused. The Old Man may have fancied
himself a scholar, but ultimately he upheld the code of the devoted comedian—he left them laughing.[2]

Fortunately for the Hiken children, their mother was a sturdy, resourceful
woman. In their village of Shlebeh on the Pripet Marshes of White Russia,
Bedona Hiken put food on the table by going into business for herself. Few re-
sources were at her disposal, but she made the best of what she had. Mixing together mud and straw, she produced bricks and sold them to her fellow
villagers in need of construction material. When they were big enough, the
children helped Bedona with her family manufacture, and over the years, they
cultivated the solid work ethic that they inherited from their mother.[3] It
helped them start businesses of their own and build a new life for themselves
when the time came to resettle in the United States.

The older sons were the first Hikens to cross over to America, arriving during the great influx of eastern Europeans between 1905 and 1910. Like many
others, they left Russia to avoid conscription in the tsar's army, a veritable
prison sentence for young Jewish men who suffered at the hands of viciously
anti-Semitic officers. After landing in New York City, the young Hiken men
moved on to the Jewish section of Chicago, and before long they earned
enough money to bring over the rest of the family.[4]

Several of the Hiken sons, although industrious like their mother, retained
something of their father as well—a talent for spinning yarns and inventing
quips, often at their own expense. Louie, one of the Hiken brothers, became
known for riding streetcars from one end of the line to the other to find audiences for his repertoire of stories. Or, at least, that was the story that other
Hiken brothers circulated through the family. Perhaps the most accomplished
raconteur among them was Max. As soon as he reached the United States, he
brought his distinctive perspective to bear on what he saw around him. As he
was fond of relating over the years, one of the first things that caught his eye
when he arrived in America was a sign for a furnace supply store that read
"Cinders for Sale." The Yiddish-speaking Max read this as "kinder for sale"
("kinder" being Yiddish for children). "What a country!" he said to himself.[5]

Many of his tales he had picked up in the Old Country. They may have
been folktales originally, but he had fashioned them to suit his own storyteller's voice. They concerned the humorous escapades of people living in a
Russian village, like his own, who grappled with human foibles and devised

clever ruses for outwitting tsarist officials. According to relatives, Max's monologues delighted their informal audiences. Years later, Max committed these tales to paper, under the title "The Village in the Woods," and even explored the possibility of adapting them for television and the stage.[6] During his early years in America, though, he could not afford artistic aspirations. He had to make a living with his hands.

Max's hands were strong and nimble, and while in Chicago he mastered the craft of using a drawknife to shape lumber into wagon tongues. Once he established a trade for himself, he was ready to take a wife and start a family. The woman he married came from the same region in Russia as he did, part of a family that had also recently immigrated to Chicago. His bride was Minnie Levin, sister of Max's boyhood friend Nat Levin. Nat had been named after a deceased uncle. Max and Minnie's only child would be named after him as well.[7]

Nat Hiken was born on June 23, 1914. At the time, Max and Minnie lived in an apartment near Chicago's Longdale district, just blocks away from Roosevelt Street, the bustling commercial center of Chicago's Jewish community. Like many children of Jewish immigrants at the time, Nat Hiken spoke only Yiddish in his earliest years. That would change after Uncle Nat Levin and his new bride moved in with the Hikens in 1917. Levin's wife, Rose, was far more acclimated to American life than either her husband or her in-laws. Descended from an earlier wave of Jewish immigrants from the Austro-Hungarian Empire, she was well educated and had taught elementary school in Milwaukee (where she had become friendly with her fellow teacher Golda Meir). Rose immediately took to the Hikens' toddler, a particularly alert and sweet-natured child with large brown eyes, who, coincidentally, had the same birthday as she did. Her devotion to little Nat quickly took the form of practical instruction. Aunt Rose taught him English when he was four and opened him up to the voices outside the Jewish immigrant enclave.[8]

The Hikens did not stay in Chicago much longer. Some of Max's brothers had already moved on to Milwaukee and had set up businesses there. Max followed with his family in 1920, when Nat was six, to begin a new venture of his own. Turning away from manual labor, he took a lease on a storefront where he opened the South Side Leather Company, a leather findings business (the supplying of goods to shoe repair shops). The new home Max found for his family was a ground-floor flat on Milwaukee's north side. Nat Hiken would remember the less than prosperous neighborhood with wry nostalgia. Years later, at an elegant cocktail party, he was asked if he and his lifelong friend Ben

Barkin had grown up in the same part of town. "As a matter of fact, no," Hiken replied. "Take Ben, for instance. He was a west side boy while I was an east side boy—Ben lived on the west side of the alley at 9th and Lloyd, and I lived on the east side of the alley."[9]

The Ninth Street and Lloyd intersection was at the heart of Milwaukee's small Jewish community during the 1920s. With delicatessens just a few blocks south on Walnut Street, kosher butchers on nearby corners, and a row of synagogues on Eleventh Street, residents had little reason to venture very far from home. The neighborhood was quite insular, recalled Nat's cousin, Vivian Hiken Gill. "Everyone was in everybody's business," as she put it.

While growing up on the north side, Nat Hiken was a quiet child. "Very shy," Vivian Gill remembered, "but always had a little wry smile on his face, always thinking of something funny." Clearly, Nat was his father's boy. At family get-togethers when Nat was about eight, Max would place his son on his lap and they would tell stories together. While Nat put his hands behind him, Max would stick his arms forward, where Nat's arms should have been, and they would perform as a sort of ventriloquist act, Max's hands gesticulating and Nat speaking the words. Another bond between them was their mutual gift for working with their hands. The two of them would spend hours together building model airplanes, tanks, and other miniature vehicles, and years later, when Nat was married with children of his own, they would collaborate on an intricately detailed dollhouse for Nat's daughters.[10]

A cousin recalled that young Nat had a keen interest in everyone around him. "He'd sit by my mother's sewing machine as she worked on a garment and he'd say, 'Aunt Bessie, what's a peplum? What's this? What's that?' All these dressmaker terms. And he'd talk with my cousin, Sam Rudnick, who was in the jewelry business, and he'd want to know in detail about his business: 'Now, these people on credit, how do you keep track of them? And how often?' He was just interested in everything."[11] Although he was not likely to be formulating a creative strategy at such an early age, this inquisitiveness would translate years later into detailed comedic characterizations in his scripts.

Curiosity about people stayed with Hiken the rest of his life and, like much about him, it seemed to originate with his father, in particular with a piece of Max's Old World wisdom. One day, in the early 1960s, while shooting a scene from *Car 54, Where Are You?*, actor Al Lewis noticed Hiken standing off to one side talking to the janitor. Lewis was puzzled. The camera was rolling and here was the producer-writer of the show, one of television's most honored talents, absorbed in conversation with the custodial help. "Afterward I went over to him," Lewis recalled, "and I said, 'Nat, why aren't you watching the scene? What're you talking to the janitor for?' He said, 'Let me tell you something my father taught me: If I become a wise man and one day I walk into town and I meet the village idiot and all his life he's only had one idea in his head—if I talk to him and he gives that idea to me, I'm already much wiser.' "[12]

The easy affinity between Nat and his father, which helped shape the writer's perspective, did not exist between Nat and his mother, Minnie. Neither, for that matter, did it exist between Minnie and Max. Their marriage, according to a family theory, might have been arranged for them, in the Old World manner. The disparity between their personalities would seem to support that conclusion. Whereas Max was a jokester, Minnie was deadly serious. Whereas Max was easygoing, Minnie was a controller, intent upon masterminding all that transpired in the family.

To her credit, Minnie was a forceful, energetic woman, admired by some relatives for her independent spirit and, in later years, for her youthful resilience. Other family members, though, observed that little of Minnie's energy was directed at understanding others' concerns. "She was just absolutely insensitive frequently, certainly to nuances of people and situations, and even didn't realize that she was manipulative," said Nat's cousin, Peter, son of Nat and Rose Levin. Years later, Nat's daughter Dana had a similar impression. "I remember my grandmother as never being a very loveable person. She just had this funny, very intense personality, somebody I couldn't see having very much insight into somebody's feelings."[13]

For Minnie, intruding upon others was simply a matter of correcting what others were liable, she believed, to do wrong. As far as the South Side Leather Company was concerned, she was convinced that Max was too relaxed and unassertive to run the business properly. In time, she stepped in and took charge of some of the operations. This might have become a sore point between her and Max. They certainly fought about something. Peter Levin recalled witnessing these arguments as a child when he came to visit. Because the bickering was in Yiddish, he could not understand what the arguments were about, but they were vehement enough to make him want to hide.[14]

Minnie could be as dogged about eccentric pastimes as she could about business. "She used to play games with herself," Levin said. "She was sure, anyplace she went, she would find a relative—cousins always. I remember one story about her in Cheyenne, Wyoming, on one of her trips across the country. She saw a name on a tailor shop—Kaminski. She went in there, for no other purpose than to establish that they were related, which she established to her satisfaction. I gather nobody else was convinced, but she was sure this was a cousin." On one such family trip cross-country, a grown Levin was driving the first of two cars, and frequently he would look back to find that the second car containing Minnie was nowhere to be seen. She was off on a side trip of her own because she had spotted a Jewish name in some small town that she was sure was connected in some way to her family.[15]

The family business and quixotic quests for cousins could take up much of her time, but Minnie's greatest passion was politics—the more uncompromising the better. Max himself was a left-winger—and was even radical enough to refuse to wear a yarmulke at family weddings and bar mitzvahs—but he was moderate compared with his wife. During their earliest years in Milwaukee, they belonged to the Workmen's Circle, the Jewish socialist organization. The Circle provided health and burial benefits as well as lectures on intellectually uplifting topics, from personal hygiene and the philosophy of Baruch Spinoza to current labor movement trends and the Jewish national question. Although the group was inspired by political radicalism, socializing could be just as important as socialism. Max warmed to this side of Circle activities. By joining the organization's local Bobruysker branch, he could fill his leisure time by chatting with *landsmen* from his region of Russia. But for Minnie mere schmoozing was grossly inadequate and far too passive. She left Workmen's Circle–style socialism behind and embraced instead the revolutionary dogma of communism.[16] In the 1930s she even traveled to the Soviet Union to witness her ideology in action. Just as she managed to find relatives where there were none, she succeeded in seeing nothing but progress and freedom in Stalin's totalitarian Russia. She returned with stories of a workers' heaven.[17]

As she did with everything else, Minnie devoted herself with unrelenting energy to the Communist cause. Lacking much sense of irony, she sometimes expressed herself like a party-line pamphlet. During World War II, for example, she mailed a wool sweater to one of Nat's friends serving in the army; with the gift she enclosed a note: "For your valiant fight against Fascism."[18]

To Nat's mind, this sort of bombast was an invitation for ribbing. When he and his friend Sid Kozak were taken, as adolescents, to Communist meetings, they spent most of their time poking fun at the ponderous speechifying. At home, when his mother engaged in heated political discussions, Nat would often needle her, finding ways to make light of her aspirations to save the world. Sometimes Minnie would get so angry that she was reduced to wagging a finger and sputtering, "Natey . . . Natey . . . you . . . you. . . ." Less amusing for Nat were the bitter political arguments that sprang up within the extended family, between Communists, liberal Democrats, and Socialists (or "left-social-fascists," as Communists regarded them). Minnie could be especially strident during these flare-ups.[19]

His mother's stridency eventually soured Nat on politics. Throughout his life he would share many of his family's left-wing concerns but not Minnie's quasi-religious fervor.[20] Minnie's political activities also subtracted from her time spent at home. Nat may have wanted a more attentive mother, but his feelings must have been mixed; at times, he clearly liked to get away from his mother's overbearing manner, as well as from the arguments between her and Max. "Very frequently—first Nate and his father, then afterwards, separately—the two of them would come down and visit us in Chicago," said Peter Levin. "Max would come down a number of times a year whenever he had a disagreement with Minnie, and Nate would come whenever he felt a need to escape."[21]

Visits with the Levins were a welcome respite, but Nat's most prized escapes came in the summer when he stayed on his Uncle Jake's farm.

Uncle Jake Levin had homesteaded in Nebraska soon after immigrating to America and, after gaining title to the property, had sold the land and used the proceeds to purchase a subsistence farm outside Bangor, Michigan. Each summer, without their parents, Nat and many of his cousins from the Levin side of the family would congregate there. Running barefoot from June to August, Nat, an only child, suddenly had plenty of playmates immediately at hand, including Peter, Uncle Jake's son Lou and, Nat's special favorite, Sandy Rothblatt, daughter of Minnie Hiken's sister Bessie. When not nurturing a reputation as a practical jokester, he helped with the chores, fetching and milking cows, toting water to workers in the fields when the time came for the area's communal threshing of wheat and oats. He treasured the carefree flow of one day to the next. Each year, as soon as spring came along, he would begin anticipating these summers away from home. He would send letters to the farm, written on wrapping paper from his father's store, alerting everyone of his imminent arrival, everyone from Uncle Jake and his sons to the cows and chickens as well.[22]

When not on the Michigan farm, Nat found other ways to explore life beyond political meetings and lonesome hours spent home alone. Round-faced and bespectacled, Nat looked like he should have been a bookworm—certainly he was interested in reading—but he was not a sedentary boy. He played baseball and basketball, and went ice skating on nearby lakes. He was especially fond of "pinners," a favorite city-boy game, known as "stoopball" in New York, a test of a player's skill at bouncing a red rubber ball off a stoop; the key was to bounce the ball off the step's corner, making the ball take off like a shot. Acute nearsightedness hampered Nat's play in any game that involved tracking a ball, but he excelled at swimming, something he practiced often at McKinley Beach along Lake Michigan. At the same time, his lifelong passion for watching sports was incubating as well. He received his introduction to professional baseball by walking a short distance uptown to Borchert Field to watch the Milwaukee Brewers (then the name of a double-A minor league team). On a more exalted level, when in Chicago, he went with Uncle Nat and cousin Peter to take in the likes of major leaguers Hack Wilson and Grover Cleveland Alexander playing for the Cubs at Wrigley Field.[23]

Young Nat's comedic sense was originally shaped by stories he had heard his father and uncles tell, but now it began to seek its own course. Helping to direct his humor's path were books he read and shows he watched. He was fond of the earthy tales of Sholom Aleichem and the slapstick he saw performed in movies and on the vaudeville stage, but he also developed a taste for more rarified English wit. He and his cousins Sandy and Jenny would attempt British stage accents as they read aloud the urbane dialogue of Noel Coward. And even more intriguing to Nat was the deft, musical patter of W. S. Gilbert. He would listen to records of such operettas as The Mikado and H.M.S. Pinafore, fascinated by the verbal precision and the nimble irony. "As we grew up we used to quote Gilbert and Sullivan back and forth to each other," Peter Levin recalled.[24]

The technique of Gilbert may have won Nat's admiration, but the English lyricist's world of foppish officers and fluttery ingenues obviously bore no relation to the life of a Jewish kid growing up in Milwaukee. For his own raw material of personalities and attitudes, Nat could draw upon the colorful convergence of ethnic types found on the north side. Standing in the middle of his own Jewish community, he could pick up the smell of hops wafting in from the nearby Schlitz and Blatz breweries, industrial landmarks of Milwaukee's German population that had played such an important role in the city's development. Also close by were Poles and Swedes, and on the corner across from Nat's apartment was an Italian delicatessen.[25] Memories differ as to how agreeable a mix this melting-pot experience was. A friend of Nat's acknowledged that many Gentile families would turn away Jewish children who sought to earn a dime or two shoveling snow off their walkways, but he also recalled that "we always managed to talk to each other and understand each other." One of Nat's cousins remembered things very differently. Growing up in a nearby German neighborhood, he was seven years old when Hitler came to power in Germany. "From there on, my neighborhood was a field of terror for me. I kept reading in the news and hearing on the radio what was going on, and my friends were going to the German-American Bund camps in the summer. It was a very paranoid time for me." As for Nat, if his later scripts are any indication, he took a more relaxed view and clearly appreciated the ethnic patchwork he grew up with. The names of the comical, endearing assortment that made up Sergeant Bilko's platoon—Zimmerman, Mullen, Paparelli, Kadowski—could easily have served as a cross-section of his Milwaukee neighborhood.[26]

In his teenage years, Nat became known by his friends as a sly kibbitzer and a funny storyteller. His perspective on people and situations was also becoming distinctively skewed, as he proved one day in high school while engaged in a debating competition. The subject was smoking. His opponent was assigned the antismoking position. Nat was supposed to argue that smoking was beneficial (at a time, of course, when there still *was* an argument that smoking was beneficial, however specious that argument might have been). Even before they began, Nat could see he stood on shaky ground. Not only was his opponent's position more valid, it was to be presented by a girl who was one of Washington High School's best and brightest students. Nat devised his own way of dealing with this disadvantage. When the time came for him to stand up at the speaker's podium, he proceeded to argue that he was in favor of smoking fish. He may not have exactly demolished his opponent's argument that cigarette smoking stunted one's growth, but his stirring defense of lox and smoked whitefish at least succeeded in throwing her off balance for a few moments.[27]

By the time Nat had reached high school age, his family's leather-findings business had started to show signs of relative prosperity (thanks in part to the go-getter assistance and business savvy of Minnie, the fierce anticapitalist). The Hikens were now able to leave the north side's immigrant enclave and move to the slightly more affluent west side, where they bought a two-story building at Center and 48th Streets. They took one of the second-story apartments for themselves and rented out the other apartments and the first-floor storefront.[28]

Nat now ventured farther from home, thanks to his father, who let him drive the family Pontiac, or "ponyak," as Max called it. Nat would use the car on double-dates with Ben Barkin, or on fishing excursions to North Lake.[29] At the same time, though, he would have to help with the family business, mind-ing the store on a regular basis while his parents were out lining up customers or, in the case of Minnie, pursuing political activities.

The South Side Leather Company was not necessarily an unpleasant place, as storefront businesses went. One relative remembered it as a clean and orderly shop, with all its cowhides and supplies neatly stored, and as a bustling store trafficked by men coming in to buy brads, heels, and pieces of leather. "I used to love to go to the place because of the smells, the smells of leather," he recalled. But Nat, obligated to spend so many of his afternoons there, was more likely to share the view of his friend Sid Kozak, who recalled, most of all, the store's wide plate-glass windows, covered with dust. "I'd go down there and visit Natey," Kozak said. "I remember him remarking on the fact that even the flies died there." [30]

To find a way of making a living more agreeable than selling shoe supplies, Nat enrolled at the University of Wisconsin after graduating from high school in 1932. He decided to study journalism. For someone skillful with words at the height of the Great Depression, training for a newspaper job was a sensible choice, much more sensible, certainly, than writing jokes and funny scripts. For the time being at least, Nat was serious about being serious.

2

The Grouchmaster

If Nat was harboring a desire to write something other than news stories, he kept it well hidden while at the University of Wisconsin. He concealed it even from his friends and relatives—at least for the first three years. He conscientiously attended journalism classes at South Hall. He acquired newspaper experience by joining the staff of the *Cardinal*, the campus daily. He even tested the waters of nonacademic reporting by witnessing and taking notes at trials at courthouses in the region. But in his senior year, the Hiken legacy began to take hold. As an upperclassman, with greater say in his assignments at the *Daily Cardinal*, he chose to write a humor column.[1]

The column was a protest of sorts against his agreeable surroundings. At first glance, there certainly was little reason to complain about life on campus in the Badger State capital of Madison. Orderly and picturesque, the university was centered in the grassy slopes of Bascom Hill, studded with a double row of elm trees and ringed with buildings constructed in Renaissance and Doric Roman styles. From the terrace fronting Bascom Hall at the top of the hill, one could look eastward and spy the capitol dome at the far end of State Street, or turn and gaze across the rippling waters of Lake Mendota to the north. Nearby on Langdon Street stood the Memorial Union, housing a refectory, a library, and a rathskeller, fulfilling three of the students' most primary needs: food, books, and beer. Milwaukee Germans might have described the campus as *gemütlich*, a congenial, cheerful place. But Nat Hiken decided to comment on university life in a column called the "Gripers' Club," a forum for complaints.[2]

In a send-up of newspaper advice columns, Nat fielded gripes from his fellow students and offered solutions to their various problems. He presented his efforts as a vital public service. "We Gripers are misunderstood," he announced in the column's first installment. Gripers are basically good souls, he went on to explain, but they are nonetheless plagued by a hypersensitivity to the smallest inconveniences. As a result, they are tedious company for all those with sunnier dispositions. Their temperament would improve, however, if they had a column where they could vent their grievances. "This club is our gesture of friendship to the student body. We no longer will buttonhole you and pour out our woes. No longer will you have to tolerate our downcast features because from now on our features are going to be definitely brighter."[3]

The gripes were supposedly delivered to Nat at the *Daily Cardinal* offices. Actually, he invented many of them himself. He assumed a host of aliases—male and female, student and teacher—and seized upon petty but irksome annoyances: out-of-order elevators, abrasive roommates, excessive belching in the rathskeller, wet, slippery steps adjoining the shower room in the men's gym ("While seasoned juniors and seniors can fall down the steps without much more harm than a few fractures, unknowing freshmen have spilled much blood on the shower room floor, making it inconvenient for persons taking showers."). Nat's suggested remedies ranged from the civil (petitioning the Board of Regents for a $1.37 appropriation to buy rubber shower mats) to the somewhat more drastic (a machine gun ambush of a noisy garbage truck driver). Occasionally, Nat, the W. S. Gilbert fancier, would try his hand at short, facetious verses to open the columns. At other times, in place of the usual catalog of complaints, he would offer absurdist descriptions of obviously fictitious Gripers' Club meetings.[4]

The column conveyed an engaging tone of good-natured kidding. Beyond that, "Gripers' Club" was still clearly the work of a neophyte humorist in need of fine-tuning his ideas and honing his craft. Robert Benchley could rest easy; his position was still secure. The column's importance only became clear after Nat graduated.

Until then, he remained a dutiful student, finishing his studies and tackling his senior year thesis. Despite a tendency to procrastinate, he succeeded in completing his paper on the formation of the American Newspaper Guild, founded by columnist Heywood Broun just three years earlier in 1933. When all the work was done, Nat did not, however, get much encouragement: he would never make a living as a writer, one of his professors advised him.[5]

Nat may have presented a soft-spoken, self-effacing demeanor, but he was tenacious enough to put these discouraging words behind him and proceed with his plans. Soon after graduation, he came up with a concept for a free-lance news-feature service. He would market Hollywood personality pieces revolving around regional angles. He would place stories in newspapers about local men and women who were now involved in motion picture production, people from the newspapers' hometowns who had gone on to become supporting actors, cameramen, chorus girls, chauffeurs for the stars—anyone connected somehow to the glamour of Hollywood. In this way, Nat reasoned, newspapers would receive copy tailored specifically for them, while at the same time movie studios would benefit from extra publicity for their films.[6]

Hiken set the scheme into motion after he contacted his cousin Sandy, then living in Los Angeles and working as a secretary at Republic Pictures. Seeing the potential for Nat's idea, she urged him to drive to California and offered to assist him with his plans by putting her movie-industry contacts to work on his behalf. Nat set out for the West Coast intent upon pursuing his journalistic venture, but ultimately it would be his old college column that would determine his future. The "Gripers' Club," originally just a collegiate whim, would soon become the launching pad for his comedy career.

◆   ◆   ◆

Although family relations defined them as first cousins, Nat and Sandy Rothblatt were better described as siblings in spirit. Among the earliest of Sandy's memories was an ordeal she and Nat shared when she was seven and he was five. Still living in Chicago at the time, they went together to the hospital for their tonsillectomies and, already quite close, they were bitterly disappointed to discover that they would not share the same room. They could, however, see each other through their respective room windows. They managed to communicate and take comfort in each other's slightly distant company as they endured their postoperative recovery, which was not nearly as painless as they had been led to believe. Through the years their relationship deepened, especially during the barefoot summers on Uncle Jake's farm. They remained close even though Sandy's family moved to California in 1920.[7]

The Rothblatts found a house in Los Angeles on Tremaine Avenue, establishing a foothold for what would soon grow into a virtual family colony. One after another, relatives moved to California and joined them, and by the 1930s, Sandy's block was lined with uncles, aunts, and cousins, both close and distant. This veritable kibbutz, as Sandy remembered it, held a special allure for Nat, who would periodically visit while growing up. As he did on Uncle Jake's farm, he savored the experience of being surrounded by so many relatives.[8]

"It was the worst piece of miscasting for him to be an only child. Family was so important to him," Sandy said. When visiting his California relatives, he would often be reluctant even to leave Sandy's house, so intent was he to remain within the family confines.[9]

While Nat's attachment to Sandy grew for purely filial reasons, there was also something else that drew him—the Rothblatts' proximity to Hollywood's entertainment industry. As a writer for the *Jewish Daily Forward,* Sandy's father would sometimes file stories on the movie scene and would take Sandy with him to film sets where she met the likes of James Cagney and Edward G. Robinson. For young Nat the Rothblatts' connection to Hollywood royalty, however tenuous, seemed awfully intriguing.[10]

By the time Nat graduated from college, Sandy had begun to explore show business on her own. Before taking her job at Republic Pictures, she had toured the country with a vaudeville dance troupe, and was now pursuing work as a singer. With some familiarity with the entertainment field—at least more than Nat had—she was able to open some doors for Nat's Hollywood feature-writing service as he made his drive from Wisconsin to California. When he settled into one of the family bungalows on Tremaine Avenue, he found that Sandy had already arranged for him to visit sets at Warner Brothers and MGM, where he could interview cast and crew members for his local-newspaper articles. Making the most of his trip to California, Nat had visited newspaper offices along the way and had sold many of them on the idea of Hollywood items that boasted hometown interest. Now, in Los Angeles, all he had to do was collect his information and write the stories.[11]

But, for Nat, the prospect of putting words to paper was a cue to put off doing any work whatsoever.

A prodigious master of delay tactics, he whiled away his time building models with one of his Tremaine Avenue nephews, or sitting around playing solitaire, preferably if a relative was nearby so that he would have someone to schmooze with while he played. Sometimes he would simply lie on the sofa, teasing Sandy, trying to coax her into running errands for him while he lazed about—"Get me a drink of water, Sandy. I'm so thirsty."—even though he must have known full well that she would refuse. On deadline days, when the articles had to be mailed to the editors, the stories still were not done. At the last possible moment, Nat and Sandy rushed out to the car, toting the typewriter with them. As Sandy drove downtown to the post office, Nat sat in the passenger seat typing the final sentences.[12]

Aided by his cousin, he continued to churn out the stories on time, just barely. At five dollars or less per article, the pay could not have been terribly inspiring, especially if Nat were not terribly inspired by the work itself, which seems likely. Given his natural comedic bent, it is reasonable to assume that his true interests lay elsewhere. Still, with the hub of the entertainment industry close at hand, he made no move to attempt something more creative; at least not until Sandy introduced him to two of her friends who worked in radio.

Roland Kibbee, who would later become a successful writer for both film and television, made a living at the time as the manager of a local radio station. Sandy met him while auditioning at the station for a singing job, then went on to meet Kibbee's high school pal, Jack Lescoulie, a disc jockey at KFWB, the radio outlet owned by Warner Brothers. In the 1950s Lescoulie would become known on television as Jackie Gleason's announcer and as Dave Garroway's amiable sidekick on the *Today* show, but in the mid-1930s he was stoking an ambition to act. At his Los Angeles high school, he had been a lead performer, until, that is, his adolescent pranks earned him a suspension from the school dramatics program. Still determined, he proceeded to win a scholarship at the Pasadena Playhouse school of performing arts and, accompanied by his friend Kibbee, even got as far as Broadway. The two of them reached the Great White Way—however briefly—when they played bit parts in a Los Angeles play and traveled with the company to the East Coast. After the play folded, they remained in New York, subsisting largely on rice and ketchup before finally deciding the time had come to return home to Los Angeles. Lescoulie now set his sights on the film industry. A six-footer with red hair and all-American looks, he managed to land roles in a handful of movies, but nothing more prestigious than "Three Mesquiteers" Westerns. As a rule he was the one brought on to say, "Let's go! There's trouble at the ranch!" or, in less stressful moments, "Going to town, Miss Lucy?" He bided his time spinning records at KFWB but remained watchful for something better.[13]

Sandy and Kibbee became romantically involved and later married, but between the three of them—Sandy, Kibbee and Lescoulie—there was another bond, a like-minded comic sensibility. They shared a taste for the madcap humor of the day, shaped by the essays of S. J. Perelman and repeated viewings of the Marx Brothers movies. Sandy was right in thinking that her friends and her cousin Nat would hit it off. Nat, Lescoulie, and Kibbee became a tightly knit threesome. When not at work, Kibbee and Lescoulie would congregate at Nat's quarters on Tremaine Avenue. They played cards, swapped stories, and, when needed, transported one of Nat's younger cousins to school in Lescoulie's Ford.[14]

At one point, Nat got around to telling his new friends about the humor column he had written in college. The column's basic premise—a public clearinghouse for people's gripes—made an impression on Lescoulie. He mulled it over, then one day appeared at Nat's bungalow to propose that the "Gripers' Club" could be adapted into an amusing radio show. If Nat would write a script, Lescoulie could probably get the program aired on KFWB. Nat saw the potential in this idea and told Lescoulie he would get to work on it.

Enthusiasm for an idea did not necessarily mean that Nat would immediately plunge into it. Lescoulie showed up a week later and asked how the script was coming. "Oh, yeah, I'm going to do it," Nat assured him, "I'm going to do it." More time passed and still Nat had put nothing on paper. Finally, Lescoulie, at his wit's end, came by to tell Nat that he had already spoken to the station manager about the show. The manager liked the idea. "We go on on Saturday," Lescoulie announced. Now, with the pressure on, Nat was motivated to work. In a single burst of effort, he completed the script for the opening episode.[15]

Entitled The Grouch Club, the show aired six mornings a week, Monday through Saturday, from six to eight o'clock. Standing in as the audio equivalent of Nat's columnist voice, Lescoulie commented on complaints about everyday annoyances (invented by Nat) purportedly mailed in by listeners. The Grouch Club began as a lowly, local program, sponsored by Sam the Credit Man, a local haberdasher, whose financial infusion left only a ten-dollar weekly salary for Nat and Lescoulie to split between them. But the show struck a nerve with Los Angeles listeners. At the time, morning radio programs relied on chipper hosts, full of unrelenting good cheer and bouncy optimism. The Grouch Club countered with unrelenting, tongue-in-cheek grumbling, officiated by Lescoulie, the Grouchmaster, the sort of host who offered heartfelt thanks to the studio audience when they responded to his opening greeting with a round of boos. For many Angelinos, the show's cranky humor was a welcome change of pace in morning listening and an amusing way to brace themselves for their depression-era workdays.[16]

Word of the program spread and The Grouch Club turned into a sleeper hit in the Los Angeles area. "You could be driving on your way to work in the morning and, if you stopped at a street light, almost everyone driving within hearing distance would be listening to *The Grouch Club* and laughing," Sandy remembered. She found that the show's grumpy comedy appealed especially to some of Hollywood's more offbeat talents. At the Republic Pictures offices where she worked, avid fans of the program included future B-movie *auteur* Sam Fuller and satiric-novelist-turned-screenwriter Nathanael West.[17]

Members of Hiken's Tremaine Avenue clan were among the last converts to the show. At first they shook their heads in dismay at Nat's oddball radio fling, convinced that he was squandering his time and any chance he might have to make a real living. Only when they noticed their neighbors clamoring for tickets to attend the broadcasts did they begin to change their minds.[18] Nat may have pursued a show business career in the most passive way possible, sidling up to the periphery without trying to find an entrée on his own. But now he found himself immersed, shouldering the daunting workload of six scripts a week. He was riding a small grassroots success that gained momentum and continued to grow.

Responding to the show's popularity, KFWB managers decided to add a new feature. On Saturdays, one of the gripes created by Nat would be dramatized in a comedy sketch entitled "Grouch of the Week." Lescoulie alone could no longer enact the entire show. Actors were needed. The expansion of the cast, though, was not accompanied by a significantly expanded budget.[19]

To fill the roles he was creating, Nat turned to the Tremaine Avenue enclave. Relatives, at least, would be willing to work for the kind of money he had to offer, which was nothing. Sandy appeared on the show, as did Nat's cousins Jenny and Zelda. When Nat could pry a few extra dollars loose, he would bring in professionals, provided that they were struggling and hungry. One week, he summoned up a princely surplus of two dollars to hire Alan Ladd, at a time when the future tough-guy star was hosting a variety show at the same KFWB studios. On another occasion Nat himself performed, quite unexpectedly. During rehearsal he forgot to assign a part to an obliging relative or underpaid actor, and when the neglected lines came up during the live broadcast, he had to jump in and deliver them himself.[20]

In 1938, *The Grouch Club* climbed to the next plateau. No longer just a Los Angeles show, it was now broadcast throughout the state by the California Radio System. No longer churned out six mornings a week, it now aired weekly, every Monday evening. The series also acquired all the basic trappings normally found in network variety-comedy programs of the day. Besides Grouchmaster Lescoulie, the regional network version featured an announcer

(Jim Berry), a musical ensemble (the Warner Brothers orchestra led by Leon Leonardi), and a crooner to provide tuneful interludes (Dan Gridley). Perhaps most important, Nat found on the Warner lot an actor who became the centerpiece of his sketches.

Arthur Q. Bryan was a well-known voice during the 1930s and 1940s. Radio listeners knew him as Doc Gamble on the popular sitcom *Fibber McGee and Molly,* and moviegoers—and subsequent generations of television viewers—knew him as the voice of Elmer Fudd, the would-be hunter and perennial patsy of Bugs Bunny in Warner's Looney Tunes. His plaintive croak made him the ideal protagonist for Hiken's sketches, which were exercises in comic frustration. He might play a suburbanite struggling to get some sleep while the neighborhood bustles with a maddening procession of noises, or a tourist searching in vain for a place to stay in New York City during the 1939 World's Fair, or a motorist pulling into an auto parts lot to replace a carburetor only to be pounced upon by unstoppable salesmen intent upon selling not just a part but an entire used car.

It is not clear whether the sketch portion of the program was initiated originally by executives at KFWB or proposed by Nat himself. Whichever it was, the decision proved exceptionally shrewd. Sketch writing emerged as Nat's true forte, and the skits he created for *The Grouch Club* quickly became the highlight of the show.

As he turned out a sketch a week, Nat developed a talent for comedic overstatement that was especially attuned to a purely audio, nonliteral medium. In one of the show's best-known skits, Bryan walks into his local library to acquire a borrower's card. Of course, this being *The Grouch Club,* the process turns out to be much more difficult than Bryan ever imagined. The librarian reels off a list of requirements he has to satisfy. He must be listed in the phone directory. He has to fill out forms in triplicate. He needs the signature of a property owner—or the sworn statements of sixteen character witnesses. Bryan leaves, then returns, ever hopeful that the card will be his. But there is always some bureaucratic detail he has overlooked. Months pass, seasons turn, and still he keeps coming back in his ongoing quest to take out a book.

In one of the funniest, and more extreme, depictions, Bryan and his wife decide to take their troublesome ten-year-old son in hand. It seems the child has always been a problem, ever since "he was old enough to slap his father in the face with a hot water bottle." The scene begins as the boy's mother talks on the phone with her neighbor: "Why do you ask me if you can water *your* lawn? . . . Oh, our Junior has the hose? . . . What? . . . He tied your son to a tree with it . . . Oh, he *hung* your son to a tree—ah, by the heels!" In a moment, Junior enters, as so many sons do, asking his mother to help him find something: "Hey, Ma!! Where's my hatchet? Mr. Schultz gave me a dirty look this morning when I let the air outta his tires. I wanna chop down his garage."

As soon as Bryan, the father, comes home, the parents decide to take action. The mother has already gotten expert advice from the family doctor. The problem, it turns out, is that Junior has been listening to too many crime shows on radio. His imagination is overstimulated. In the evenings, he should listen instead to soothing radio bedtime stories.

Junior returns from his latest outing ("What a neighborhood—me with my BB gun and not a cop in sight."), and the family snaps on the radio in accordance with the doctor's prescription. Over the air come the sweet sounds of violins playing "Rock-a-Bye Baby." The bedtime program begins. Uncle Sleepwell, the honey-voiced host, instructs his moppet listeners to close their drowsy little eyes before he ever so gently continues the story of little Josephine in Gooby Looby Land. Junior howls for his father to let go of him so he can get away from this nursery school drivel.

Little Josephine, Uncle Sleepwell begins, was menaced by a big bad tiger last episode, but all is well now. Her courageous little skunk friend has driven the nasty beast away. But now, Uncle Sleepwell continues, little Josephine enters Gooby Looby Land's rank, slimy jungle. Two horrible eyes gleam at her through the darkness. The tiger is back! Josephine flees, but no matter how hard she runs, the beast keeps apace. Soon she is cornered. A vicious lion joins the tiger. They close in for the kill. The story builds to a terrifying crescendo of screams and roars—only to dissolve suddenly into the lilting "Rock-a-Bye Baby" refrain. Uncle Sleepwell signs off.

The story has reduced Junior to a quivering, stammering wreck. His mother is not much better off. As she tries to put the hysterical child to bed, Bryan calls the radio station responsible for the broadcast. He demands to speak to Uncle Sleepwell and gets the bedtime host on the line. Bryan begins as if about to lodge a complaint but then quickly implores Uncle Sleepwell to reveal what will happen to poor little Josephine. His voice breaks into his best Elmer Fuddish tremble. "I won't sleep tonight!" he cries.[21]

The Grouch Club created enough of a noise for *Variety* to take note. Appraising the program in the show business paper's telegraphic style, the reviewer wrote, "On night caught, it was one long howl in the audience and just socko off the set."[22] During the show's regional run, Warner Brothers saw additional possibilities for the fan-following that Hiken's sketches were attracting. The studio inaugurated a *Grouch Club* series of short films. The one-reelers starred Bryan (who, it turns out, actually looked like Elmer Fudd) and reprised such material as the library card skit. Among the titles were "Tax Trouble," "No Parking," and "Trouble in Store." For the first time, *The Grouch Club* reached audiences outside California as Warner Brothers distributed the films throughout its circuit of theaters. The program, though, reached its highest rung a year later. NBC picked up the series and began broadcasting it coast to coast.

In 1939, network radio was thirteen years old. The concept of aligning stations across the country into a single entity had originally been championed by David Sarnoff, then a young executive with RCA. He orchestrated a system of leased telephone lines that could reliably transmit sound across great distances. On November 15, 1926, this system allowed RCA's newly formed subsidiary, the National Broadcasting Company, to go on the air for the first time, originating its broadcast that day from New York City but also incorporating segments from Chicago and Independence, Kansas. Two years later, William S. Paley followed suit by forming the Columbia Broadcasting System and offered some stiff competition. Still, Sarnoff's NBC remained for some time the dominant broadcasting force. Sarnoff's network was so big, in fact, that it encompassed two networks—NBC Red and NBC Blue. Only in 1943 did the FCC finally coerce parent company RCA into relinquishing one of its radio chains. It sold NBC Blue, the less prestigious of the two, which soon evolved into the American Broadcasting Company.

When *The Grouch Club* joined NBC Red in 1939, comedy programs accounted for much of network radio's popularity. Jack Benny, aided by sidekicks Don Wilson and Eddie "Rochester" Anderson, had been making radio listeners laugh for seven years and was already one of the medium's great institutions. Listeners could also find amusement with Bob Hope, Eddie Cantor, Burns and Allen, and Edgar Bergen and Charlie McCarthy. Predecessors to television sitcoms were also on the air, the first and foremost being *Amos 'n' Andy*. The show's blackface antics would likely induce apoplexy in politically sensitive audiences today, but in the late 1930s it was still a radio staple, with candy bars and toys officially merchandised in its name. Other sitcoms of the day drew audiences by focusing on foibles in other segments of American life, from the small-town squabbles of *Fibber McGee and Molly* to the barroom imbroglios of *Duffy's Tavern* and the ethnic strivings of *The Goldbergs*.

Hiken's *The Grouch Club* was to join this array of comedy in the six-thirty slot on Sundays, as the lead-in to no less a powerhouse than *The Jack Benny*

Show. In just two years Nat had gone from would-be journalist to creative participant in the most potent mass medium of the day. Exhilaration must have
fueled his efforts for the upcoming season, but intensified pressure also frayed
his nerves. To help him with the weekly scriptwriting chores, he recruited
Roland Kibbee, now married to his cousin Sandy. Kibbee, who was losing patience as he waited for a play of his to be produced, agreed quickly to come
aboard.

Kibbee not only helped Nat with work, but also collaborated with him in
avoiding it. With a much larger salary at his disposal, Nat could be more creative in this area. To get away from writing for the airwaves, he now took to
the air. With Kibbee he learned how to fly, and together they earned their
pilot's licenses. Any available time the two of them had they spent flying their
newly purchased Waco, a four-seater biplane. Not all of that time was, strictly
speaking, available, according to Sandy. She was devoting herself during that
period to the serious-minded pursuit of left-wing causes and tended to take a
dim view of the aerial capers that captivated her cousin and her husband. "I
was disapproving, because I was so busy saving the world, and here they were
going off flying. And they weren't coming in until ten or twelve at night to finally write the scripts."[23]

Despite what seemed to be all their efforts to the contrary, Nat and Kibbee
completed the scripts on time. *The Grouch Club* first aired coast to coast on
April 16, 1939, bankrolled by the program's first major sponsor, General Mills'
Kix cereal. The *Variety* review was lukewarm, describing the opening episode
as "hit 'n' miss."[24] Over the course of the season, though, the program continued to improve, as Nat and Kibbee injected the scripts with a *Hellzapoppin'*-
style energy.

The series was not widely reviewed during its two-year NBC run, but more
important than any assessment by a newspaper critic was the appraisal of one
man already firmly established in the broadcast business. Now that *The
Grouch Club* could be heard in New York, it was noticed by someone generally
considered to be the sharpest-tongued humorist of the airwaves. The show
had caught the ear of Fred Allen, and on the basis of what he heard, the
renowned radio comedian hired Nat and Kibbee to join his writing staff. He
sensed a kindred spirit between these two young men and himself, to be found
in *The Grouch Club*'s acerbic humor and flights of absurdist fancy. Or as Allen
himself put it, "If they're going to steal my style, I might as well put 'em to work
for me."[25]

3

Fred Allen Writes His Own Material

Like most comedians of his generation, Fred Allen emerged from the ranks of vaudeville. He spent his formative professional years barnstorming across the country, sometimes across the seas, learning his craft while performing between the likes of Wormwood's Monkeys and Rose's Royal Midgets. In this variety show format—the great mass entertainment vehicle of the early twentieth century—comedians like Allen fine-tuned their own distinctive style as they enacted their routines over and over again from one theater to the next. They learned to sharpen their verbal delivery and perfect their physical mannerisms. The best of them—Allen, Jack Benny, Bob Hope, George Burns—also learned the fine art of working with partners, how to listen and feed straight-lines and follow unexpected changes in routines. They became not only joke slingers, but also skilled comedic actors, who went on to movies, radio, and eventually television.

Allen could not claim a loveable mug as part of his basic equipment. With his angular features and hooded eyelids, he presented a harsh demeanor, even as a young man, before age and worry added bags under his eyes. With little chance to endear himself to the audience, he had to rely purely on cleverness and a quick wit. These qualities kept his career going even as vaudeville began to fade in the 1920s, overshadowed by the rise of motion picture entertainment. He moved onto the Broadway stage, contributing to a series of revues as both performer and writer, and when the legitimate theater also began to encounter problems, as the Great Depression struck, Allen shifted again and decided to take a chance on the young medium of radio. That was in 1932. The gamble turned into an eighteen-year engagement.

In 1932, radio was about to enter its greatest years of popularity and influence. When Allen premiered in *The Linit Bath Club Revue*, he was following in the footsteps of such vaudevillians turned broadcasters as Ed Wynn, Al Jolson, Eddie Cantor, and Jack Benny. His show, underwritten over the years by various sponsors and sporting an assortment of program titles, stirred together a mix of topical patter, sketches, amateur acts, and mock news reports. As the show developed through the 1930s, it became most famous for two things: the comedian's ongoing, on-air feud with Jack Benny (actually a good friend) and Allen's droll sense of wordplay.

As a teenager, Allen had worked in the Boston Public Library, where he developed a keen interest in the books he was toting from the stacks to the pickup desk. With that interest came an appreciation for the deft use of language that would inspire so much of the material he wrote for radio. Soon he began to stand out among broadcast comedians as the darling of the intelligentsia and literary humorists. Numbered among his admirers were Ring Lardner, John Steinbeck, Gibert Seldes, and James Thurber.[1]

As his popularity grew Allen also developed a reputation as a broadcast industry curmudgeon. He was continually at odds with sponsors and executives who meddled with the content of the show. If Allen made reference to a mythical Long Island town called Dirty Neck, executives would object—what if this name offends residents of real Long Island towns such as Little Neck or Great Neck? To Allen's mind, these corporate office-holders made demands and suggestions just to hear their own voices or see their own memos. A favorite target of his was a breed of advertising vice president that he called a molehill man, "a pseudo-busy executive," Allen later wrote, "who comes to work at 9 A.M. and finds a molehill on his desk. He has until 5 P.M. to make this molehill into a mountain. An accomplished molehill man will often have his mountain finished even before lunch."[2]

For Allen, an especially vexing development in the broadcast business was the migration of talent to Hollywood. In the mid-1930s, listener complacency indicated that radio needed to inject greater glamour into its programming. To accomplish this, broadcasters based more of their shows in Hollywood, where movie personalities could be easily recruited for appearances on the airwaves. Soon, all the major radio comedians were originating their shows in Los Angeles. All except Fred Allen. He had already spent some time in California to appear in some highly forgettable films, and he was not pleased with the lifestyle he found there. "The people here seem to live in a little world that shuts off the rest of the universe and everyone appears to be faking life," he once wrote. He found the setting particularly troublesome for someone in his line of work. "Hollywood is no place for a professional comedian," he concluded. "The amateur competition is too great." In his most famous assessment of West Coast life, he conceded that California was a fine place to live "if you happen to be an orange."[3]

In the summer of 1940, when Hiken and Kibbee went to work for him, Allen was appearing on the CBS network in a weekly hour-long show. Coming up with material for the earlier half-hour incarnation of his program had been difficult enough, but the current writing demands—one hour, thirty-nine times a season—were especially burdensome. The show always bore the Allen stamp but the comedian had long given up on the idea of writing it entirely on his own, as he had done in the very beginning. First, he had hired one young writer, Harry Tugend, to help him assemble the scripts, then a few years later he had taken on two, Arnold Auerbach (who would later write for such television comics as Milton Berle and Jackie Gleason) and Herman Wouk (the future author of *The Caine Mutiny*). Still, Allen wrote the bulk of the show and was the final arbiter of comedic taste and discernment.

When it came to phrasing and choice of words, he had few equals. Once Herman Wouk came up with what he considered a fairly deft *bon mot*, or at least it seemed that way until he shared it with Allen. In the news at the time was an incident in Mexico where, one morning at the break of dawn, actor Lee Tracy concluded a night of boozing by urinating off the terrace to his room. Below him, and directly in the line of fire—or rather, liquid—was a Mexican general, who was understandably miffed by the whole experience. Wouk seized upon the title of a film currently in release—*The General Died at Dawn*—and came up with a line: "The General Dodged at Dawn." When he told the joke to Allen, the comedian immediately corrected him. "No, Herman," he said, "The General *Dried* at Dawn." For Wouk, the single word change demonstrated Allen's mastery of the quipper's art.[4]

It was this reputation of Allen's that had intrigued Hiken and Kibbee when the comedian had contacted them. Allen had not, as it turned out, been the only radio star to take an interest in their work on *The Grouch Club*. Eddie Cantor had also made them an offer. But they decided they had to work for Allen, the medium's great wit.[5]

◆   ◆   ◆

When Nat joined Allen's show, he was making a leap across two dimensions in his life, traversing the continent to relocate from Los Angeles to New York while also bounding from marginal network broadcasting to the heights of big-time radio. Any trepidation he felt at negotiating these two formidable changes was eased somewhat by having his cousin Sandy and his partner Kibbee alongside, making the transitions with him.

At first, Nat's exposure to New York life was circumscribed by his new boss's social habits. This meant that Hiken did not immediately come into contact with the glamorous Gotham nightspots that were so often highlighted in newspaper gossip columns. After work, when Allen would take Nat, Roland, and Sandy to dinner, the comedian tended to stay away from the noisy establishments frequented by other show business personalities, and he had no interest in the Stork Club or any other fashionable emblem of New York's so-called café society. Instead, he would bring his writers to Louie Gino's, a small Italian restaurant on the east side, or the comfortably informal House of Chan on Seventh Avenue off Times Square. On the way to these favorite Allen haunts, Nat would have been likely to witness the comedian's legendary generosity. Allen's habit, before leaving home, was to stuff his pockets with loose one-dollar and five-dollar bills so that he would have handouts at the ready for the panhandlers he would meet on the street, many of whom he knew by name.[6]

While chatting at dinner, Allen tended to turn to the past. Hiken and Kibbee, embarking on a new professional adventure, were focused on the challenges immediately before them, but Allen, after years of feuding with broadcast executives, would often be more interested in talking about his old vaudeville days. He would regale his new writers with stories about the towns he had played and the acts he had followed. "He worried about whatever happened to all those people. He said he wondered what happened to Swayne's Rats and Cats," Sandy remembered. She believed this was a trait shared by Allen and Nat, an instinctive interest in and curiosity about people they encountered, no matter how indirectly. She recalled a time when she and Kibbee had just leased a house from a man named Gorman who was about to be transferred to a new job in Cleveland. After Sandy and Roland had moved in, Gorman's transfer fell through and his family was left without a place to live in New York. "Fred heard about this, and every time he'd see me he'd say, 'Now what happened to the Gormans? Did they find a place?' These people that he never met."[7]

Nat found that his interests intersected with Allen's in other ways, too. These intersections included a love of sports. Boxing was a particular favorite with both men. This was the time of such illustrious champs as Tony Zale and Joe Louis, as well as hard-hitting newcomers such as Jake LaMotta, Sugar Ray Robinson, and Rocky Graziano, who would recharge the sport with a new excitement in just a few years. The worlds of boxing and show business often overlapped at that time, as they had for decades. Back in his vaudeville days, Allen would often travel along the same routes taken by barnstorming fighters. The best known of them—Jack Johnson, Gentleman Jim Corbett, Jack Dempsey—would even appear on the vaudeville stage, either in exhibition bouts or novelty comedy acts.[8] Later, in Hollywood during the 1930s, when movies had left vaudeville in the dust, fighters such as Max Baer and Slapsie Maxie Rosenbloom would make a living as character actors on the screen. New York's Times Square was another junction. With theaters dominating the area and Madison Square Garden a block away on Eighth Avenue, show business people and fight-game mugs would congregate and mingle in the area's nightspots. Allen's passion for pugilism may have been reflected in some of his more pugnacious and bruising one-liners, but Hiken was intrigued by the fighters themselves. In his later television years, he would spin some of his best comedy off their broken-nosed personas.

Hiken and Allen's interest in boxing differed in another significant way. Nat was merely a spectator. Allen would put on the gloves on a regular basis. Each Tuesday he would go to the YMCA on Sixty-third Street and spar with professional boxer Joey LaGrey. His regimen at the gym also included handball, jogging, and medicine-ball tossing. This was his antidote to the pressures of weekly broadcasts, and a safety valve for his escalating blood pressure, an ongoing worry throughout his radio career.[9]

The most important quality Hiken and Allen shared was their approach to comedy, incorporating a wry outlook and an attention to detail that allowed their sensibilities to complement each other. Not all writers assigned to Fred Allen's staff were able to carve a niche for themselves, even some of those who later proved themselves capable on other shows. It was difficult to duplicate the comedian's distinctive approach and meet his exacting standards of excellence. Hiken, despite his modest manner, was able to succeed where others failed and established his position on the program quite early.

Belying his appearance, Nat had his own way of asserting himself in the brash world of broadcast comedy. As a later associate noted, "Nat was quiet but he demanded attention. He realized his own worth and insisted upon getting his due, but he did it nicely, he did it quietly." Terry Ryan, who became part of Allen's writing staff in the mid-1940s, remembered that it was the sharpness of Hiken's ideas itself, rather than his way of presenting his thoughts, that grabbed the attention of those around the writers' conference table. "Nat was extremely creative and fertile," Ryan said. "I remember telling my parents once, 'Jeez, he just began talking like he had only a germinal idea and then sat there developing it as Fred took notes.' He was very spontaneous." [10]

Allen called Nat "The Tramper," a derisive reference to his attire (Nat was known to show up at work in corduroy pants and plaid shirt, hardly *de rigueur* for an up-and-coming Manhattanite). But at the same time Allen's respect for the young writer was growing, and he began to solicit his judgment on crafting the show's sequences. [11]

When not at work and learning the Allen way of putting comedy on the air, Nat continued to pursue a pastime from his Los Angeles days. He piloted his Waco from the West Coast to New York and kept it hangared at Floyd Bennett Field on Brooklyn's south shore in between recreational flights. Before long, though, his time away from the show would be devoted to something else. On his visits to the Kibbee house in Queens, he came to know a pretty, petite young woman named Ambur Dana Salt. [12]

Ambur Dana was born in Kansas but was raised in Los Angeles from the age of six. As a young woman, she found work, as Sandy did, at the nearby movie studios, landing a job in the MGM script department, then moving on to the office of producer Joseph L. Mankiewicz. Like Sandy once again, she was also active in political causes, and it was through these activities that her close friendship began with Nat's cousin. Through politics she also met Nat for the first time, but rather obliquely. One night, while working on *The Grouch Club*, Nat accompanied Sandy to Ambur's house for a meeting of a committee to aid indigent agricultural workers. Ambur was married at the time to MGM screenwriter Waldo Salt. Although the meeting was held at her home, Ambur had to leave early because she received word of her mother's death and was summoned by the sanitarium where her mother had been a patient. "When Waldo and I came back," Ambur recalled, "there was a man in the living room and he was trying to put the remains of a Christmas tree into the fireplace because he was apparently freezing." The man was Nat, but Ambur was too preoccupied to pay him much attention. "The next thing I knew he was lying down on the couch trying to sleep. The committee members were in the other room, in the dinette. I decided it was cold so I got a throw and put it on him. I don't think he ever knew." Understandably, she did not develop much of an impression of him, aside from his striking disinterest in his activist surroundings. Her true meeting with him occurred after her divorce from Salt and after Nat had moved to New York.[13]

She wrote to Sandy about the end of her marriage and the anguish she was going through. Sandy replied by inviting her friend to come stay with her. When Nat would come by to work with Kibbee on the Fred Allen scripts, the four of them would spend evenings together.[14]

It was typical for Nat to meet dates through his cousin Sandy, who described him as lazy when it came to romance. "When he was living with us in California, he went out with every friend of mine, and then he'd complain if I wasn't bringing somebody over that he might ask out for a date. He'd tease me." She added, "But it was *Ambur*. I'd never seen him so smitten with anybody." No longer did Nat needle Sandy about bringing girlfriends for him to meet. He and Ambur married in October 1941.[15]

The couple moved into a single room at the Plymouth Hotel, then took a studio apartment above a travel agency on West 46th Street just a few months later. As enamored as he was with his bride, Nat was not able take his mind off work for very long, especially while groping for some way to make a Fred Allen gag work. When he had finished procrastinating, and the time for the actual writing had come, he would begin his workday at dawn. First, before even rolling out of bed, he would reach for his eyeglasses so that he could find his cigarette pack. With the first of his many smokes for the day, he would be ready to sit before the typewriter. Typical of this period, Ambur recalled waking up early one morning in their single hotel room, roused by the clacking of typewriter keys. She turned to Nat and, even as she struggled to peel her eyelids open, he greeted her with "Hey, does this sound funny?"[16]

Nat's responsibilities on Fred Allen's show increased, but recognition did not always come with the job. In general, the public rarely knew the names of radio comedy writers; the Allen mystique, though, could make the problem especially acute. For Nat, nothing dramatized this more than an incident during one of his cross-country flights. He was on summer hiatus at the time, flying his Waco with a friend, en route to visiting his relatives in both Milwaukee and Los Angeles. During the Milwaukee-to-Los Angeles leg of the trip, while flying past the Grand Canyon, Nat encountered a severe storm. He searched for a place to set down along the desolate, rugged landscape. Finally, up ahead, he spotted a flat stretch that resembled an airstrip. He brought the plane in for a landing, but the ground was muddy and, as the plane swerved, he plowed into a tree. He found himself stranded in the middle of the Walapai Indian reservation, on a patch of land that had just been cleared for an upcoming rodeo. Fortunately, he and his companion soon met up with a group of Walapais who were eager to help. When they were brought to shelter, the stranded fliers sat and talked with some of the tribal elders, one of whom asked Nat what he did for a living. "I write for the Fred Allen show," he said. One of the Walapais snickered. What was so funny, Nat wanted to know. The Walapai answered, "Everybody knows Fred Allen writes his own material." [17]

This story became a favorite along Broadway where it was often retold and embellished. For people in show business, the anecdote became part of the lore concerning the writer's plight. For Hiken's family, though, the incident had a much less humorous dimension. Not only did Nat fail to arrive in Los Angeles on schedule but he was unable to reach a telephone and let his relatives know what had happened. The Los Angeles branch of the family was wracked with worry and remained so until Nat and his friend finally reached the city, looking, according to Ambur, "like Jesus and John the Baptist, bearded and completely unkempt by that time." [18]

To his family's relief, Nat's flying came to an end soon after his wedding, but it took the outbreak of World War II to do it. As part of his civic duty, Nat donated his Waco to the Army for use in civilian reconnaissance as the nation guarded against Axis activities along its shores. How much further his duties as a young male citizen would take him remained an open question for nearly two years. His writing partner, Kibbee, was inducted into the Army Air Force, where he became both a pilot and flight instructor. With his own flying experience, Nat might have followed a similar route, but his acute nearsightedness disqualified him. For some time, it looked like he might not become part of the war effort at all; he was repeatedly called in for physicals and judged unfit for service. Finally, in the summer of 1943, while he and Ambur were vacationing in Los Angeles, the Army decided to look him over once more and concluded that they had some use for him after all. He was inducted on September 10. His branch of service turned out to be the Air Force, but he would not come anywhere near a cockpit. Instead, his service on the front lines amounted to working as an advance man for a Broadway musical. [19]

The Army assigned Nat to work as one of the publicists for *Winged Victory*, a show produced by the Air Force as both a morale booster and fund-raiser for Army Emergency Relief. The play, written and directed by Moss Hart, focused on members of a bomber's crew, from their induction through their training and first mission. As was also the case with many war films of that period, *Winged Victory* featured a regional cross-section of freedom-loving Americans—a farmboy from Oregon, a rustic from Texas, a kid from Brooklyn named Irving—who all learn to pull together as a team, although Hart's warriors learn to pull together between an occasional rousing show tune concocted by Hollywood composer David Rose. The male actors were recruited from the air force ranks. Some, such as Lee J. Cobb and Alan Baxter, were already established performers, while others, such as Edmund O'Brien and Red Buttons, were still unknowns.

The play opened at New York's Forty-fourth Street Theatre in November, just two months after Hiken's induction. His job as public-relations man could not have been terribly taxing. Because the play was, in effect, a military operation in wartime, journalists did not need much coaxing to give the show favorable coverage. The reviewer for the usually circumspect *New York Times* was especially effusive. He described *Winged Victory* as "a stirring, moving and, what is more important, a most human play," and frequently took the opportunity in his critique to praise the larger war effort, commenting that the Air Force was "obviously breeding group acting along with well coordinated bomber crews." [20]

On occasion, Hiken would have to travel, acting as advance man for the road company version of the show. Mostly, though, he remained in New York with much time to spare. And what exactly he was doing while on duty was sometimes unclear. "Don't ask what he did," said Nat's cousin, Peter Levin, also in uniform and posted in New York at the time. "As a matter of fact, *he* couldn't tell me what he did." Nat's schedule was so loose, in fact, that beginning in December he had time and approval from his superiors to continue writing for Fred Allen. The absurdity of his distinctly unmilitary military service was not lost on Nat. He was fond of telling the story of how the *Winged Victory* troupe would arrive for the day's performance. To maintain at least a semblance of martial discipline, they would march, in uniform and in formation, down Broadway toward the theater. As the procession surged by, women would watch and weep, under the impression that the boys in uniform were marching off to war instead of to the Broadway footlights. [21]

The war ended without making much of a dent in Hiken's life. He was discharged, as a sergeant, five months after Japan's surrender, on January 3, 1946. His work on the Allen show, meanwhile, had undergone some significant changes.

First was a matter of format. After eight years as an hour-long program, the show had reverted to a half-hour length in the fall of 1942. With the change in duration had come the debut of the radio star's most famous invention, Allen's Alley. This segment combined Allen's flair for topical humor and his appreciation of ethnic and regional types. Each week he would stroll down the Alley with a question on his lips about some current concern, from the postwar housing shortage to the breakup of Benny Goodman's band. Knocking at each door, he would solicit comments on the issue from the Alley's residents, an incongruous assortment of people who could only live together in the imagination of radio listeners. The cast of characters evolved over the years but the most famous Alley residents were Mrs. Nussbaum (played by Minerva Pious), a Yiddish-accented housewife; Titus Moody (Parker Fennelly), a dry, tight-lipped New Englander; Ajax Cassidy (Peter Donald), a ne'er-do-well Irishman; and Senator Claghorn (Kenny Delmar), a blustering, filibustering Dixiecrat, whose idiosyncratic speech pattern ("Somebody, I say, somebody knocked!") would be popularized for later TV generations in the form of Foghorn Leghorn, a Loony Tunes rooster modeled after the windbag senator.

Allen's Alley helped revitalize interest in a program that had already been attracting more than 20 million listeners. The Alley provided a thread that wove through the series from one season to the next, presenting characters that could elicit laughs by merely making an entrance. In the process, Allen's Alley introduced catchphrases into the national idiom, primarily courtesy of the ever-voluble Claghorn, who would be featured on recorded songs ("I'm in Love, That Is") and in films (*It's a Joke, Son*). A cloud, though, hovered above this renewed success: Allen's health. His blood pressure climbed to such an alarming degree that his doctor ordered him to take a sabbatical from the airwaves for the 1944–45 season. Still, the show returned a year later—on its original network, NBC—as popular as before, part of a memorable Sunday night lineup of NBC programming that also included Jack Benny and Edgar Bergen.[22]

As the new format took hold, Nat's standing on the Allen show solidified, not only while putting together the script but at rehearsal as well. The scripts typically ran long, and at rehearsals Allen would have to decide where to cut. His writers sat in the control booth, ready to offer suggestions. Grey Lockwood, on hand as an NBC page boy at this time, observed that "Fred Allen was always talking to Nat. He leaned on him."[23]

During script meetings, Hiken contributed ideas to all portions of the program, but writing the closing sketch became his primary responsibility. Although Allen's Alley stood out as the program's signature segment, the sketches, drafted by Hiken and revised by Allen, would typically deliver the biggest laughs. In another sign of the stature he had attained, Nat was given the task of reworking material turned in by the show's less experienced writers before they would be relayed to Allen for final polishing. Like his boss, Nat became known for his ability to add a seemingly small element to a routine that would make it shine. Whereas Allen focused on the choice of words, Nat would often think in more conceptual terms. Looking back on his days as an Allen staff writer, Aaron Ruben recalled that he could become frustrated by his inability to keep up with Hiken's ingenuity. Once, he and another junior writer were working on a routine about a crackpot inventor who has designed skyscrapers to be built downward into the ground—*earth*scrapers, in other words. "We turned in our stuff to Nat and he looked it over and he added a joke. He said, 'You construct buildings downward, then if somebody dies you just throw him out the window.' When I heard that, I said to myself, 'Damn it, why didn't I think of that.' I found myself saying that quite often. He just had this oblique way of looking at things."[24]

Brainstorming for an episode would begin on Saturday morning, eight days before airing. Allen and his writers would meet the next week's guest star and then convene at Allen's Alwyn Court apartment on West 58th Street to outline ideas for Allen's interview with the guest and the sketch that would follow. Over the next few days, they would all collect news clips with joke potential, which would be pooled together at the NBC offices on Wednesday. Out of this topical material would come Allen's opening remarks, his patter with Portland Hoffa (his wife and long-standing costar), and the Allen's Alley gags. These segments would be compiled by Allen based upon suggestions from his staff and, of course, his own consummate comedic judgment. By Thursday, the staff turned in their pages, and on Friday morning Allen's final version of the script would be discussed and fine-tuned. Rehearsal took place later in the day. Here, Allen, ever the stickler, would seize upon the slightest imprecision in phrasing. "Adjectives! Jesus, we'd go over a script and he'd really consider each and every little word," remembered Terry Ryan. When all adjectives met with the comedian's approval, Allen and his cast would be ready to broadcast the program at Radio City's Studio 8-H. Recorded shows and tape delays were not an accepted practice at the major networks at the time, so the cast would broadcast the show once at 8:30 for the East Coast and again at 11:30 to supply a live rendition for West Coast prime time.[25]

When he was not at meetings, Nat's work method was, as always, an exercise in creative brinkmanship. He had to deliver his draft of the sketch to

Allen's apartment by noon on Thursday. He did not actually start writing until earlier that morning. Ruben was flabbergasted by this approach. "I'd say, 'Jesus, how can you work against such a tight deadline?' And he'd say, 'Well, I've been thinking about it.' I know now how that works. You think about certain jokes and then they kind of form in your mind, but you still haven't written it. Thursday morning he'd get up at six o'clock and finally start working on the damn sketch. A terrible procrastinator. but what came out was brilliant."[26]

With Allen's writing as an example to follow, Hiken sharpened his satiric edge and refined his talent for devising sketches. It is easy to imagine where the common ground lay between Allen the caustic wit and Hiken the *Grouch Club* creator. At the collaboration's fiercest was a 1946 parody of cheerful morning radio shows, exactly the sort of program to which *The Grouch Club* originally served as a counterpoint.

For this skit, Allen and his guest Tallulah Bankhead portrayed the stereotypical morning-airwaves couple of the day, broadcasting from their picture-perfect home, oozing endearments for each other while surrounded by their frightfully adorable family. Allen arrives at the breakfast table, waited upon by his solicitous wife, Bankhead. Every comment about their wonderful life together is accompanied by a related, and transparent, commercial plug: Allen mentions how well he slept ("Thanks to our wonderful Pasternak pussywillow, factory-tested mattress!"); his precious little girl gushes over her single gleaming tooth ("I brushed it with Dr. Pratt's homogenized toothpaste!"); Bankhead notices how happily their canary chirps ("He knows that the newspaper on the bottom of his cage is New York's leading daily!"). Once this scene is played out, Allen and Bankhead reprise the routine, demonstrating how the couple would act in the real world. The husband and wife fire murderous insults at each other as well as their sponsors, from the very second that Bankhead badgers Allen out of his fitful night sleep. The hate-fest only gets worse and within a minute Allen is smacking around his little girl and gunning down both his wife and canary. A vivid reminder that irreverent broadcast humor did not begin with *Saturday Night Live*.[27]

Although this skit may be a definitive example of the Allen show at its most acerbic, most of Hiken's work was not nearly as aggressive. Typically, he would come up with smart, playful slants on current trends or guest stars' personas. When austere concert violinist Albert Spalding appeared on the show, for instance, he auditioned for "Lum Allen and His Barefoot Bobcats," Fred's new hillbilly band. When Edward Everett Horton guest-starred, Allen discovered the masterfully prissy character actor living in a flophouse on the Bowery.

As the scene unfolds, Horton declares that his seedy surroundings are merely part of a calculated career move. He announces that he can no longer tolerate playing prim floorwalkers with gardenias sprouting from his lapel. Instead, he intends to transform himself into a tough guy, another Bogart. The sketch ends with an enactment of Horton's dream vehicle: *Nasty Eddie—Beast of the Underworld!* "Stick them up, fellows. Reach for the murals," Horton entreats his gangland rivals in what he considers a hard-boiled highlight.[28]

Hiken seized upon the appearance of Russian actor-director Gregory Ratoff as an opportunity for some cross-cultural incongruity. In the final portion of the program, Ratoff and Allen present typical American radio shows as they would be adapted for Russian audiences. Among the parodies is a gossip report featuring Waldovich Winchelkovich. Portrayed by Allen in the rat-tat-tat style familiar to all listeners of Walter Winchell, the commentator enthuses about "the blessed event" visited upon the former Miss Collective Farms 1937; in a salacious blind item, he crows, "What assistant district manager of what tractor combine is making a fool of himself over that little blond steel puddler from Kachov?" Also included in Hiken's transpositions is a radio soap opera. Because this is a Russian serial drama, the laughably puny suffering found in American programs of this kind would be grossly inadequate. Only Russian-sized suffering would be in order for the soap opera entitled "Just Plain Mischa."

Accompanied by the weary strains of "Volga Boatmen," Mischa (Ratoff) visits his sweetheart Mascha (Minerva Pious) in her crowded hovel of a home. He is told that her family is waiting. "Waiting for what?" Mischa asks. "The inevitable," Mascha replies matter of factly. "In Russia what else is there to wait for?" Mischa gets a full review of the nagging troubles faced by his girlfriend's family, from Grandpapa's habit of sitting with his legs in the fire for the simple pleasure of keeping warm, to the regrettable necessity of eating beloved Uncle Igor for dinner. At this less than opportune moment, Mischa springs some news. Naturally, the news is bad: he is giving Mascha up for a much richer woman. Mascha responds, quite nonchalantly, by getting her former beau to drink a glass of poisoned tea. Once he has imbibed the lethal liquid, Mischa objects: How dare she serve tea in Russia without lemon? He tells Mascha to drop dead—which she promptly does, without giving the matter so much as a second thought.[29]

In one of the *Fred Allen Show*'s most famous sketches, Hiken managed to dovetail baseball and Gilbert and Sullivan, two of his great passions. The guest this week in the fall of 1945 was Leo Durocher, player-manager for the Brooklyn Dodgers. Hiken recast Leo the Lip, perhaps the most argumentative and abusive baseball figure of his day, as the star of a new operetta entitled "The Brooklyn Pinafore." Durocher, paralleling the role of *Pinafore*'s Captain Corcoran, opens the presentation by addressing his men in song. Allen the narrator describes the tableau: the players kneel around the Lip in a semicircle beside home plate, the infielders holding lavender bats, the outfielders strumming mandolins with mother of pearl picks. Before long, Durocher discovers his beloved mystery girl in the stands, portrayed by Allen-show regular, and future Tony and Oscar winner, Shirley Booth. In a variation of Little Buttercup's introductory ditty, she announces herself and her love for the Dodger captain in a Brooklyn accent as thick as mustard on a Nathan's hot dog: "I'm called Little Bobby Sox—sweet Little Bobby Sox/My heart for you, Lippy, could boist . . ." But romance in operettas is never simple and "Brooklyn Pinafore" is no exception. Social propriety prevents Durocher from marrying Little Bobby Sox—her father, it turns out, is an umpire! Worse, her father is Cockeye Allen, the Lip's most hated enemy. In the end, though, true love triumphs, aided by a song from Allen in which he explains himself to his future son-in-law. Borrowing from the Rt. Hon. Joseph Porter's autobiographical tune, Cockeye confirms every Brooklyn fan's suspicions about his profession with the opening lines "When I was a lad I could not see/A hand held up in front of me." In a later verse:

> As the years went by I grew up a schnook,
> My eyes were so bad I couldn't read a book.
> The Army took me but they sent me back
> When I tried to kiss the general because I thought he was a WAC.
> I'm still half-blind with no physique,
> That's why I'm an umpire in the National League.[30]

Sketches like these earned Hiken a reputation in the broadcast industry, even if his contributions to the show were invisible to the public. Allen appreciated him perhaps most of all. By the mid-forties Ambur could see the comedian's reliance on her husband during off-hours. "I remember those long telephone calls. We would go to a movie and I got awfully used to waiting outside the telephone booth because that was when Nate was supposed to call

Fred and talk about what the next week's show was going to be." Articles written about the show at the time may not have acknowledged it, but Hiken had become, in effect, Allen's head writer. Further bolstering the connection between the two men was Nat's choice of lawyer, Arthur Hershkowitz, who was married to the sister of Allen's wife, Portland.

Hiken and Allen would occasionally socialize, eating at Allen's favorite restaurants, sometimes playing low-stakes poker at Allen's apartment, or, at Nat's suggestion, going downtown to the Second Avenue Yiddish Theater to see the great Jewish comedian Minasha Skulnick. Although the friendship between them primarily revolved around their work, the relationship was nevertheless close, according to other writers on the show. It was close enough, in fact, that observers drew upon a father-son analogy when describing the star and head writer. The analogy becomes especially apt if it encompasses the tension that can sometimes develop between fathers and sons. Nat was quick to give his boss due credit, telling his wife that Allen would have been perfectly capable of writing the entire show himself if the weekly grind had not placed too much of a burden on him. As for the popular perception that Allen created the show on his own, Nat professed that he did not care; he was in it only for the money, he would say. But he must have rankled at the situation to some extent. For Allen's part, there was some ambivalence as well. "Fred was quite dependent on Nat and I think he resented that," commented Aaron Ruben. "There was never any open hostility between them—I certainly didn't see any—but underneath I'm sure the resentment was there because Nat came in with those brilliant parodies. They were really the best part of the show."[31]

Exactly how Allen's resentment was expressed is not clear, but Ruben's experience as a writer on the program provides a glimpse of the testy side of the star, a generous, admired man whose name was often coupled with the adjectives "dour" and "prickly" when described by acquaintances. Ruben's entrée to the program originated with his marriage to Nat's cousin Sandy, recently divorced from Roland Kibbee, who had left the Allen show for other radio work. Ruben and Nat struck up a friendship that led to Nat's encouraging his cousin-by-marriage to pursue comedy writing. When there was an opening on *The Fred Allen Show* staff in 1945, Nat suggested that Ruben should fill the position, and Allen went along with the idea. But not without offering an Allenesque appraisal. Upon Ruben's arrival, he cracked, "What're we going to do when Sandy runs out of husbands?" This set the tone for what was to come.[32]

Early on, Ruben learned about Allen's unswerving loyalty to those comedians he liked and his fierce antagonism toward those he did not. One of Allen's favorite guest stars was George Jessel, whom he considered a true wit. Another favorite was Doc Rockwell, an old friend from his vaudeville days and a fellow New Englander, who specialized in absurd, pseudoscholarly lectures (and whose son turned out to be the considerably less amusing George Lincoln Rockwell, the American Nazi leader assassinated in 1967). Eddie Cantor, on the other hand, Allen hated. He dismissed him as "the dean of bad taste," a hack comic who relied solely on tired schtick, which was also how he characterized Milton Berle. Once, Ruben made the mistake of suggesting a comedian named Jimmy Savo as a potential guest. "A cute little guy," Ruben recalled. "He did parodies and he really was a nightclub favorite. I mentioned his name and I almost had my head taken off." Allen's reaction may have been exacerbated by the perception that Ruben was a nepotistic hireling, but the intimidating manner was not uncommon. Soon, Ruben got into the habit of keeping his mouth shut. Allen made no effort to draw him out.[33]

Ruben regarded his boss as the radio comedy master, but his association with the man did not last long. "Even before the season was over," Ruben remembered,

> Fred said to Nat, "I want to try some new writers," which meant, "You got to let Aaron go." So Nat came to me, feeling absolutely terrible about it, and he said, "Fred wants to try somebody new, but you can stay for the season." I said, "I'm leaving at the end of the week, are you crazy?" Several years later, when I was doing pretty well—I'd come up with the Henry Morgan show and a couple of other things—Fred said to somebody, "I'm surprised he's doing well because he was very quiet at the table. He never opened his mouth." He simply didn't know what terror he could instill in people.[34]

Nat's experience was not nearly as severe, although on at least one occasion it was vexing enough that he threatened to quit. For the time being, the prestige that went with writing for the Allen show was sufficient compensation for whatever annoyances he had to tolerate. Besides, he had found ways to divert himself from the rigors of the show's deadlines and the nettlesome manner of his mentor. He was cultivating a rich social life centered in the bustling Broadway scene—even if he was reluctant to mention it in Allen's presence. (The comedian would brood if he learned that his writers, unlike himself, did something else other than crafting jokes for next week's show.)[35] The gathering spots Nat frequented, and the camaraderie he found there, were not only a re-laxing respite but also a stimulant for his comedic ideas.

◆   ◆   ◆

Twenty years had passed since Damon Runyon had first mythified the Great White Way in such stories as "Little Miss Marker" and "Bloodhounds of Broadway." Even so, by the mid-1940s, enough of the old Times Square lin-gered to warrant describing much of it as Runyonesque.

At 51st Street and Broadway there still stood Lindy's delicatessen, a setting for so many of Runyon's tales, ever so thinly disguised by the author as "Mindy's." Under the stewardship of Leo Linderman, the place continued to attract a boisterous crowd of entertainers, columnists, publicists, and sports figures, as well as an assortment of other characters whose livelihood was not quite so obvious. Also remaining on hand were the waiters famous for their snappy quips (although one patron, writer-actor Heywood Hale Broun, main-tained that the waiters were more rude than witty). A comparable bastion of culture could be found a few blocks uptown at the area's great educational in-stitution. Stillman's Gym, on Eighth Avenue above 54th Street, reigned as the prizefighters' Sorbonne, where both champs and upstarts honed their slug-gers' craft. For aficionados of Times Square ambience, it also held another dis-tinction. With its clientele of pugs and gamblers, trainers and mobsters, sporting nicknames like Whitey, Beau Jack, and Racehorse, the place could pass for a living setpiece from *Guys and Dolls*.[36]

For more gaudy tastes, the area still pulsed with a garish nightlife. New York was in the midst of its great nightclub era, and along Broadway the delirious mix of alcohol and entertainment could be found at such legendary spots as Billy Rose's Diamond Horseshoe and the Latin Quarter. There, customers could take in such headliners as Milton Berle and Mae West during intervals in the procession of shimmy dancers, Apache dancers, gymnasts, and nearly naked showgirls. Also perpetuating the Times Square style were the renowned Broadway restaurants, known better for their atmosphere than their food: Sardi's, the definitive theatrical meeting place; Toots Shor's, a favorite come-dians' hangout; and Jack Dempsey's, the fight-game watering hole.[37]

Nat would schmooze with friends at Lindy's, the Stage Deli, and, after Sun-day night broadcasts, at Shor's. When at Lindy's, though too much of a new-comer to rate inclusion at this point, he would have been within earshot of the celebrated "Long Table," where conversation amounted to a contest of comedic one-upmanship, a sort of Borscht Belt equivalent of the Algonquin Hotel's Round Table.

When not patronizing his favorite hangouts, Nat and his friends would unwind with games of poker and gin. His friends generally were those people who amused him. Some were fellow comedy writers, such as Jay Burton or Goodman Ace. Many of them were press agents.[38]

By the mid-forties, the occupational title of public-relations counsel was coming into vogue for many in the publicity field, but the flacks that Nat palled around with did not have much use for such gentrified terms. As one unabashed press agent of the old school once explained, "A public relations man has an office. For a press agent, a phone booth is his office." Some press agents were aspiring gag writers whose job was to invent funny quotes for their clients. Other flacks were funny unintentionally. Always hustling to get their clients' names in print, they were often driven to oddball extremes. Comedy writer Leonard Stern zeroed in on what it was about press agents that appealed to Nat and struck him as so amusing: "Their pronounced desperate behavior. It was very apparent. The eyes always searching for a story. They couldn't cloak their anxieties."[39]

Much of the desperation was focused on Walter Winchell, the lord almighty of Broadway columnists. Get your client mentioned in his column and you were golden. Cross him somehow and you landed on his Drop Dead List, nothing less than professional Siberia. As Neal Gabler makes clear in his biography of the columnist, Winchell-toadying knew no bounds in those days. Sid Garfield, one of Hiken's closest press-agent friends, was sitting with Winchell in a night club one evening, when he noticed the columnist admiring a couple on the dance floor performing the rhumba. Winchell mentioned how much he enjoyed watching them. Garfield piped up with, "Look, Walter. I'm enjoying them too." A Hiken acquaintance named Jack Tirman figured into another well-circulated Winchell tale. Tirman found himself one day among a group of fellow press agents who had the nerve to swap complaints about the columnist king. Tirman grew fearful. Looking heavenward, he cried, "I'm not listening, Walter!"[40]

Underscoring Winchell's near supernatural reputation was an anecdote from Coleman Jacoby, one of many publicists who later graduated to comedy scripting. Jacoby and another press agent had just finished a night's work in Brooklyn promoting a Sheepshead Bay seafood restaurant and were riding back to Manhattan in a cab.

It's three in the morning and it's a rainy night that's like something out of an English murder story. The other guy said, "Coleman," and he drops his voice, "I heard something today about Winchell you won't believe . . . " And he looked around the cab and he looked out the back window, and then he told some piece of scandal about Winchell, all the time dropping his voice. I don't know *what* he was thinking. Did he think Winchell was sitting on the trunk of the cab?

Jacoby added, "These are the kinds of stories Nat would listen to and he'd *kvell.*"[41]

Jacoby observed that it could be both colorful antics and small quirks of behavior that would delight Nat and nourish his ideas for funny characterizations. Milton Berger was a press agent who drew Nat's attention on both counts. First, Nat appreciated the shamelessly fraudulent tactics that Berger employed. A flack of the old order, Berger was one of the last to rely on outlandish publicity stunts. Once while representing Charles Atlas, king of the bodybuilding correspondence courses, Berger met a married couple on the verge of breaking up. Someone else might have seen the tragedy of the situation. Berger saw an opportunity. He offered to pay for the couple's divorce, and in return, the couple cited Atlas as the cause for the split-up: after getting a glimpse of Atlas's he-man physique, the wife simply could not have anything further to do with her shrimp of a husband.[42]

Besides the press agent's outrageous scams, Hiken was also amused by Berger himself. One day, Jacoby accompanied Nat to Berger's office, where Hiken considered subletting a portion of the press agent's space. "Berger overdid everything—that was his problem," Jacoby recalled. "When Nat first came to talk about renting the office, Berger says, 'Nat, give me your coat. Here, take off your shoes. I got shoe trees.' He's got shoe trees! That made Nat's day. Berger was always bending over backwards. He was the kind of guy, if the Nazis took over, he'd say, 'I *used* to be a Jew.' "[43]

The press agents closest to Nat were those who were aware of their idiosyncrasies and were able to rib themselves. Sid Garfield, the flack who was so eager to agree with Winchell, was known as an ebullient man with a quick mind that he put to work for such clients as Paramount Pictures, bandleader Artie Shaw, and, in the 1950s, CBS Radio. His wry acknowledgment of his nervous kowtowing and his compulsive gambling endeared him to Nat and the rest of his Broadway cronies. Other publicists in Hiken's circle of friends were more overtly humorous, masters of the snappy comeback so closely associated with Times Square banter. Bernie Green, a rep for Warner Bros. and various Broadway cafés, was considered enough of a wit to emcee events sponsored by press-agent organizations. Among friends and acquaintances, he had a reputation for brittle impatience. Once his patience was sorely tried by another publicist named Paul Benson.

Whenever he had someone to listen, Benson would rave about his dog, which he named Boy. Always there was a new story about this remarkable creature of his, and each one rankled the querulous Green, who, according to Jacoby,

> had a very low threshold for that sort of thing. Bernie had been hearing about Boy for so long and finally he'd had it up to here with it. One day, they all met at Lindy's and got around Nat to listen to his stories, and Paul came in. He started talking about Boy, and Bernie Green pulled out a picture of his twelve-year-old kid. "Oh by the way, Paul," he said. "This is my poodle. He's going to be barmitzvahed next Saturday." Benson never talked to him again.[44]

Hiken and his friends could be a prankish bunch. One of their targets was Richard Himber, a well-known bandleader of the day. Himber moved in rarified circles, performing at the most elegant social occasions and living at the upper-crust Hotel Pierre on Fifth Avenue. What was most important to Nat and his friends, though, was Himber's reluctance to admit he was Jewish. They placed an ad in the *Daily Forward*, the Yiddish Socialist newspaper. The ad read: "Wanted—Jewish types to appear in Broadway show. Apply R. Himber, Hotel Pierre." The response was immediate. The next day, the Hotel Pierre lobby was mobbed with Yiddish types waving copies of the *Forward*, crying, "Meester Himbair . . . Meester Himbair. . ."[45]

Mostly, though, Nat and his friends passed the time sitting in restaurants, swapping stories about baseball, boxing, show business, real-life misadventures (embroidered perhaps for maximum effect). Aaron Ruben, only an occasional guest at these sessions, discovered one day at Lindy's that conversation could become almost ritualistic. One of the men at the table began a story, one that Ruben had heard him tell before. Ruben made the mistake of saying as much. "Nat put his hand on mine, very quickly. He shook his head, as if to say, 'No, don't, don't. Sure we heard it but what difference?' The idea was to tell the stories as many times as you needed to." But not all tales were equal in Nat's eyes. If the talker tried his patience, he was not shy about letting him know. In an instance that would be recounted within Broadway circles, an acquaintance once cornered Nat with an exceptionally long and pointless anecdote. When the long-winded raconteur paused for an instant to take a breath, Nat quickly put in, "What's the matter, cat got your tongue?"[46]

Nat himself would often indulge in verbal reruns of his own when out with Ambur, Sandy, and Aaron. Ambur, no doubt embarrassed by his apparent forgetfulness, would sometimes point out that he was repeating himself. "But he'd love to tell a story over and over again," Ruben recalled. "And it always got better in the retelling."[47]

◆   ◆   ◆

By 1946, Nat realized that if he were going to tell his own stories over the airwaves, he would have to make a decision about his long-standing partnership with Fred Allen. Like Arnold Auerbach and Herman Wouk, two earlier Allen favorites, he came to believe that he had gone as far as he could on the Allen show. Auerbach had left to pursue screenwriting prospects in Hollywood. Wouk had moved on to try his hand at dramatic plays and novels. Hiken wanted to create and control his own radio program. Beyond the creative satisfaction, he was also eager for a boost in pay. A year earlier his first child was born, a daughter named Dana, and the family was likely to get larger. Besides, as he put it to Ambur, "Seven years as an indentured servant is enough."[48]

When he learned that other producers were interested in his services, Hiken decided the time had come to let his boss know that he intended to leave the show. The prospect of broaching the subject with Allen could not have rested easy on Nat's mind. The waspish comedian's reaction could be difficult to face. But when Nat finally met with him, Allen was quite understanding, truly like the benign father figure he often appeared to be. He sympathized with Nat's desire to be his own boss and encouraged him to move on to his next challenge. If Nat had any doubts about Allen's sincerity, they were dispelled in the spring of 1947, on the night of his last show. As usual, to commemorate the completion of a successful broadcast, he accompanied Allen to Toots Shor's. There a sportswriter, friend to both Nat and Fred, stepped over to their table and said that Hiken was making a mistake leaving the Allen program. Allen would not hear of it. "Oh no," he said, "he's got to go on to the next thing. He's doing what he has to do."[49]

As amicable as it all seemed, Allen was capable of powerful, bitter brooding. Auerbach, who had worked closely with the comedian for five years, noted in his memoir that Allen, a childless man, nurtured and defended his show as if it were his baby. When a trusted lieutenant left the program, he did not merely upset Allen's routine; he "jarred the pram." Months later, after starting work on his new show, Hiken learned for himself exactly how strong these quasi-parental feelings could be.[50]

He was headed toward the RCA building to attend a cast reading of his latest script. With him was Aaron Ruben, his writing partner. "As we approached the revolving doors," Ruben recalled, "Fred was coming out. Nat smiled and said, 'Hi, Fred.' And Fred walked right past him. Cut him dead."[51]

Not Quite Mr. Television

In 1947, when Nat Hiken set out on his own, a revolution in broadcasting loomed on the horizon. A new technology was about to bring an unprecedented visual dimension to electronic communications and overhaul the way information and entertainment could be transmitted instantaneously to millions of people.

Nat was not impressed. Neither were many other creative people in radio.

Television had first been showcased, to spellbound crowds, eight years earlier at the New York World's Fair. World War II had compelled broadcasters to put their marketing campaign for the new medium on hold, but now, with peace and potential prosperity at hand, the networks forged ahead once again. Even though progress was slow—in 1947 only 135,000 sets were in use—broadcasters were at least beginning to find ways to fill their schedules and reach a variety of audiences. Stations offered *Howdy Doody* for babyboom children, *Kraft Television Theatre* for drama aficionados, and pro wrestling for connoisseurs of artful mauling. Still, most broadcast people thought in audio terms.[1]

Like most writers and directors in the field, Nat saw radio as an entertainment vehicle already refined by years of creative trial and error, a form for serious-minded craftsmen. For him and others like him, television was nothing more than a gimmick. Radio stars had even more reason to stand pat. After years on the air, performers such as Jack Benny and Fred Allen had relied on their voices to etch their winning personas into the public's mind; they were not inclined to tamper with success.

For adventurous creators in the business, television may have offered a bracing challenge, but Nat was content to embrace a task on more familiar terrain that was perhaps just as formidable. He went to work for Milton Berle.

At this point, even the future Mr. Television was still angling for high ratings over the audio airwaves. In a year, Berle would dominate and energize the new video medium, but for now he, along with his sponsor Philip Morris, was searching for a successful radio format. Hiken's challenge was to conjure up a hit for a comedian bedeviled by eleven years of broadcasting flops.

At thirty-nine, Milton Berle was a headliner both on stage and in nightclubs. A few years earlier he had starred in the latest Broadway edition of the vaudeville-style *Ziegfeld Follies,* and he had recently performed for a record forty-six weeks at New York's Carnival Club. Described by the *New York Times* as "an after-dark idol in Broadway social circles," he could have easily continued on the nightclub circuit and made a handsome living at it. But he was intent upon establishing himself in radio, no matter how ill suited his comedy style might have been for the audio medium.[2]

In his vaudeville and club acts, he was brash and breezy, constantly on the move, careening from wisecrack to take to double take. He had to be seen to be appreciated. Whenever he tried to filter his physical comedy through the radio microphone, the results were distinctly less uproarious. Of course, the concepts of his radio shows had not helped much either. At their best, they could be merely insipid. *The Gillette Original Community Sing,* for instance, amounted to nothing more than a series of jokes alternating with audience sing-alongs led by a duo called the Happiness Boys. At their worst—namely, *Let Yourself Go*—the concept could be a colossal misjudgment. For this broadcast curiosity, Berle invited contestants to come on stage and act out whatever stunt they had always secretly wanted to perform, no matter how outrageous. Typically, the contestants would *do* something—such as cracking an egg on Berle's head—as opposed to *saying* something. In short, a radio show based on sight gags. It did not last long.[3]

When Hiken contracted to create a new program for Berle, the comedian had compiled an unbroken string of six radio failures. These defeats did not discourage the ever competitive Berle; they only made him more determined than ever to conquer the broadcasting field. In fact, he turned down an engagement at the Roxy Theater, paying $25,000 a week, to appear for around one-sixth of that price on his new Philip Morris show.[4]

For Hiken, the new series promised a long-awaited creative independence. His status as the top hired scripter on *The Fred Allen Show* had been known only among show business insiders, but on *The Milton Berle Show*, he was clearly recognized as the head writer and was given the power to mold the program as he saw fit. To help him with his new task, he brought in Aaron Ruben.[5]

Berle turned to Hiken because of the former Allen-show writer's reputation. But, anxious as the comedian was to win raves and ratings with this show, he might very well have been dismayed if he had witnessed how Nat actually went about crafting a formula for success. Often he and Ruben would meet at their office to schmooze at length about a wide variety of subjects, none of which included the show. As Ruben recalled it, "By now it's suddenly four o'clock and Nat says, 'Well, it's too late to do anything, maybe we'd better meet tomorrow.' " Often they would come up with sketches—such as one involving Ruben imitating President Truman as a Yiddish-speaking New Yorker—but only for their own amusement, not anything that could possibly be put on the air.[6]

Even though verbal detours seemed to derail office sessions, the back of Nat's mind somehow remained on track, and the Berle show began to take shape. Nat steered clear of the sort of labored gimmicks that had typified previous Berle programs such as *Let Yourself Go*. Instead, he focused on adapting a conventional comedy-program format to showcase the aggressive comic at his funniest. Unlike Fred Allen, Nat was amused by Berle and appreciated his headlong approach. As Ruben saw it, "One of Nat's great talents was how versatile he was. He could write for a brilliant satirist and wit like Allen, and then he could also write for somebody like Berle, who was sometimes very burlesquey. Not that it was lowdown—just a different order."[7]

As with the Fred Allen and Jack Benny shows, Hiken's format for Berle opened with banter between the comedian and his announcer, followed by interaction with recurring characters (including a variation on Allen's Alley called Forum Tonight, in which fictitious audience members questioned the star on the topic of the week). This was succeeded, in turn, by a musical interlude and then a closing sketch. From the outset, Nat engendered some sympathy for the star by pitting him against an announcer who was constantly demeaning. Frank Gallop was known for his austere introductions to the New York Philharmonic broadcasts, delivered in deep, funereal tones. On the Berle show he fired one acerbic shot after another at the star, declining to address him as Mr. Berle or as Milton, but merely as *Berle*, as if it pained him to let the name pass his lips. Few other people could have made the manic, combative comedian seem like an underdog.

and I used one of my favorite James Thurber lines from one of his cartoons where this guy says, "It's a young, naïve, domestic burgundy but I think you'll be amused by its presumption." Ruth burst out laughing—and that was all Milton had to hear, a laugh that he did not create. So he whipped around and said, "What? What? What did he say?" I knew this was not the kind of joke that was up Milton's alley, so I said, "No, nothing, Milt." "C'mon, c'mon, what'd you say?" So I repeated the line to Milton and, without a smile, he just tapped on the table, he said, "Get it on paper, kid. Get it on paper." [11]

Even without Thurber's help, Nat created a show that justified Berle's confidence in him. The series, which premiered on NBC in March 1947, got off to a slow start as far as ratings were concerned, but the star could see that this time he had a program that was genuinely funny, "the best radio show I ever did," as he later wrote in his autobiography. He went on to point out, quite rightly, that the high point was the closing sketch, entitled "At Home with the Berles." [12]

For this section, Nat recast some of his old *Grouch Club* material, including the library sketch and the skit revolving around the overstimulated child who gets a prescription of radio bedtime stories (with Stang, of course, as the hilariously horrendous whelp). Other sketches had a similar *Grouch* bent, taken to a new absurdist extreme. In one episode, Berle and his wife take a Caribbean cruise at a special discount—eighth class—which lands them deep in the ship's hold, locked behind bars, with a stack of hay for a bed and a cow for company. In another, Berle takes his son to a Brooklyn Dodgers game and ends up missing at least two or three rallies every time he turns away from the field, whether it is for five minutes or five seconds. No matter how he tries to focus on the game, there is always a distraction: he has to fetch a hot dog for Junior; he has to say hello to an acquaintance in the back row; he has to hide under his seat when an unpopular call by the umpire sets off a hail of small-arms fire from the Brooklyn fans. [13]

Critical reception was lukewarm at first, as if reviewers were unwilling to shed the idea that Berle and radio were necessarily a mismatch. Writing in the *New York Times* after the first two episodes aired, Jack Gould conceded that, compared with Berle's previous radio efforts, "the program is an improvement," but went on to say that the comedian "still has his work cut out for him in fully adapting his ways to the microphone." By the 1948–49 season, though, the critics became more appreciative. The *Variety* review of the season's opener declared that Berle's problems with the medium had been overcome.

"The important facet of the initial layout seems to be the fact that Berle, after several previous tries, has a format and staff that is capable of producing high powered radio results."[14]

Despite increasing praise and growing attention, the Berle show never became a top-rated series. Undermining the show to a great extent was the comedian's segue into television.

Berle's great opportunity came in 1948 when Texaco bought his radio show, replacing Philip Morris as sponsor. The company moved the program from Tuesday nights to Wednesdays, and from NBC to ABC. More important, Texaco also planned on testing the infant television market with a new variety show. Berle, intrigued by the new medium, auditioned with several other performers for the host's role during a series of pilot editions of the program that were aired over the summer. He won the job on a full-time basis and began his legendary run on *Texaco Star Theater* that fall.

On television Berle did not need finely crafted scripts and inspired supporting characters. Now that the audience could see him, he could merely cut loose with the frantic, physical act that had drawn so many sell-out crowds in theaters and clubs. He was back in his natural element.

Nat had no interest in joining Berle in the upstart medium. The radio show continued, now running concurrently with the comedian's TV series, but Hiken's efforts suffered in comparison to the visual Berle. This was especially true in the minds of critics, who now revived the old complaints about Berle's limitations on radio. The quality of the writing did not matter. Stang, who worked with Berle on both radio and TV, did not believe that "the material he was given on television was half as good as what he got on the radio show." In the end, the comparison boiled down to something very simple: in grabbing the audience's attention, there was nothing that could compete with the comedian's outrageous costumes and his raucous video slapstick while butting into other people's acts.[15]

Nat's radio version of *Texaco Star Theater* coexisted with Berle's television series until mid-1949. It was then canceled, before it truly had a chance to build an audience, and before it had run through the entire number of episodes originally stipulated in the Texaco contracts. But Nat ended up with a comfortable financial cushion, because of some shrewd bargaining at the time that Texaco had taken over the program. Through the efforts of his lawyer, Arthur Hershkowitz, he had gained part-ownership of the series and had negotiated a clause stipulating that he would be paid for all the episodes, whether they were aired or not. As a result, he left the series with another year's pay coming to him.[16]

At a time of upheaval in the broadcast business, he had time to weigh his options.

◆　　◆　　◆

There was one thing about the suddenly booming television business that must have appealed to Nat: the industry was clearly a New York phenomenon.

Network radio production, which had also begun primarily as an East Coast business, had already moved most of its operations to California, leaving Nat, like his mentor Fred Allen, as part of a relatively small group of New York holdouts. But now television revived broadcasting in his adopted city. Corporate headquarters were in Manhattan; much of the research and development for the technology had taken place in the area; and the networks' original array of stations had been concentrated almost exclusively on the eastern seaboard. Television production naturally gravitated to the area, and Berle's meteoric success reinforced the trend. Between 1948 and 1949, the number of TV sets in use had jumped from five hundred thousand to more than double that amount, largely because of the popularity of Berle's show, a New York program in both location and flavor. For an established comedy writer eager to stay on the East Coast, the prospects were promising.[17]

Even though he got his professional start in Los Angeles, Nat was now a thoroughgoing New Yorker. His family—recently expanded to four with the birth of his second daughter, Mia—was comfortably ensconced in an apartment on West End Avenue, and his parents had also come east to live nearby on West 101st Street. As for work and much of his social life, Broadway remained the focal point.

He found inspiration in an office inside a rundown walk-up on West 48th Street, just off Broadway and just a couple of blocks from Lindy's, where Milton Berle and his entourage now reigned at the coveted Long Table. The office's three-story building "certainly was basic," as Ambur described it with considerable understatement. Comedian Alan King was more blunt. "Looked like a porn shop," he recalled.[18]

Although not listed in any tour books of the area, 156 West 48th Street was considered by many a Times Square landmark. It was a place filled with history, at least the sort of history that connoisseurs of the area would appreciate. The building's residents had included the Broadway bard himself, Damon

Runyon, as well as the formidable Times Square chronicler Walter Winchell, heavyweight champ Jack Dempsey, and famed restaurateur Toots Shor. The ground floor had originally been a tavern, owned at one time by a wise guy named Billy Duffy. In the early 1930s, Duffy and his racketeer associates had trained a six-foot-seven Italian strongman named Primo Carnera in an up-stairs apartment and finagled the light-hitting giant into a heavyweight title-holder (a story later fictionalized by Budd Schulburg in the novel *The Harder They Fall*, which in turn was made into a Humphrey Bogart movie). By 1949, the first floor had been turned into an Italian restaurant named Zucca's, but the building's main attraction was the top-floor apartment/office of a press agent named Eddie Jaffe.[19]

An orphan from Cleveland, Jaffe had drifted into New York in the 1930s after a stint as a carnival shill, useful undergraduate study for anyone entering the flacking profession. At first he mostly represented strippers, though some of his early, better-dressed clients also included Adrienne the Psychic, Zorita the Snake Charmer, and a conjuror named Think-a-Drink Hoffman, whose act consisted of magically producing any cocktail suggested by his audience. In time, Jaffe moved onto more prestigious customers, from United Artists and Warner Bros. to Tony Bennett, Jimmy Durante, the Andrews Sisters, and Dorothy Dandridge. The small, wiry-haired Jaffe was an inexhaustible pro-moter and a good-hearted, generous adviser, but he always had difficulty hang-ing onto clients. Like Woody Allen's Broadway Danny Rose, he would help entertainers when they were young and hungry, then watch them move onto big agencies when their careers finally took off.[20]

Jaffe was known as the world's ugliest press agent. He was known that way because he billed himself that way. For him ugliness was merely a distinction that could land him in newspaper columns. Coleman Jacoby remembered that Jaffe was always open to suggestions when it came to new ways of putting him-self down. "He used to say to me, 'Coleman, I need some jokes for Winchell—Jaffe's so ugly that . . . ' One time he had his apartment done over. I looked at it, and Jaffe said to me, 'Coleman, have you any ideas on how to improve the looks of this place?' I said, 'Stay the hell out of it.' He said, 'Great!' And he started writing it down."[21]

At the time Nat sublet his third-floor office from press agent Jack Tirman, Jaffe's place was already known as a round-the-clock hangout. When Nat would cross the hall to visit, he was likely to find a rare collection of charac-ters: strippers, politicians, tap dancers, rodeo cowboys, cops, hookers, com-posers, showgirls, comics, trade-union muck-a-mucks and Hollywood stars.

Among the regulars at one time or another were Milton Berle, Gwen Verdon, Victor Borge, Jackie Mason, John Wayne, and assistants to Vice President Henry Wallace. In one corner of the main room was a rock pool and near that a tinny-sounding piano and in another corner an ongoing gin rummy game. To one side was a broken-down sofa, at quieter times a surrogate motel bed for guests looking for lusty interludes. In the center of the room, and the hub of all the bustle, was a round table on which were two telephones nestled amidst a layer of litter. The phones rang constantly, answered by a pair of secretaries. The secretaries were employed by Jaffe, but most of the calls they fielded were intended for his guests. If Nat happened to wander in sometime between two and four in the afternoon, he might have had the pleasure of witnessing Jaffe's grand entrance. This was the time of day that the press agent woke up. He would emerge from his bedroom still garbed in his bedclothes: a red fez, a maroon smoking jacket, and nothing else. He would work through what remained of the day and on through to the early hours of the morning, churning out his press releases, whether he managed to clear out the freeloaders or not.[22]

For Nat, a collector of stories, the Jaffe madhouse was an ideal backdrop for his work. Of the legion of anecdotes about the press agent's hangout, one of the best came from Coleman Jacoby, the supplier of insults about Jaffe that Jaffe craved. One night, without much to do, Jacoby dropped by to see what was going on and was met at the door by the apartment's tenant. "What the hell brings you here?" Jaffe said by way of greeting. Jacoby replied, "A lapse in my good taste," which naturally sent the press agent scrambling for pen and paper. The place was full that night. Among the luminaries were Peter Lorre and Errol Flynn. Also in attendance was Jacoby's boss, publicist Irving Zussman, accompanied by a pretty, virginal young woman. The air was blue with ribald stories, the most outrageous told by Lorre, who was determined to amuse the worldly Flynn.

"He's telling a joke, it was unprintable, involving bestiality and an innocent girl," Jacoby remembered. "The girl with Irving was in shock. And, of course, Flynn was amused by the little guy Lorre telling this terrible story and amused by the girl's reaction. She was practically fainting. I said, 'Irving, get her the hell out of here. Don't you see she doesn't belong in this crowd?' " Jacoby took it upon himself to escort the young woman home, for which she was thankful, thankful enough that she invited him into her apartment, where she lived with her sister. As the three of them sat around and talked, the young woman spoke about her experiences in Manhattan since moving there six months earlier. She explained that she had met this wonderful guy and, after a whirlwind romance, they had gotten married, then quickly split up. It turned out that Jacoby recognized the name of her estranged husband.

> He owned a checkroom concession for a Broadway nightclub I was working for at the time. He was a gangster. A real Murder, Inc. guy. The real thing. She said, "Now the man is carrying a torch for me and he's following me around. He's haunting me." I said, "He's following you around?" I said, "Would you excuse me please?" I got out of the house. I came there like the bon vivant, like the Scarlet Pimpernel, I'd saved the girl from ruin. I left like someone in the movies where you see the guy hugging the wall."[23]

There were times when Jaffe's place was not filled to capacity. He might be sitting quietly with a client, listening to his or her troubles, or simply going about his business while lending space to Times Square denizens down on their luck. Not just a ragtag Gatsby of the Broadway scene, Jaffe could also be, in his way, a patron of the arts. Sammy Cahn and Jule Styne are reputed to have composed a Broadway score on Jaffe's piano; Ed Tryczinski slept on the apartment's couch while waiting for someone to produce his play *Stalag 17*; and young press agent Ernest Lehman used Jaffe's office to write much of his novella *Sweet Smell of Success*, a fictional exposé of Walter Winchell and later a film starring Burt Lancaster.[24]

Some of Jaffe's open-door policy rubbed off on Nat and his own office space. The work environment that he found so congenial consisted of a single room, subdivided into a front area—uncarpeted and just barely furnished with a typing stand, a desk, a couch, and a filing cabinet—and a bedroom area in the rear set off by an archway. No matter how seedy, it still was inviting enough to become a flophouse for the overflow from Jaffe's digs. People would spend the night both in the bedroom and on the office's bare floor. All Nat asked was that they clear out by the time he started work in the mornings. Sometimes there was an overlap. Al Lewis remembered sitting with Nat one day years later, talking about a TV project, when "a guy would come in there with a seabag. He'd walk right through. And Nat'd say, 'Don't talk to him, he only talks Greek.' 'What?' 'Only talks Greek. That's it. Forget it.' The guy would go into the other room and I don't know why he was there." Other freeloaders had more auspicious prospects. In the forties, one of those using Nat's office as a hostel was Marlon Brando, a Jaffe-place regular on the verge of Broadway stardom in *A Streetcar Named Desire*.[25]

In 1949, Nat made his own entrance on the legitimate Broadway scene. Among the productions performed on Times Square stages that year were the classic musicals *Kiss Me Kate* and *South Pacific*, the gritty drama of *Detective Story*, the modern tragedy of *Death of a Salesman*, and the fast-talking comedy of Phil Silvers in *High Button Shoes*. Hiken became a part of this memorable season when he contributed to a revue called *Along Fifth Avenue*, starring two promising newcomers, Jackie Gleason and Nancy Walker.

The producer, Arthur Lesser, commissioned Nat to write a sketch and the lyrics to two songs. The sketch, written with Charles Sherman, was an unexceptional burlesque-style routine that did not measure up to Hiken's best radio work. The first of the songs, "The Fugitive from Fifth Avenue," was performed by Gleason and was generally well received by critics, but it was the second musical number that attracted genuine raves.

Sung by Walker and entitled "Chant D'Amour," the tune was a sendup of the sort of impassioned torch song—like the *Showboat* ballad "Bill"—in which the hopelessly smitten chanteuse describes her love for her less than ideal man. As scripted by Hiken, Walker proclaimed undying devotion to her beloved Irving, who, she concedes, is really nothing special:

> He's just an ordinary guy
> No superman, no whiz.
> Why, in a crowded subway
> I can't tell which hands are his.

Even reviewers who were unenthusiastic about the show praised the song and Walker's performance. Walker especially appreciated the tune and went on to make it a staple of her cabaret act in years to come. For Hiken, the play proved to be an entrée to theatrical revue comedy that would become a sideline of his in the 1950s and an outlet for some of his most clever work.[26]

Nat's enthusiasm for theater and for New York was not necessarily confined to the Great White Way. He especially enjoyed trips downtown to the Lower East Side for a night at the Second Avenue Yiddish Theater. Performances by such great comics as Menasha Skulnik and Molly Picon were nostalgic excursions for him, reminding him of his early Yiddish childhood. Just as important, and completing the cultural outing, were the culinary preambles that began across the street.[27]

Moskowitz and Lubowitz belonged to the old breed of Jewish restaurants. Waiting on the table as customers entered was a serving of sliced black radishes and chicken fat, or *schmaltz*. Following that was a flavorful parade of cholesterol, from chopped liver, knishes, and stuffed derma to weighty desserts guaranteed to add just a little extra ballast to the customers' bellies as they heaved themselves out of their chairs. "That restaurant possibly killed more Jews than anything else," Ruben said.[28]

For Nat, a trip to Moskowitz and Lubowitz was no ordinary dining experience. While working on the Berle show, he would spend the entire week anticipating his Friday night order. Once, Ruben remembered, he rhapsodized in particular about the restaurant's chicken soup with kreplach, or Jewish meat dumplings. As soon as the Hikens and Rubens were seated that Friday, Nat immediately placed his soup order, only to be informed that the restaurant was out of kreplach. "I thought Nat was going to cry," Ruben recalled. "He looked at the waiter and he said, 'What? You're not serious.' The waiter said, 'No, no, we're out of them. We don't have any kreplach.' Nat said, 'Go in the kitchen, look behind the stove. Maybe one of them fell down there.' "[29]

Other attractions normally associated with New York culture did not have quite the same allure for Nat. Ambur, a devotee of opera, ballet, and art museums, would take on the cultural education of their daughters, escorting them to such events as Leonard Bernstein's celebrated afternoon concerts for young people and, for her own diversion, would freqently attend the opera, usually accompanied by friends who stood in for her reluctant husband. For Nat, the phrase "poetry in motion" described Joe DiMaggio patrolling center field, not Erik Bruhn executing an entrechat. Even Ruben, a steady Hiken companion, could find Nat's sports-minded crowd somewhat limited, too constrained to include his own interests in classical music and political causes. But there was another side to Hiken that was not likely to surface at his table at Lindy's or amongst the menagerie at Jaffe's.[30]

When visiting Peter Levin in Connecticut, he would often hold forth on world events, launching into satiric riffs and elaborate scenarios based on political inanities of the day. "It was a conversation game he played," Levin recalled, "and, of course, you couldn't beat him at it." Privately, Nat also embraced esoteric literary interests. He was especially fond, for instance, of James Boswell's biography of Samuel Johnson and the diaries of Samuel Pepys, a detailed, multivolume portrait of seventeenth century Restoration London that would have certainly confounded the boys at Toots Shor's, not to mention a good many other people as well. Ultimately, this other, more cultivated side of Hiken would play a role in his next project.[31]

◆　　　◆　　　◆

After his brief sabbatical from broadcasting, Hiken decided to deal with the television issue by, essentially, hedging his bets. He developed a series for radio, but he also took on his first TV assignment at the same time. Of the two, the audio project was clearly his favorite.

NBC Radio's *The Magnificent Montague* was Hiken's first half-hour situation comedy and his first stint as a triple-hyphenate, serving as producer as well as writer and director, performing a virtual one-man show behind the scenes. Seven months into the series, he acquired his only significant partner on the show, Billy Friedberg—a press agent, and cousin to lyricist Lorenz Hart—whom Nat hired to work with him on the scripts. The series was a striking departure from the Berle show. After writing for a brash burlesque comic, he now spun a comedy around the central character of a Shakespearean actor, played by former Yale drama professor Monty Woolley.

Edwin Montague is the scion of a long line of classical tragedians, while his wife, the refined Lily Boheme (from Cleveland), is also a leading light of the legitimate stage. Montague never entertains any doubt that he is the world's greatest actor. The strength of this conviction is matched only by the vehemence of his contempt for the current theater scene. To him, anyone starring in anything other than Shakespeare or Ibsen is nothing more than a chorus boy. As explained in the premiere episode's introduction, "In the last eight years, he's turned down any play in which he did not have the starring role. In the last eight years, he's refused to be in any drama in which he did not have the privilege of re-writing and directing personally. In the last eight years he hasn't worked."[32]

The consequences of unemployment finally hit home when Montague realizes he must settle on domestic instead of imported kippers for breakfast. This forces him to do the unthinkable—take a job in radio, "the lowest point a man can sink to and still stay out of jail," as Montague puts it. And not just radio but radio *soap opera*. The curmudgeonly actor takes the title role in "Uncle Goodheart," in which he must drool syrupy platitudes to the troubled and world-weary five afternoons a week. Making the job even more burdensome, Montague now has to live a double life. If he should reveal how he is making a living, he will be drummed out of his beloved Proscenium Club, gathering spot for New York's proudest, and longest unemployed, thespians.[33]

The Magnificent Montague premiered in the fall of 1950 as a "sustaining" show. (This meant that the network was airing the program even though it had not found a sponsor, a now nearly forgotten broadcasting practice that allowed offbeat shows to find both an audience and a financial backer at the same time.) Quickly, *The Magnificent Montague* established itself as unique. Its satiric jabs at radio set it apart from most comedies on the air, almost as much as its references to George Jean Nathan and Eugene O'Neill and its snatches of soliloquies from *Hamlet, MacBeth,* and *The Merchant of Venice.* (The truly erudite might have also noticed, incidentally, that the main character's name was a paraphrase of Edward Montagu, the benefactor of diarist Samuel Pepys.)

Nat's casting of Woolley was a natural—the bearded sixty-two-year-old actor and the Shakespearean he portrayed on the air made a perfect fit. Woolley had first achieved fame eleven years earlier as the impossibly arrogant Sheridan Whiteside in the Moss Hart/George Kaufman comedy *The Man Who Came to Dinner.* Nat met him a few years later when the former Ivy League professor had appeared as a guest on *The Fred Allen Show.* Although not quite as much as Montague, Woolley harbored a bit of the ham himself. He could boom his lines to the upper rafters and could intone his words as exquisitely as any other man infatuated with the sound of his own voice. Off-stage and off-mike, he also nurtured a reputation for irascibility that would have made even Montague proud. Once, when pressured into making a publicity appearance at a children's party, he replied, "Very well then. I shall attend, and I shall pat the little darlings on the head—until they are dead."[34]

Counterbalancing Woolley's trademark snobbery was the Berle-show alumnus Pert Kelton. She appeared as Agnes, the Shakespearean's wisecracking maid, who engages Montague in an unending war of verbal thrusts and parries. The show's most consistent scene-stealer, though, was a young Art Carney. The future Ed Norton, then a radio character-for-hire, appeared in a variety of roles, sometimes more than one per episode. His best was the part of Montague's father, the overpowering theatrical patriarch and the only person who can reduce the bombastic Edwin to a mumbling, foot-shuffling schoolboy.

With *The Magnificent Montague,* Hiken earned the most enthusiastic reviews of his radio career. "Written, produced and directed by Nat Hiken, one of radio's better scripters, 'Montague' emerged as a refreshing, brittle and sparkling comedy," wrote *Variety*'s reviewer, "and to boot it lampooned radio (in a mature, intelligent and funny fashion) as perhaps the medium has never been lampooned before." Even the more guarded *New York Times* concluded that a "program that indicates an effort to throw off radio's yoke of lethargy, as this one does, must be applauded."[35]

Perhaps the most perceptive review came in June 1951, seven months after the show had first gone on the air. *Christian Science Monitor* critic Robert Lewis Shayon described the series as "radio's single attempt at the difficult form of farce. On the whole, it is a successful attempt, due chiefly to the work of Nat Hiken, a writer-director who created the program and who carefully marks each episode in the series with his 'regisseur' talents." Shayon distinguished farce from what he termed "zany comedy." In farce, he pointed out, writers propel their characters into improbable situations but must always keep the misadventures credible; "otherwise the illusion, always tenuous, is immediately shattered and the comic experience degenerates into meaningless anarchy." In focusing on this quality of *The Magnificent Montague*, Shayon was noting a new direction in Hiken's comedy. Previously, Nat had been known for fast and loose parodies and travesties. Now sustained comedic plotting would be his goal.[36]

Heard today, *The Magnificent Montague* seems strained at times during the obligatory bickering that goes on between Montague and his maid Agnes, as if most of the best put-downs had been used up in the early episodes. But the situations that Hiken devised still build to big laughs, as when Montague and a fellow tragedian rehearse the battle scene between MacBeth and MacDuff in their old actors' athletic club. Unbeknownst to them, the place has been taken over by Curly Novak Professional Wrestling Promotions. Novak (played by Carney) thinks the twosome are a grappling team and is flabbergasted by their originality. "Talking Shakespeare and fighting at the same time! It can't miss!"[37]

Based on the reviews, *The Magnificent Montague* should have been Nat's most successful radio show. It merely turned out to be his last. By 1950, comedy audiences were simply not listening to radio anymore. Uncle Miltie and his competitors had made sure of that. *The Magnificent Montague* found sponsors within a month of its premiere but it never found its listeners. The final episode aired a year after the show had begun.

Nat never quite accepted the commercial failure of this series. He continued to have a special affection for the show and in the late fifties he attempted to produce it once again as a television program. It never aired. In the early sixties, he tried once more and still could not place it on a network lineup. One of Nat's associates on the television versions of *Montague* believed that it was the culture-clash comedy of the program that appealed to him so. "Nat was very much into the class structure and the way some people behaved as a result of feeling superior to everyone else. He loved poking fun at the grandeur of people who, for instance, thought in terms of Shakespeare. He respected that, and at the same time he could see the humor in it."[38]

The Magnificent Montague may have been a commercial miscalculation, but Nat's strategy of pursuing both radio and television simultaneously proved to be a wise maneuver. While Montague garnered the glowing reviews, it was his television project that set him on course toward his greatest success.

Book Shows

Hiken made his entrance into television as a head writer on the staff of *Four Star Revue*, a new variety series developed by NBC. Whatever misgivings Nat may have had about the new medium, he must have appreciated that he had landed at a TV network well suited to his talents. Under new dynamic leadership, NBC in 1950 offered an agreeable setting for creative people in general and creative funny people in particular.

Pat Weaver signed on as NBC's vice president of television the year before. He arrived at an uneasy time for the network. Milton Berle's *Texaco Star Theater* had given NBC an early lead in attracting the new television audience, but the notorious "Paley raids" had already succeeded in turning the tables. Beginning in 1948, CBS head William Paley had lured away several of NBC's biggest comedy stars, acquiring the radio shows of Jack Benny, Burns and Allen, Edgar Bergen, and Freeman Gosden and Charles Correll, the principals of *Amos 'n' Andy*. All of these programs made a successful transition to television. By 1949, *Texaco Star Theater* was NBC's only series rated in the top ten, and the network's executives feared that Paley might capture Berle as well. Weaver provided the network with a badly needed knack for programming.[1]

Weaver had gotten his start in broadcasting as a radio comedy writer and later continued along the same lines as producer for Fred Allen in the mid-1930s. He acquired his executive experience at advertising agencies, where, during the heyday of radio, most of the programming decisions were made. Because a single sponsor would underwrite each show, the advertiser exercised ultimate control over the program's content. Despite his advertising background, Weaver was questioning the wisdom of this arrangement by the time he reached NBC. He also brought with him a respect for talent and a set of innovative ideas on programming strategy.[2]

Weaver planned to recruit advertisers according to what he called a "magazine concept." A magazine publisher sells many ads per issue, and NBC, Weaver reasoned, should follow this example by lining up more than one sponsor per program. In this way, the network would find it easier to raise money for a form of production that was much more expensive than radio programming. At the same time, the network could retain control of its shows because no single sponsor held the purse strings. He believed that broadcasters were better suited to creating diverse, compelling programming than advertisers, who were more concerned with selling their products. This theory proved to be correct—provided that the broadcaster was an enlightened executive like Weaver.[3]

Weaver developed the concept of the *Today* show, one of the longest-running broadcast institutions. He promoted live dramas such as *Philco TV Playhouse* and *Hallmark Hall of Fame*. He launched NBC's *Producers' Showcase*, a series of specials that included a production of *The Petrified Forest* starring Humphrey Bogart, Lauren Bacall, and Henry Fonda; a musical version of Thornton Wilder's *Our Town* featuring Frank Sinatra; and the original historic broadcast of *Peter Pan* showcasing Mary Martin in the title role. Weaver even attempted to interrupt the drone of afternoon soap operas with a serious daytime drama series entitled *Matinee Theater*.

True to his gag-writing roots, Weaver was especially keen on humorous programming. In fact, he regarded it as the linchpin of his prime-time schedule, in which the eight o'clock slot every night would be set aside for comedy. The thinking was that funny shows such as *Texaco Star Theater* would attract the entire family until nine o'clock, at which time parents would put their small children to bed and stay tuned for the dramas that would follow. Weaver also made sure that there would be something amusing on the air to wrap up the evening's viewing. At first, this late-night slot was filled by *Broadway Open House*, alternately hosted by comedians Jerry Lester and Morey Amsterdam. Replacing this program in 1954 was another Weaver-instigated institution, the *Tonight* show.[4]

When Weaver came aboard, Tuesday nights at eight were already the domain of Milton Berle. For other eight o'clock slots, the NBC vice president invited Groucho Marx to adapt his radio show *You Bet Your Life*, and brought in the team of producer Max Liebman and comics Sid Caesar and Imogene Coca for the brilliant revue *Your Show of Shows*. On Sundays, he assembled a set of four hosts to alternate as headliners on *The Colgate Comedy Hour*. *Four Star Revue*, Hiken's assignment, was another version of the same idea. The *Revue*'s four stars were Jimmy Durante, Danny Thomas, Ed Wynn and Jack Carson, each appearing once a month in a rotating pattern known as a "wheel." Nat was hired to write for Carson.

Like many other performers in the early days of television, Carson was a marginal film actor who looked upon the new entertainment outlet as a chance to rejuvenate his career. For years, the burly character actor had turned in amusing portrayals of oafs and blowhards in such movies as *The Male Animal*, *Strawberry Blonde*, and *Arsenic and Old Lace*. Almost always a supporting player, he now could get top billing in a vehicle tailor-made for him.

In crafting a format for Carson, Hiken enjoyed considerable leeway, with virtually no meddling at all from network executives. Weaver's involvement with the production of shows generally ended once he hired the creative talent. Gary Simpson, a *Four Star Revue* director, considered Weaver unique in this regard. "I worked under six vice presidents in charge of television at NBC, and of all of them Pat was the supreme person in terms of coming up with ideas. He put out the things that he wanted to accomplish, but he stood back and let other people bring it about. I've known so many people who tried to get in and interfere, but it was always at the wrong time and they didn't have the skills to really improve things."[5]

Comedy-variety shows such as *Four Star Revue* were all the rage at the time as the networks scrambled to duplicate Berle's video-vaudeville success. Hiken tinkered with the standard formula found in most of these programs. Instead of a grab bag parade of acts, he devised story lines to connect the hour's worth of sketches and musical numbers. This idea may have originated with Carson. According to an interview he gave at the time, Carson explained to his producer and director that, as an actor rather than a stand-up comic, he would need some sort of narrative if he was going to carry an entire hour. Certainly, Nat would have encouraged the idea as well, because comedic storytelling, as opposed to joke writing, was his forte.[6]

Carson and Hiken were not the only ones to pursue this so-called book-show concept at the time. In his installments of *The Colgate Comedy Hour*, Eddie Cantor strung together his various routines with a thread of a story, but it was a mighty thin thread, at times only barely perceptible. Hiken's plotline,

on the other hand, was noticeable and inventive enough to earn some qualified praise from critic John Crosby. "As ideas go," he wrote, "this is hardly
wildly original but no one else has done it."[7]

Hiken's collaborator once again was Billy Friedberg. This show, along with
the concurrent *The Magnificent Montague*, was the beginning of a long partnership between the two that would continue on and off into the 1960s. Of all
of Nat's press-agent pals, Friedberg might have been the least overtly funny, or
at least the most quiet of the bunch. He remained reserved when he was away
from the table at Lindy's and when working with Nat. "Nat was definitely in
charge," a *Four Star Revue* director observed. "Billy was just sort of there. Every
time I saw them, Nat would bounce stuff off of Billy." But Friedberg functioned
as more than a sounding board and an editor. When producing script after
script for an ongoing series, Nat often needed a sidekick to motivate him, and
Friedberg was an accomplice especially attuned to his sense of comedy.[8]

The scripts Hiken and Friedberg wrote were broadcast live, as was true of
most prime-time network programming, a practice carried over from radio.
The nerve-racking task of coordinating and airing a complex variety show required a studio that could house both a Broadway-style extravaganza and an
electronic transmission facility. The site NBC chose for shows such as *Four
Star Revue* was the Center Theatre located in Rockefeller Center. Designed
years earlier as a sister showcase to Radio City Music Hall, the Center had always been overshadowed by its legendary neighbor. It had failed as both a legitimate theater and as a movie house by the time NBC leased it in 1950, but
the place certainly could not be faulted for a lack of opulence. The theater
boasted a seating capacity of thirty-two hundred, a six-ton chandelier sus-
pended overhead, a fountain that could generate elaborate water effects, a machine that could create a theatrical ice rink, and a huge stage measuring 130
feet wide and 60 feet deep. Impressive as the place already was, the network
still had to spend $300,000 to convert it into an origination point for their
broadcasts.[9]

A section of seats had to be uprooted to make room for a control booth, and
runways and platforms had to be constructed for the massive video cameras.
The ice-making machinery was also removed. Early variety spectaculars may
have been lavish, but not so lavish that they required the ability to create ice-
skating production numbers on a regular basis. A feature that the network
kept was the mechanized stage. Three sections could be elevated ten feet
above the stationary portion of the stage or lowered twenty-five feet below,
where performers and scenery could be picked up and raised back up for the

next number. There was also a thirty-eight-foot circular section that could be
rotated like a turntable. The gadgetry provided directors with intriguing production toys. Other people were not so thrilled.[10]

Many comedians, such as Cantor and Berle, refused to broadcast their
shows there. They felt that the vast stage dwarfed their small-focus routines,
and they also found the thirty-two-hundred-member audience distracting
when they were attempting to keep their comedy intimate enough for families
huddled around the small screens at home. While an abundance of space
posed some difficulties during the performance, another problem emerged for
the exact opposite reason. Rehearsal space in the city was at a premium. With
so many programs vying for so few halls, the Carson-show cast could not settle
into one site, alternating instead between various dance studios and hotel
ballrooms in the Times Square area.[11]

This sort of arrangement was typical of early New York television production. Congested midtown Manhattan did not lend itself to motion picture
work, and the networks had to cobble together an ad hoc array of facilities.
Underused theaters like the Center ranked as premier choices and were reserved for the most spectacular broadcasts. Aged movie studios such as the
Vitagraph in Brooklyn, which had been gathering dust since the final exodus
of the movie industry to Hollywood in the early thirties, were now cleaned out
and resurrected. Other sites had a less obvious connection to show business
production. CBS set up studios above Grand Central Station. Even less likely,
Dumont, the fourth network, founded by TV manufacturer Allen Dumont,
housed its operations in Wannamaker's department store. When broadcasting
a foot-chase for a program such as *Rocky King, Inside Detective*, cameramen
had to move in close enough to the actors so that viewers would not be able to
detect that the exciting, gutter-tough action scene was actually taking place in
the housewares department.[12]

While preparing a Carson show a month, Hiken was still producing, writing, and directing *The Magnificent Montague* once a week. His focus was split,
and his pet radio project commanded most of his concentration. This may account for the Carson show's variable results and mixed reviews. Even so, in
some installments he succeeded in demonstrating the book-show concept's
potential for blending funny sketches into a larger, amusing premise. In the
premiere, for instance, Carson takes the stage for his grand season debut only
to find that NBC has already expended the entire *Four Star Revue* budget on
the three other hosts. He has to mount his show with no props, and when the
time comes for him to perform his big singing number—originally to be ac-

companied by a full orchestra—he has to make do with the Bessarabian string trio.[13]

Of the series' material that worked, the best usually revolved not around Carson but one of his supporting players, Betty Kean. A streetwise and physical comedienne, she was the key performer in what became known as "The Phone Sketch," the series' most memorable segment. The skit begins with Carson, stranded in Brooklyn, trying to make a call at a bank of pay phones. Here, Kean is calling a friend about her upcoming party, which, she is sure, will "usher in the Red Hook social season." She dragoons Carson into answering a call in the next booth from another one of her friends, and before long, she has him marching from phone to phone, fielding a rash of questions about the conspicuously lowbrow soiree. The sketch is a finely orchestrated piece of footwork and clamorous dialogue, rightly described by Variety at the time as "a gem in timing."[14]

Another important member of the supporting cast was Billy Sands, an early recruit in what would eventually become Hiken's stock company of actors. Nat had worked with him on The Milton Berle Show and valued him for his sharp-voiced, deadpan delivery that seemed to elicit laughs so effortlessly. Just as valuable was his trouper's ability to think on his feet. This talent, honed on the burlesque stage and at Catskill resorts, proved especially useful in the unpredictable world of live television. Writers and directors would often discover near the end of a broadcast that the show was running too long, or perhaps too short. Hiken and the director would turn to Sands to make the on-the-spot adjustments. If they needed to cut, Sands would supply the instant transition across the deleted section to the next scene. If, on the other hand, Carson found himself on stage bidding farewell to the audience with still a minute or two left to fill, Sands would enter and launch into one of the many blackout skits in his comic's repertoire. After relying on Sands's skills in a succession of shows, Nat eventually installed him as part of that remarkable collection of faces and personalities that made up Sergeant Bilko's platoon.[15]

For behind-the-scenes personnel, assignments on Four Star Revue could be fluid, allowing writers, directors, and technicians to move from one star installment to another. After a year on the Carson show, Nat took advantage of this flexibility so that he could work with a new member of the Revue roster. He was still intrigued by the idea of a variety show with a story line and, even though he regarded Carson as a true professional, he now had the chance to develop the concept for a comic with extraordinary potential. His new star of choice was Martha Raye. Like Carson, she was another Hollywood castoff.

Stardom had managed to elude Raye despite years of pursuit. A vaudeville baby, she started performing at the age of three when her parents worked her into their barnstorming song-and-dance act. As an adult, she retained singing and dancing as part of her routine but concentrated instead on comedy, beginning on stage then moving on to nightclubs and radio. At every turn she avoided subtlety like the plague. Renowned for her big, sea-bass mouth and accompanying hog-holler voice, she constantly reached for big laughs, through mugging, pratfalls, knockabout roughhousing, and crude asides. At her best, she seemed to be the second coming of Fanny Brice. At worst, she seemed merely desperate.

Raye's good moments were enough to earn her a Paramount Pictures contract in the mid 1930s. Hollywood never figured out what to do with her. She clearly possessed an explosive broad-comic talent but her comedies never made the most of it. She also had a shapely build, and her features were quite attractive—when, that is, she was not twisting them into some mad-comic contortion—but an attempt by studio executives to turn her into a glamour girl was obviously doomed to failure. No one was about to confuse her with Lana Turner.[16]

Only one filmmaker truly capitalized on her talent. In 1947's *Monsieur Verdoux*, Charlie Chaplin portrayed the title character, a Bluebeard amassing a fortune from the inheritances left somewhat prematurely by the wives he murdered. Serving as writer-director as well as star, he cast Raye as one of his spouses. Chaplin allowed her to be both elegant in appearance and rambunctious in manner as the willful Annabella, a most inconvenient wife with an annoying habit of staying alive, despite Verdoux's best homicidal efforts to the contrary. Critics praised her hilarious performance, but few other people saw the film. Red-baiters were hounding Chaplin at the time for his leftist sympathies, and right-wing picketing and negative press helped ensure the movie's early closing.[17]

Raye's movie career was effectively over by the time she got her chance to headline in NBC's *All Star Revue*, the renamed and recast version of *Four Star Revue*. Most of her recent activity had been confined to nightclubs. There, her act was often uproarious, but it also lacked taste and judgment. According to Herb Ross, "her nightclub act was disgusting . . . She would do things like pick her nose and flick it at the audience. It wasn't pretty." As head writer, Hiken had to figure a way to tap into Raye's prodigious energy and, at the same time, transmute her vulgarity into an engaging earthiness.[18]

Hiken set Raye on the right course in the show's first installment, while also proving how viable the book-show concept could be. The character he created for Raye was manic, aggressive, and man-hungry but also sweet-natured and vulnerable. In stark contrast to glossy variety shows of later years, the program revolved around Raye's rat-trap apartment in Flatbush, where her neighbor was a frowzy Jewish hausfrau named Mrs. Storecheese. Hiken defined Raye's love life in her first scene, when a friend calls to fix her up on a blind date. The audience hears only Raye's side of the conversation: "About his eyes ... Never mind the color. How many?"[19]

The friend happens to be the maid of Ezio Pinza, the dashing Metropolitan Opera star who had recently found more pop-oriented fame in *South Pacific*. Tired of the glitz and superficiality of the Stork Club and 21, the lonely Pinza has told his maid that he yearns for the company of an unspoiled, down-to-earth woman. Raye does not know her date's name, even as he shows up at her tenement. While they make small talk, the unimpressed Raye shoots a quick aside to the audience, "Here's a new bit. This guy looks like Ezio Pinza." In the next moment, when she learns that he is, indeed, Ezio Pinza, she flops to the floor in a show-stopping face-first faint. From there, Hiken carries out another variation of his favorite culture-clash theme, as Pinza squires Raye to a posh nightclub and Raye reciprocates by escorting him to Schultz's Stable, the bucket of blood where she works.[20]

Critics responded enthusiastically. *Variety* described the plotline, slight as it might have been, as "a welcome relief from both the vaudeo and revue type broadcasts 'All Star' has carried," and in a critique of a later episode in the same season, described the program as "an excellent fusion of Miss Raye's talents with good writing and imaginative production." *Variety* was so admiring, in fact, that it even lauded the commercials. This is not quite as strange as it might seem. Many of the commercials in early variety shows were not separate entities. They were integrated into the proceedings on stage, and deft writers such as Hiken could find ways to work a laugh or two into the huckster interludes.[21]

The success of Raye's show in 1951–52 ensured its return the next season. As Nat proved he could adapt to a visual medium, he was rewarded with more money and greater responsibilities, becoming not only head writer but also director. He now regained the sort of creative control that he had enjoyed in his final programs in radio. He was poised to do his most uproarious and acclaimed work.

◆   ◆   ◆

Nat's old boss was also venturing into television during these early years. After eighteen years on the air, Fred Allen's radio show had been canceled in June 1949, the victim of a dwindling radio audience and changes in public tastes. To compete with television, radio producers had begun to rely more on gimmickry, especially the gimmick of giveaway quiz shows. One of the most successful of these programs, *Stop the Music,* hosted by Bert Parks, had eventually knocked Allen out of his time slot. At fifty-five he was now forced to adapt to sudden changes in the broadcasting business. As is to be expected, the crotchety comedian took a dim view of the new, cockamamie industry of television. "The reason why television is called a medium," he said, "is because nothing on it is ever well done." But the old comedy warhorse was not quite ready to get out of harness just yet.[22]

In June 1950, Allen, along with Eddie Cantor, joined the roster of stars on *The Colgate Comedy Hour.* Never one to let by an opportunity to bristle, Allen must have been aggravated at the very thought that he would be alternating on the program with the comic he had once dubbed "the dean of bad taste." Still, this could not have galled him nearly as much as the fabulous television success of Berle, another one of his bêtes noires. Within months, Allen's failure on TV only fueled this disgruntlement.[23]

His first *Comedy Hour,* guest-starring the former Montague, Monty Woolley, was a bleak precursor of things to come. After some bright opening banter, Allen moved ineffectually from one misfired routine to another. At one point, he tried to manufacture a visual version of Allen's Alley, in which Mrs. Nussbaum, Senator Claghorn, and the others were portrayed by hand puppets. The result was peculiar, strained, and unamusing. The *New York Times* called the show "the season's first major disappointment." In a paper that had once referred to the comedian as "that great man," the reviewer criticized Allen for not seeming "to be trying very hard, which is not the trouper's way of showing loyalty to an audience that wants and expects to be entertained."[24]

Deteriorating health may have caused this apparent listlessness. High blood pressure had continued to dog Allen over the years, and during the summer of his radio cancellation, he had suffered a minor stroke. There may have also been a basic incompatibility between the comedian and television. He had proven himself as a successful visual comedian in the past, during his early vaudeville days, but theater audiences had appreciated him from a distance; now that video cameras magnified the baggy eyes and the severity of his features, Allen did not present a friendly visage that viewers would be likely to welcome into their living rooms. In this respect he served as a striking contrast to his longtime friend and sham rival, Jack Benny, who was remarkably videogenic.[25]

Allen left *The Colgate Comedy Hour* in December, just three months after his first installment. He cited his worsening health as the reason for his departure, although it is also likely that the stress of an obviously failing show had helped damage his physical condition. Pat Weaver, nonetheless, remained convinced that Allen could succeed in the new medium. He had been a great admirer of the comedian since the 1930s and now believed that it was only a matter of finding the right vehicle to transform Allen into a video star. One of Weaver's thoughts was to feature the comedian in a talk-show format that would have exploited his gift for impromptu repartee, something like Groucho Marx's *You Bet Your Life*. A plausible idea, but Allen never had the chance to test it. In 1952, he suffered a heart attack, which left him alive but weakened. From then on, except for appearances on the panel of *What's My Line?*, his television experiment was effectively over.[26]

◆   ◆   ◆

During this period, as Nat secured his foothold in the television business, his favorite method of getting away from work was a weekly gin rummy game. Held at the Park Plaza Hotel, the game's show business participants included composer Jule Styne, CBS executive Oscar Katz, press agent turned producer Irving Mansfield, comedy writer Leonard Stern, and then–Broadway star Phil Silvers. "It was more a group catharsis than a card game," remembered Stern. "Through screaming and yelling we were all finer people the next day."[27]

As Stern explained it, no other game but gin would do. "In poker you're responsible for your own hand. Gin allows you to castigate everyone. That was a requisite of the game." Four or five men would play as partners, which meant that once a player's hand was finished, he could continue to criticize those on his side who were still in the action. The game was a great leveler. Any player would feel free to lash into anyone else, regardless of how important the target might be outside the hotel room. Only occasionally would fist-fights break out.[28]

The most vocal and combative of all may have been Phil Silvers. A compulsive gambler, he would tolerate no chitchat between hands; idle talk merely held up the game and the chance to place his next bet. Once the cards were dealt, he then launched into nonstop patter in his distinctive comedic rhythm as he constantly shepherded the game forward or verbally assaulted a partner for betting too timidly.[29]

Quieter members of the group might be overshadowed in terms of sheer volume, but yet they, too, would hold their ground. They still would find some way to defend their card-playing decisions in a game that was "essentially a matter of declaring your territorial rights and making a vain attempt to maintain human dignity," as Stern wryly put it. Taking a different tack was Jule Styne, the great appeaser. Typically, he would agree with whatever argument had just been voiced, even if that meant contradicting the last argument he had so graciously agreed with.[30]

The tumultuous give-and-take made the game such a good show that one man, press agent Kurt Weinberg, would attend merely to watch and keep score. He would sit in a canvas director's chair, slightly elevated above the rest, almost like a tennis match judge. In time, the players regarded him as an integral part of the experience, and on more than one occasion, they delayed games because Weinberg was late in arriving. They would not start without him.[31]

Coursing through all the talk, along with the furor, was a steady stream of dry wit. Nat, in his laconic fashion, was one of the prime sources. His comments were spare but pointed. In meeting him for the first time during one of these games, Stern was struck by his bemused quality. "I sensed that while he had the ability to be involved in the game, he was a detached observer at the same time. He wasn't among the vituperative. When he was upset, he was excessively witty."[32]

Like the others there, Nat relied on the game as an outlet for the frustrations and anxieties stirred up by the entertainment business. There was always a deadline looming just ahead, sometimes two of them overlapping, and also the stress of manufacturing hilarity on cue. And then there was the fear that audiences would not laugh when the gags arrived and, of course, the trepidation about ratings and reviews. These worries would have been enough to set any person on edge. But then also, during this time, there were other forces at work, exerted from outside the business. More than merely making life difficult, they could make a career disappear altogether. The efforts of a handful of industry watchdogs had taken their toll on a number of people, and Nat would have to face the same threat himself.

◆　　　◆　　　◆

On June 22, 1950, Nat's name appeared in a booklet that included citations on 151 broadcast professionals. The publication, entitled *Red Channels*, set out to expose Communist influence in radio and television. It soon became the blacklister's bible.

The publisher was American Business Consultants, an outfit founded in 1947 by three former FBI agents, Theodore Kirkpatrick, John Keenan, and Kenneth Bierly. While serving in the bureau during World War II, the three men had bristled at people's reluctance to confront the Communist menace in America, seeing this willful apathy not only among the general public but also within the government. After leaving the bureau behind, Kirkpatrick, Keenan, and Bierly gathered together to wake America up. They sought to alert businesses about possibly subversive employees and began publishing a newsletter, whose title reflected the fierceness of their beliefs. It was called *Counterattack*.[33]

American Business Consultants settled on broadcasting as its primary target at a time when the cold war was reaching a critical stage. The Russians had detonated their first atomic bomb the previous August; Soviet spy Klaus Fuchs had been arrested in January; Communist North Korea invaded South Korea just three days after *Red Channels* was published. Other fields of battle in the cold war were more demanding than the entertainment business, and others actually had something to do with national security and the antitotalitarian cause. But few could produce such dramatic results so quickly.

The House Un-American Activities Committee (HUAC) had already proven this three years earlier, in 1947. The committee's investigation into Communist influence in Hollywood had quickly garnered headlines and had put alleged subversives on the run or out of work. *Red Channels* now echoed that campaign in radio and television.

The booklet's cover illustration featured a hand about to grasp a radio microphone. Those inclined to pick up on symbolism would have noticed that the microphone was tilted to the left. Less subtle was the picture of the hand: it was colored red. *Red Channels'* introduction, written by an American Business Consultants ally named Vincent Hartnett, stated that the booklet indicated "the extent to which many prominent actors and artists have been inveighed to lend their names, according to these public records, to organizations espousing Communist causes." A hint of the pernicious mischief that *Red Channels* would set in motion could be gleaned from Hartnett's opening remarks. Not only did he subscribe to the dubious idea that the broadcast appearance of a Communist actor posed a threat to the republic, but his definition of those people deserving pillory in the booklet was alarmingly loose. According to the introduction, the booklet listed people who lent their names to Communist causes "regardless of whether they actually believe in, sympathize with, or even recognize the cause advanced."[34]

Beneath the name of each person included in *Red Channels* was a list of allegedly subversive activities. Three citations appeared beneath Hiken's name. He was listed as a sponsor of two May Day parades and as a sponsor of the "Scientific and Cultural Conference for World Peace," a transposition of the Cultural and Scientific Conference for World Peace held at the Waldorf-Astoria Hotel in 1949. The event had been a meeting of intellectuals organized primarily by pro-Soviet activists, but also including some liberal anti-Communists such as Norman Cousins and Norman Mailer.[35]

Ever since he had first learned to skewer his mother's heavy-handed radicalism, Nat, unlike those around him, had only skirted the fringes of left-wing activities. As Ruben put it, "Ambur was involved and I was involved and Sandy was involved, but Nat wasn't." By 1950, his political viewpoint had evolved to the extent that he had become an admirer of Harry Truman, the original architect of the policy of Communist containment. Still, Minnie's politics may have left some imprint upon him. He retained a lingering sense that he was not doing his share when it came to issues such as civil rights or aid to the poor. Sandy, for instance, would ask Nat to sign petitions or donate money to various left-wing causes, and she would find him ready and willing to help, as if he might have felt guilty about his usual political inactivity. This sort of involvement brought him to the attention of the *Red Channels* compilers. Sandy recalled, "He'd write the check and he'd say, kidding, 'Remember, when you're up there before the tribunal, when they drag me in, you're going to speak up for me.'"[36]

Red Channels exerted an influence on the broadcasting business almost immediately. Its widely flung net pulled in Communists, casual supporters of Communist-front activities, people *mistaken* for casual supporters of Communist-front activities, and casual supporters of events misrepresented as Communist-front activities. Within two months of the booklet's publication, jittery executives at General Foods, then sponsoring *The Aldrich Family* on television, fired *Red Channels* listee Jean Muir from the show's cast. Soon, others cited in the booklet also suffered, including Philip Loeb, who was dismissed from his long-standing role on *The Goldbergs*. According to an entertainment lawyer commenting on the situation at the time, "Everyone of them [the *Red Channels* listees] has been affected. A few don't even know it, but they've *all* lost some shows. A majority have lost a great many jobs, and a good-sized minority just aren't working at their professions anymore."[37]

Nat saw the blacklist undermining the careers of people all around him. In Hollywood, Nat's *Grouch Club* collaborator, Roland Kibbee, was coming under suspicion and would eventually have to testify before a HUAC investigator, while Ambur's first husband, screenwriter Waldo Salt, suddenly found his services unwanted because of old political affiliations. In New York, Pert Kelton was another victim. Since working with Nat on radio, she had moved on to Jackie Gleason's *Cavalcade of Stars*, where she created the role of Alice Kramden in the original "Honeymooners" sketches. In 1952, at a time when she was fending off accusations stemming from her listing in *Red Channels*, Kelton suffered a heart attack and had to be replaced by Audrey Meadows. Whether or not the political pressures contributed to her health problems is a matter of conjecture, but what is certainly clear is that the blacklist prevented her from working on television throughout most of the 1950s. Comedian Jack Gilford, who appeared on Hiken's Jack Carson show, was also named in the 1950 booklet. His politically manufactured unemployment began abruptly when a network executive announced his dismissal on the set of a Fred Allen variety show. Allen fumed and protested, but to no effect.[38]

Striking perhaps closest to home were the struggles of Coby Ruskin, producer-director of the Carson show. While working together on *Four Star Revue*, he and Nat had become friends, discovering in time that they shared not only a gift for theatrical humor but also an interest in golf and a passion for cuisine that was easy on the taste buds and hard on the arteries. Coincidentally, their wives met at a dance class about the same time, and the families grew close. When Ruskin's four citations in *Red Channels* made him unemployable on prime-time variety extravaganzas, he was compelled to work without credit for several years as director of Arthur Murray's dance show. When Murray could no longer perpetuate this dodge, Ruskin had to go to England to find his next television job. Nat was privy to these troubles as the noose continued to tighten around his own career.[39]

Hiken's problems began to simmer with the release of *Red Channels*, but ultimately, as with many other targeted broadcast people, it took a grocer from Syracuse to bring the issue to a boil.[40]

Laurence Johnson, the owner of four supermarkets, was already past sixty when he decided to fling himself heart and soul into the anti-Red crusade. Determined to cleanse the airwaves of every Communist-tainted actor, writer, and director, he forged an alliance with his local American Legion post and drummed up an ideological army of stout-hearted food retailers designated as the Veterans Action Committee of Syracuse Supermarkets, commanded by Johnson's highest-ranking fruit and vegetable buyer. Hardly a formidable array of forces at first glance, but broadcast executives were somehow awed. When Johnson and company agitated, networks and sponsors trembled.[41]

If Johnson learned that a TV show was employing a performer with a suspect background, he rallied his troops and ordered a barrage of phone calls and letters. Network and advertising executives took the protests seriously, as if they constituted a widespread, spontaneous groundswell of outrage, even though most of the letters bore the same postmark and many of the notes tended to use the same phrases. Johnson also vowed to jeopardize sales of products advertised on supposedly Red-infiltrated shows. The products might be relegated to sections of stores that customers would not readily find, or, even worse, they might be displayed beneath signs proclaiming that the product's manufacturer sponsored programs employing "Stalin's little creatures." Johnson flaunted his position as an officer in the National Association of Supermarkets, hinting that his influence spread far beyond his little bailiwick in central New York, but this power was never demonstrated. The reason for this was simple: broadcasters were too timid to call his bluff. Instead, sponsors shuddered on cue at the grocer's every threat. Major corporations sent emissaries to Syracuse to appease Johnson. New York executives curried the grocer's favor when he traveled to Manhattan. The success of Johnson's blacklisting career serves as a lasting testimonial to the television industry's capacity for panic.[42]

Once Johnson began to target him, Nat knew that he had only two options: let the grocer's campaign run its course and drive him out of the business, or find some way to clear himself. If he let Johnson do his worst, he would have to turn to the theater for a livelihood. The blacklist had little or no influence on Broadway, but writing plays did not pay nearly as well as television scripting and paid very little indeed if the play closed early. As for blacklist clearance, Nat faced a possibly daunting and dicey proposition.

Clearing oneself involved some form of denial of or explanation for past indiscretions, accompanied by a convincing display of anti-Communist zeal. Guidance could come from various self-proclaimed clearance experts and agencies, including the Anti-Defamation League of B'nai B'rith, the American Legion, screening officials at advertising agencies and networks, and a handful of influential conservative journalists. Sometimes advice on how to escape the blacklist could come from blacklisters themselves, such as American Business Consultants.[43]

According to one clearance method, people who had fallen under suspicion would need to testify before HUAC to cleanse themselves of any reddish hue. This was particularly distasteful, because a witness would be expected to name friends and acquaintances who then might lose their jobs as a result. Roland Kibbee, testifying in 1953, managed to name only those people who had named him and was able to plead forgetfulness about everyone else, but this sort of tightrope act was the rare exception to the rule.[44]

Perhaps most onerous of all the procedures was the one outlined by Aware, Inc., a right-wing watchdog organization employing *Red Channels* author Vincent Hartnett. As far as Aware was concerned, naming names before HUAC was just a beginning. If alleged subversives were truly sincere about turning over a new leaf, they should also be willing to compose written confessions of their political sins and cooperate with other investigative agencies, such as the FBI and the Internal Security Committee. Not only that, they should agree to pronounce their new anti-Communism at union meetings and engage in whatever anti-Communist activities that Aware deemed worthwhile. The clearance process, whatever the route taken, could last as long as three years, during which time the suspected person would not be able to work in his or her profession (this was the case, for instance, with actress Kim Hunter). Sometimes the process would fail to clear the person altogether.[45]

To explore relatively acceptable avenues, Nat consulted with an attorney. Through Peter Levin's wife, Alice, he acquired an entrée to Frank E. Karelsen Jr., a high-powered New York lawyer, well connected with the state Democratic Party and, at the time, vice president of the Public Education Association. Karelsen arranged a meeting with Hearst columnist George Sokolsky, who sometimes acted as intermediary for people seeking clearance. Sokolsky had been pro-Communist himself when he was a young man, until he traveled to Russia at the time of the Bolshevik revolution and witnessed Communist tactics firsthand. The force of his disillusionment propelled him well to the right across the political spectrum—landing him in the camp of vigorous cheerleaders for laissez-faire capitalism. By selecting Sokolsky as a go-between, Karelsen was making perhaps the best of available choices. Unlike some of his colleagues in the clearance business, Sokolsky did not charge a fee for his services and looked down upon anyone who did. He also lacked the vindictiveness of other right-wing journalists, something he later proved when he denounced the rabid rhetoric of Hollywood columnist Hedda Hopper.[46]

Karelsen was able to strike a deal. If Nat would publish a letter in *Variety* that established his anti-Communist convictions, Sokolsky would intercede on his behalf with Laurence Johnson. In the letter, Nat would state that he was not, and never had been, a member of the Communist Party, and he would go on to denounce all that communism stood for. Compared with other clearance procedures, this was fairly benign, but it was not painless, and Nat was not sure at first that he would comply. He resisted the idea of playing along with the blacklisting/clearance process. He may also have been uneasy about denouncing the political beliefs of his mother and other relatives, no matter how far he had distanced himself from their ideology. "He went through hell trying to decide whether or not to do it," Ambur recalled. Finally, he made his choice.[47]

"He called me one day," his cousin Sandy recalled, "and he said, 'You're going to be reading something in *Variety*, and I don't care what people are going to say, but I care what you think about it.' And already my skin was beginning to tighten, because the times were so tough." He told her that this was something he had to do because his job was on the line. When Sandy said that he could always write for Broadway, Nat replied that he did not think he could support his family that way.

> He said, "I have to do it because I've been having dreams that my daughters were going from door to door begging for food." I guess maybe in the end—I have no right to conjecture—but in the end he might have felt, why should I take a rap when I really happen to be, by birth, surrounded by all these communists?
>
> But I wasn't prepared for my reaction. I was on my way home to Larchmont on the train one day, and I picked up this *Variety*. I was turning the pages, like I didn't want to see it, but finally there it was. And my heart just dropped to my stomach.[48]

Other members of Nat's extended family did not try as hard to understand his predicament and over the years would continue to take a dim view of Nat's choice. Levin recalled, "My Aunt Pearl and my Aunt Bessie used to cluck their tongues whenever that thing was brought up." As for Nat's mother, Minnie, easily as staunch a leftist as her sisters Pearl and Bessie, it is not clear how she reacted, although the tension between her and Nat certainly did not ease any after his decision to clear himself.[49]

Nat's own response may not have been much different from Sandy's dismay. The deal arranged by Karelsen allowed him to continue on *All Star Revue* without further harassment. He was truly in the clear. But neither he nor Ambur would ever mention the *Red Channels* episode to their children.[50]

Clown Queen

For all the praise the program received its first season, *The Martha Raye Show* was already starting to coast. After the outstanding first installment, the situations on the show did not always provide Raye with opportunities to develop a viable comedic character, the sort of character that needed only to react naturally to her surroundings to generate laughs. Raye compensated the one way she knew how: she fell back on old schtick. She started to rely on trademark lines—"Thanks large" or "Dis must be da place"—and lapsed too often into wild mugging, grasping for an easy laugh whenever she feared the material would not carry her through. For the program's initial batch of episodes, at least, Raye's manic clowning had been enough to please both critics and audiences, but the appeal was likely to wear thin without some fine-tuning.

Now that Hiken was director besides head writer, he had more authority to introduce changes that might reinvigorate the series, and a five-month summer hiatus gave him some time to consider what those improvements might be. In the end, his most important directorial decision was triggered by serendipity. If it is true that people make their own luck, then Nat manufactured this piece of good fortune by choosing his lowdown workplace wisely.

One day, early in the summer of 1952, he was working in his dingy single-room office on West 48th Street, while across the hall, as usual, there was a crowd going full throttle at Eddie Jaffe's place. The hurly-burly sounds drifted throughout the building, but Nat managed to resist the distraction. Too many assignments were piling on his desk. Not only did he have to prepare scripts for Raye's fall episodes, but he was also writing sketches for revues both on Broadway and television. With all the celebrities and eccentrics that paraded through the building on a regular basis, it would take an especially distinguished visitor to lure him from work. One arrived that day who was sufficiently distinguished, at least in Nat's eyes.

He received news of the visit when one of the Jaffe freeloaders stuck his head through the doorway. Rocky Graziano was across the hall, the man said, adding that Eddie thought Nat should know. Hiken, the avid fight fan, quickly left his desk.[1]

The former middleweight champ had been brought there by Marlon Brando. Unfamiliar at that point with the Jaffe experience, Graziano was treated to a flavorful first taste. As the boxer described it in his autobiography, *Somebody Down Here Likes Me, Too,* men yapped excitedly into Jaffe's telephones, a big white poodle lapped up water from the corner rock pool, a couple of showgirls decorated the piano with multicolored stickers, a tap dancer knocked himself out showing off his newest routine for anyone who would watch. Brando, meanwhile, made himself at home, sprawling on Jaffe's bed to peruse some magazines, then stationing himself at the little piano, demanding that people listen to the one-finger composition he claimed to have written that morning. Nat paid little attention to the clamor around him as he approached Graziano. The boxer could not help but notice the star-struck look on Nat's face. As he later put it in his autobiography, "I t'ink he's gonna get sick when he spots me."[2]

Adulation was something Graziano was used to. Although he had held the middleweight title for only a year, he was one of the most popular boxers of his day. A child of the Lower East Side slums and a former teenage hoodlum, he fought with an animal-like, brawling style guaranteed to warm the hearts of all true fight fans. As a boxing gym owner so succinctly puts it in one of Hiken's scripts for *Car 54, Where Are You?*, "One fighter in a thousand has that viciousness, that killer instinct, that sheer brutality that makes this whole business worthwhile." In all, Graziano the slugger racked up fifty-three knockouts in eighty-three bouts. And he could take it as well as he could dish it out. As he prowled relentlessly after his opponents, looking for his chance to unleash a pulverizing right, he typically absorbed a fearsome barrage of counterblows, as evidenced now by the broken nose and puffy eyelids that coarsened his once youthful, handsome features. Graziano's manner outside the ring further endeared him to his fans. Despite his brutal upbringing and his pugilistic ferocity, he projected an ingratiating boyish quality that always made good sports-column copy.[3]

Nat spent only a short time with Graziano that day, mostly schmoozing about the fight game, but the germ of an idea began to form in his mind. The idea took more definite shape soon after that when, watching TV at home, he caught an appearance by Graziano on a late-night talk show hosted by Broadway columnist Nick Kenny. Something about the boxer's manner on screen convinced Nat that he could use him on *The Martha Raye Show*. He imagined featuring Graziano, under his own name, as Raye's boyfriend. Handled properly, Nat figured, the fighter's natural personality could succeed despite his lack of experience and could provide a valuable element to the show.[4]

Nat opened negotiations at Stillman's Gym, one squalid flight of stairs up from Eighth Avenue. Walking past the sparring rings and the clutches of gamblers and promoters, he located Graziano and his manager, Irving Cohen. Nat explained that he wanted to feature Rocky on Martha Raye's first show of the season. All Cohen wanted to know was how much money was involved. Graziano had questions of his own, doubts really, but he kept them to himself for now.[5]

Graziano knew he had to find some new line of work. He had lost his title four years earlier to Tony Zale, in the last of three electrifying bouts between the two fight-game gladiators. Since then he had managed to polish off a string of lesser opponents, but when Sugar Ray Robinson knocked him out in just three rounds in the spring of 1952, he realized his boxing days were numbered. While preparing for an upcoming fight against Chuck Davey, he fielded offers of other ways to make a living. He did not lack for propositions. Entrepreneurs, both legitimate and shady, were eager to cash in on Graziano's fame, but nothing particularly appealed to him. As for the proposal from Hiken, he found it hard to imagine an uneducated mug like himself making it on a bigtime TV show. For the time being, though, he figured he had nothing to lose, and besides, there was something about the bespectacled writer-director in the rumpled suit that appealed to him. "I could tell by how soft an [sic] slow the guy talked that he's a right guy," Graziano would later write. "You could see he likes people."[6]

Nat brought the boxer to his office a couple of days later to show him *The Martha Raye Show* script. He could see a look of dismay spread across Graziano's face as he skimmed through the pages. In another moment, Graziano turned the offer down and was heading for the door. He was alarmed by the number of lines he would have to memorize. Mindful of his reputation as a one-time champion, he was sick with fear at the possibility of making a fool of himself. Hiken's casting experiment was about to evaporate before it even had a chance to be tested.[7]

Nat assured the fighter that he would have enough time to prepare before going on air, but Graziano's anxieties still had the best of him. He was no comedian, he said, and he was afraid that his fractured Lower East Side dialect would not even be intelligible. Nat tackled this objection straight on. "That's just it," he said. "It's the way you say things. It's the guy that delivers the lines that makes them funny. All humor comes from your own character. All you got to be is yourself."[8]

Nat continued to explain that it was Graziano as he was that he wanted, not someone trying to be funny. Finally, he persuaded the boxer to give the show a try. Rehearsals began in October, after Nat had the chance to polish the script and after Graziano had lost a ten-round decision to Davey in what would turn out to be his last fight. From the start Nat could see that his hunch had been on the mark. There was an engaging, offbeat chemistry between the former champ and the lusty comedienne. Graziano's awkwardness and difficulty with lines were no impediment; in fact, they proved to be an asset. As molded by Hiken's writing and direction, Graziano came across as artlessly disarming. And the boxer's stillness, a product of his not knowing exactly what to do with himself, was a perfect counterpoint to Raye, the burlesque cyclone. Despite Graziano's hard-slugging past, Raye became the combative one of the couple. When impatient with him, she would smack him across the chest. And no ladylike love tap either. She let loose with a hearty wallop, while Graziano, one of the most feared battlers of his generation, just sat there, his head ducked slightly to one side like a sheepish little boy.

From the first day of rehearsal, Raye referred to Graziano as "goombah," Italian for godfather, which Hiken incorporated into the show as his star's pet name for the boxer. Graziano's flubs also became part of the program. Guest-starring with Graziano was celebrated soprano Risë Stevens, whose first name, as all opera aficionados knew, was pronounced "reesa." Graziano, who did not quite fit the profile of the typical *Opera News* subscriber, pronounced her name simply as "rise." After the laughter in the rehearsal hall subsided, fellow cast members corrected him, but Hiken, seeing an opportunity for laughs, corrected the correction. He instructed Graziano to call Stevens "Rise" throughout the episode.[9]

The addition of Graziano also allowed Hiken to create a comedic love triangle. At one of the triangle's points was Graziano, the dese-and-dose mug, and at the opposite point was guest star Cesar Romero, the suave Hollywood leading man. Rocky may been Raye's steady beau, but she swooned for Romero and longed to throw herself at him. (With Raye, of course, the phrase "throw herself" was no figure of speech.) The situation focused Raye's inspired clowning in a way that had been missing from most of the first-season installments.

Romero comes into Raye's life through a misunderstanding: he mistakes her for his leading lady while he rehearses a scene for his upcoming film version of *Dr. Jekyll and Mr. Hyde* in her apartment (relocated now from Flatbush to an equally disheveled flat on Second Avenue). As the dapper Dr. Jekyll, he sweeps her into his arms and declares his undying, passionate love for her. Raye faints at her sudden good fortune. Later, without her knowing, Romero transforms himself into his Mr. Hyde guise. He grabs her, tries to force himself upon her. Trapped in his clutches, she recoils at his monstrous features. "No! No! No!" she screams. Then, as an aside to the audience, "Me say no? Never thought I'd live to see the day."

When Raye learns that this has all been a big mix-up, her real troubles begin. She makes a date with Romero, her living dream, forgetting that she already has a date with Graziano. When all three show up at the saloon where she works, Martha does not have the heart to reject Rocky outright. Instead, she reminds him of their solemn, unbreakable agreement: if Rocky should ever hit a man outside the ring, they would be finished. She then immediately eggs Romero into insulting the former champ. No matter what Romero says—and no matter how much of a negative spin Raye puts on what he says—Graziano never rises to the bait. Until, that is, Romero brings up the subject of Percy Shelley, whom he describes as "a bit esoteric." Rocky explodes, lunging at him, about to uncork a haymaker.

The slapstick highlight occurs when Raye and Graziano are invited to join Romero and Stevens at a gala benefit dinner held at the Ritz Plaza Hotel. Uneasy about fitting in with the benefit's upper-crust crowd, Martha and Rocky decide that they will copy exactly what Romero and Stevens do at the dinner table. At the same time, Romero and Stevens decide they should go out of their way to make their guests feel at home: they will duplicate whatever Martha and Rocky do. The scene begins with a staring contest and tentative gestures on both sides, then gradually escalates, with cockeyed logic, to salad-flinging pandemonium. The skit, as described by the *New York Times*, "was hilariously silly business, thanks chiefly to faultless staging and timing."[10]

Variety raved about Martha Raye's second-season premiere, the first TV program both written and directed by Hiken. The reviewer characterized the

All Star Revue installment as "a show which should be a landmark on this series." The article cited the episode as far and away Raye's funniest work on television, "an amalgam of big time production, miming, casting, writing and direction," and in particular, marveled at the contribution of Graziano, "the thespic surprise of the occasion." [11]

In a quote appearing in another paper, Nat provided his own wry analysis of Graziano's newfound gift: "Nature and Tony Zale made Rocky's face a thing of endless interest to all. People love him on sight. Rocky Graziano acquired the complete Actors Studio technique soon after he began to walk. He was born mumbling." Nat originally hired Graziano for just the one show, but he now saw the greater potential. By the end of the season, he had installed the boxer as a regular performer. [12]

With this piece of casting, Hiken's reputation acquired a new dimension, as a sort of comedy-business Pygmalion. Not only could he craft outstanding material for established comics, he also now proved that he could take a non-actor and fashion a character for him that would tap into unrealized comedic possibilities. This process was an extension of what he had done on *The Grouch Club*, when he had written parts for nonactor relatives. But that, of course, had been merely a matter of making do within a spartan budget. In the case of Graziano, he cast a nonprofessional by choice and discovered he could enhance the show as a direct result. Bernie Seligman, a William Morris agent involved in the show, recalled hearing Nat explain his casting philosophy: "He said he cast people who brought two pages of dialogue to the show by virtue of their personalities and who they were." [13]

For the time being, Nat's unorthodox casting was confined primarily to the boxing world. Once he was established on the show, Graziano approached Hiken about finding work for his pals at the gym, many of whom were down on their luck now that their fight careers were fading. Nat went along with the idea and used many of them as extras. Of the bunch, the only one with any show business experience was one of Graziano's managers, Jack Healy, a sort of poor man's George Raft, a tough guy turned dancer who had never quite gotten beyond small-time vaudeville. The rest—including Walter Cartier, Frankie Gio, and Willie Pep—were pure pug, lending an earthy, colorful quality to the show. [14]

Inadvertently, Nat hired performers from another profession as well. A publicist acquaintance of his, who fancied himself a part-time talent agent, was lobbying Nat to hire some of his clients. Nat was leery. The press agent was known for his fondness for prostitutes. In fact, the gibe making the rounds on Broadway was that he met the buses at Port Authority to recruit young women from out of town. After putting up with the agent's repeated pitches, Nat finally agreed to hire some of his actresses, but with a stern proviso. "No professionals," he insisted. The publicist replied, the picture of innocence, "Oh, no, Nate. What do you mean? I wouldn't do that." Soon, after using some of the actresses as extras, Nat learned that his suspicions had been warranted after all. He confronted the press agent, who immediately denied everything. They argued. Finally, Nat stalked off. At which point the publicist hollered, "Listen, I don't tell you how to write scripts—don't you tell me about whores!"

Among the performers recruited from Stillman's talent pool, the most significant find, aside from Graziano himself, was Jake LaMotta. Like Graziano, the Raging Bull could boast of both a past middleweight title and an earlier prison record. Together the two boxers brought what must have been a new peak of gritty realism to the musical-variety genre. In one of their scenes together, they were supposed to go through the motions of a simulated bout but, anxious to put on a good show, they began pounding away at one another, leaving themselves bruised and battered for the sake of light entertainment. In another, conspicuously less brutal sequence, they enacted one of Hiken's most memorable sketches in the series.[15]

The setting is a dressing room where the two former champs prepare for a televised fight. The audience sees them from the point of view of the mirror as the two mugs preen themselves at the makeup table, exchanging tips, in their unmistakable street-tough accents, on hair styling and the proper use of Elizabeth Arden Pancake Number Five. In the midst of their primping, someone calls from outside the door, announcing that they have only ten more minutes. "Ten minutes!" Rocky screams. "And I haven't got my lips on yet!" In a flurry of tweezers and mascara brushes, the two bruisers scramble to finish, only to be interrupted once more, this time with grave news. A doctor, barely able to contain his tears, hands Rocky the results of his medical examination. The fighter reads the report, then buries his face in his hands, sobbing uncontrollably. "They just found out about my blood!" he moans. LaMotta asks what is wrong with his blood. "It don't show up on television!" Rocky wails. LaMotta tries in vain to comfort him.[16]

Nat referred to Graziano as his good luck charm. He believed that the pug's persona was largely responsible for the popular and critical success of the show. The two men were an unlikely pair—one a bookish-looking Jewish kid from Milwaukee and the other an Italian street-gang brawler from the Lower East Side—but they grew very close. According to Greg Garrison, who knew them both, "Rocky was Nat's best friend. He felt more comfortable with Rocky than anybody." Nat was fascinated by Rocky's stories about the fight game and his mobster acquaintances, and like so many people, he was taken with Graziano's unspoiled Dead End Kid manner. As Ambur remembered it, "Rocky was so outgoing and so generous that it was hard to avoid becoming involved with him."[17]

Nat would take Graziano to Lindy's for lunch, an eye-opening experience for the boxer who claimed he had never gone out to lunch before in his life, his midday repasts having been strictly confined to oily homemade sandwiches devoured during the odd break from workouts at Stillman's. In turn, Rocky introduced Nat to redolent downtown eateries, such as the Grotta Azzura tucked away in a cellar in Little Italy. The weekends were a time for golf, as it could only be played by Graziano. Perhaps even more important and more entertaining for Nat than the pleasure of the game itself was getting onto the courses. Each week they drove to a different place, typically an exclusive club in sequestered sections of northern New Jersey and New York's Westchester County. The fact that neither Nat nor Rocky was a member was of no concern. Nor did it matter if the club was restricted, meaning that it was completely off-limits to Jews. They would simply drive up, and Rocky would ask, "Excuse me, where da pro?" Once the club pro recognized the interloper, he escorted the champ and his party to the first tee.[18]

In coming years, Hiken's penchant for casting nonactors would bring him as much distress as success, as beneficiaries of his talent did not always appreciate what had been done for them. In the case of Graziano, though, it was a blessing, both professionally and personally. The former champ was grateful to Nat for masterminding a second career at a time when his future was uncertain, and he fully realized that it was Hiken's judgment and skill that had made it all possible. Like others who worked with Hiken, Graziano came to regard him as a kindly parental or avuncular figure. In describing his attitude toward Nat in his autobiography, Graziano evoked memories of his harsh childhood. When something happened in the mean streets that made him cry, he would run home to his mother, and she "would wash my face and comb my hair and then fix a piece of bread with olive oil an [sic] vinegar on it, and it was the greatest thing I ever eat [sic] in my whole life. That's the way I sometimes feel about Nat Hiken. He washed my face and combed my hair and gave me a piece of oil and vinegar bread."[19]

◆   ◆   ◆

With his own children, Nat did not always fit so easily into an attentive parental role. To an extent, the problem had to do with the long hours spent on a daunting work schedule. Besides writing and directing *The Martha Raye Show*, Hiken at this time was scripting for *The Buick Circus Hour* and *The U.S. Royal Showcase* and was creating a television pilot for Betty Kean and her sister Jane. He was also translating into English his father's Yiddish stories for possible adaptation to the stage or television. After all the day's work was done, there was not much time left to unwind at home and focus on his daughters, Dana and Mia.

"When I was a child we had our difficulties," recalled Dana Hiken Buscaglia, the older of the girls, who was six years old when *The Martha Raye Show* first went on the air. "He was often in his own world, or when he had free time he'd want to play golf with his friends." Dana knew that her father cared for her and her sister, but she was also aware that he had little patience for sitting and playing with a child for any length of time and little inclination to take his daughters out for afternoon jaunts. Beyond that, there could also be a feeling that he was high-handed. "There were times when he was harsh and he was unfair," said Dana, "but I think he was just under a lot of pressure and it was difficult to have demands made of him." Both daughters and Ambur agreed that Nat was not at ease in relating to girls. "He was okay with it when we were little," recalled Mia, "but Mom said that it was difficult for him to accept the fact that we were growing older. He really didn't know how to handle it. I think if he had had sons it might have been easier." [20]

What both daughters remembered fondly were the stories Nat told about growing up in Milwaukee and starting out on radio in Los Angeles, anecdotes usually about ordinary experiences made hilarious by his unique perspective. Often he would spin these yarns at the dinner table, and sometimes he would hold forth at social gatherings. If the Hikens were at a party dominated by comic extroverts such as Mel Brooks and Carl Reiner, Nat would be content to remain in the background, laughing with the others, but in quieter settings he emerged as a compelling raconteur. "I always wanted to hear what *he* had to say because it was always entertaining," Dana said. "I was always very impressed with him, obviously." [21]

Along with her father's facility with words, Dana was also intrigued by his ability to create with his hands, a gift passed on from Max Hiken that Dana herself inherited and would put to use years later in her work as a skilled jewelry maker. She would watch her father build model sailing ships, crafted from balsa kits that required sanding, excising minute pieces with a razor blade, attaching a miniature cotton rigging, masking off, and painting the boat's fine details. The ship might be his own project, or one that he bought for Dana but had to construct for her because she was too young to master the intricate handiwork. "I used to watch him for hours. We didn't talk. I'd just watch him."[22]

Perhaps mindful of what he would have done had he had sons, Nat occasionally took his girls to see baseball games at Yankee Stadium. If he had intended to teach them the fine points of the game, he would quickly forget, getting so wrapped up in the play on the field that he would neglect to explain the most basic rules of the sport. As far as Mia was concerned, she was watching nothing more than men in uniform running haphazardly around the field. Even so, she appreciated the experience. "It was a way to be with my dad, it was a way to get some attention."[23]

◆   ◆   ◆

All the work that Hiken devoted to *The Martha Raye Show* helped fashion the program into a vital part of a remarkable phenomenon. Often taken for granted at the time, and sometimes characterized in its day according to its lowest common denominator rather than its heights of inspiration, television evolved in the first half of the 1950s into what is now known as its Golden Age. The term is misleading to an extent. The word "golden" certainly could not be applied to all programming from the era; much of it was pretty dismal. What the term does accurately describe is the spectrum of vibrant drama and exuberant comedy that was only possible in a medium that was still defining itself. Under the stewardship of executives such as NBC's Pat Weaver and CBS's Hubbell Robinson, the networks allowed room for excellence on their daily TV schedules, sandwiched between the likes of *Rhythm Rodeo* and *Bonny Maid Versatile Varieties*.

Seizing upon this opportunity for excellence was a handful of astute New York drama producers. First stood Fred Coe, the great pioneer of live television theater; arrayed not far behind were Worthington Miner, Martin Manulis, David Susskind, and Herbert Brodkin. The now legendary collection of writers cultivated by these men, including Paddy Chayefsky, Horton Foote, Reginald Rose, and Rod Serling, created a series of diverse plays, often memorable, sometimes extraordinary, many of which—such as A *Trip to Bountiful* and *Marty*—went on to even more successful incarnations on Broadway and in the movies.

Not only the doyen of TV drama, Coe was also a comedy innovator, producer of Mr. Peepers, one of the earliest sitcom successes. Starring Wally Cox as Peepers, a mousy high school teacher, and featuring a young Tony Randall as his arrogant rival, the series, performed live once a week, projected a wry, easygoing portrait of small-town life, fashioned with a dramatist's eye for characterization. At the same time, on the opposite coast in California, Lucille Ball and Desi Arnaz were producing industry milestones of their own. They eschewed the live-broadcast methods favored in New York and recorded their hugely popular I Love Lucy directly on film, in the process laying the groundwork for a type of television production that, within just a few years, would transform the business.

Because broadcasters were feeling their way across uncharted territory, they were still relatively open to offbeat experiments. In 1953, more than ten years before I Spy established the formula on a national network, WOR-TV, a New York station, was willing to air Harlem Detective, a half-hour crime series featuring a pair of plainclothesman heroes, one white and one black. Broadcasters at the time also made room for the anarchic, surreal comedy of Ernie Kovacs. Although no network was ever willing to make a home for the comedian for very long—his approach was far too iconoclastic to fit comfortably into any corporate setting, no matter how tolerant—he still managed to remain on the air almost constantly throughout the decade.

The comedy-variety format that Hiken worked in was clearly more conventional. The genre's confines, though, encompassed a range of individual styles, buoyed by the boisterous spontaneity of live performances, from the brash video-vaudeville of Berle, Gleason, and Martin and Lewis to the electronic Broadway revue of Sid Caesar's Your Show of Shows and the artful self-mockery of Jack Benny. Making it all possible was a remarkable set of comedy writers, particularly those headquartered in New York, "the big-laugh people," as Leonard Stern dubbed them. Besides Hiken, they included Larry Gelbart, Mel Brooks, Mel Tolkin, Neil Simon, Tony Webster, Carl Reiner, Lucille Kallen, Goodman Ace, Hal Kanter, the team of Everett Greenbaum and Jim Fritzell, and Woody Allen. Stern, who also belongs in this group, speculated on what accounted for this flowering of talent in New York during the 1950s. "We were all the beneficiaries of having listened to radio," he said. "We became collaborators in a sense when we were kids because in radio you created the ambience, you visualized what the characters looked like. That seems to be similar to all of us, explaining why this disparate group from so many places all created humor that reflected each other. There was a commonality to the funny bone." Al Lewis, an active television performer during this period, believed that the theater was the other compelling influence for those who learned their craft in New York rather than Los Angeles. "These writers came out of that background, whether they worked in it or not. And in theater you have to have *writing*."[24]

Adapting a tradition from the Broadway stage, Hiken used his book-show approach to bring his own distinctive stamp to the variety format. At the same time, behind the scenes, he was beginning to establish a reputation for guiding performers to stardom. He demonstrated that he could turn a relatively unheralded comic into show-business royalty, functioning in this case as a veritable queenmaker of comedy.

Martha Raye's prominence during this period has been largely forgotten. Not only did her show receive consistent critical praise, she herself was singled out as a premier TV comedienne, typically rated as high as Lucille Ball, sometimes higher. Just a few years earlier her career had reached a new low. Under Hiken's guidance, she achieved her greatest fame, prompting *Variety* to designate her "the funniest lady buffoon on TV."[25]

In the years since her heyday, two factors have dovetailed to consign Raye's accomplishments to obscurity. First was her show's means of delivery. As live broadcasts, her programs went out over the airwaves to reach their enthusiastic audiences, and then, in effect, drifted out into the ether. Videotape would not be invented until 1956. That meant that the only way to preserve a broadcast such as *The Martha Raye Show* was to film the picture displayed on a video monitor as the program was being aired. The result, known as a kinescope, was a grainy, inferior record, whose visual and audio qualities were not crisp enough for the rerun market. After years of disuse, gathering dust in network storerooms, many kinescopes were simply discarded, lost forever. In contrast, Ball's filmed antics on *I Love Lucy* were continuously repeated throughout the fifties and are still on the air today.

The second factor that weighed against Raye was longevity, or lack of it. Her tenure as a TV star, rousing as it was, ended up lasting less than five years.

Her trajectory reached its peak during her second and third seasons. Consistently, Hiken developed situations that showcased her best, most rambunctious talents. In the opening to one installment, Martha, working as a cigarette girl, stumbles onto an opera stage during the production of *La Bohème*. Believing she has merely wandered into an Italian neighborhood, she attempts to hand out smokes at the sidewalk-café tables. She notices the tragic characters beginning to cry and soon starts bawling uncontrollably herself in sympathy. In an another especially memorable slapstick sketch from another episode, Martha agrees to give her neighbor, Mrs. Storecheese, a home permament, only to discover halfway through the procedure that she has been reading instructions off the back of an instant cake-mix box. And, in an installment guest-starring Zsa Zsa, Ava, and Magda Gabor, Hiken ventured into high-concept plotting with the comedic conceit that Martha is, in fact, the lost, fourth Gabor sister.[26]

At the beginning of the third season, *Variety* proclaimed that Raye's "partnership with director-writer Nat Hiken is one of the most potent comedy liaisons on video." Even more to the point from Hiken's perspective, in terms of the challenge he faced at the outset of the series, were the comments made by Jack Gould of the *New York Times*. While applauding the most recent episode, Gould noted Raye's previous propensity for coarseness, then concluded, "Apparently, a gentleman named Nat Hiken is to be credited for the theatrical discernment in preserving the more winning qualities of Miss Raye and weeding out the less desirable ones."[27]

Further burnishing Hiken's reputation at this time were his accomplishments on Broadway. The sketch he and Friedberg wrote for the Bert Lahr revue *Two on the Aisle* was singled out as a highpoint of the show by the *New York Times Magazine*, whose editors were so impressed with the piece that they ran a nine-panel photo-and-caption re-creation of the skit. "Schneider's Miracle," an oblique little satire of the go-getter business culture of postwar America, featured Lahr in the title role as a Central Park litter picker, a faithful, longtime employee, who, as he is proud to point out, was a six-bag man in his day. But the rat race is nipping at his heels. Piper, a young whippersnapper in the garbage game, has set his sights on Schneider's job and is moving in on his territory—from North Lagoon to South Comfort Station. What's more, an officious young inspector berates the old-timer for not being sufficiently productive. Schneider is up against it—either he brings in a full bag by six or he will be demoted to the indignity of dump detail. At the end of the frantic day, Piper bests Schneider through underhanded means, snatching from him that litter-picker's prize, a complete Sunday *New York Times*. "It's all over the park, Schneider," Piper crows. "You're through, I'm telling you, through." All seems truly lost, but then Schneider stumbles upon a suitcase jammed full of stolen money. "Thousands!" he exclaims. Happily, he tears up the bills and fills the rest of his bag. "It's a miracle. No dump for Schneider!" he says.[28]

The sketch Hiken wrote with Friedberg for Bette Davis's *Two's Company* did not attract the sort of glowing reviews that greeted their work for Lahr, but ultimately it acquired a considerable afterlife. The skit is set in a cluttered tenement apartment, inhabited by Helen, a blowsy wreck of a housewife (Davis), and Stanley, her truck driver husband (David Burns), who is convinced that every man is lusting after his bedraggled mate. The play as a whole was buffeted at first by unfriendly reviews and was then terminated just three months later when the star was incapacitated by a severe bacterial infection. But the "Jealousy" sketch survived. Actors were eager to sink their teeth into the dynamic interplay between Helen's frumpy indifference and Stanley's passionate mania, and over the years producers repeatedly licensed the sketch for a variety of theatrical settings. Among the more enthusiastic performers was a young Carol Burnett, who took the "Jealousy" skit with her from summer stock to her early days in television.[29]

As *The Martha Raye Show* developed a following among viewers, the program became a favorite, too, among NBC personnel, especially those who also worked for Milton Berle, regarded by many as an abusive martinet. Lee Pockriss, an NBC songwriter, said that shifting from Raye's show to Berle's was "just like going from *Lives of the Saints* to Krafft-Ebing." Like others, Pockriss found life on the Raye set to be demanding but also free-wheeling, full of hilarity and Runyonesque characters, an atmosphere that he affectionately compared to both a circus and a betting parlor.[30]

Graziano and his Stillman's crew, of course, accounted for much of the ambience, assisted by the cast's burlesque and Borscht-belt performers, but the quirky Runyon aura surrounded others as well, including former Metropolitan Opera star Ezio Pinza. A semiregular foil for Raye, the great *basso profundo* savored the limelight that followed him after his success in *South Pacific* and relished his new role as a Broadway character. His largesse, though, did not always measure up to his grand, sometimes grandiose, manner.

Greg Garrison remembered going to Lindy's one day with both Hiken and Pinza, where he was treated to the sight of the great man in all his glory, a larger-than-life individual with enormous appetites and, it seems, a special fondness for referring to himself in the third person. Seated at the table, he ordered one dish after another—"Pinza wants this . . . Pinza wants this . . ." When the gargantuan meal was all over, Nat and the singing star argued over who would pick up the check. Pinza finally relented; he would allow Nat to pay but only if he did his part by leaving the tip. This did not augur well for the hired help. "The check was for maybe twenty dollars, which was a lot of money, and Pinza puts down a dollar," Garrison recalled.

We walk out, Pinza gets his hat from the hat-check girl—"Pinza!" he says—and he gives the girl absolutely nothing. Nat turns to me and says, "Just a second, I forgot a paper at the table." He goes back, he puts two or three bucks down on the table, because he didn't want Pinza to look bad. "But everybody knows Pinza's bad," I said. "What did you do that for?" He said, "Well, this one time maybe it would help him out a little."[31]

Nat regarded his colorful assortment of performers with a watchful eye, always poised to take advantage of their talents and idiosyncracies. Something about his manner reminded Pockriss of a Jack Russell terrier, a sprightly little dog with a tendency to size up people out of the corners of its eyes. "Nat had a funny, sly, sideways kind of thing about him. I always felt he was sort of amused with me in some way and I don't know why." When directing, Nat did not resort to explosions of temperament, but he clearly exerted control and demanded the best. Quiet and droll as Nat may have been, the show's choreographer, Herbert Ross, could also see that he was "tense and intense."[32]

Sticking to form, Nat could be relied upon to deliver scripts late, sometimes leaving costume and scenery people imploring him for the most rudimentary idea of what they should be putting together a mere ten days before broadcast. Partly, this foot-dragging had to do with Nat's preference to work with the actors before finalizing a scene. For the dressing-room sketch with Graziano and LaMotta, for instance, he went to the two fighters with an outline of the skit and asked them to try out various lines to let him ascertain exactly which beauty product names sounded the most amusing coming out of their mouths and what reactions would best heighten the incongruous exchange. Often his tweaking of material would continue to the last day of rehearsal. According to Grey Lockwood,

He always made it sound like he didn't know anything about what he was doing. Which, of course, was quite the opposite. He was so withdrawn, he would say, "Maybe if you say. . . ," and he'd put in a word. And that one word would make the thing funny. It wasn't funny until then. That's what I call being a genius. He could just pluck a word out of the air and put that in and everybody would say, "My God, it's just one word and it's a laugh now." Little things like that which were in his soul, his technique.[33]

As choreographer, Herbert Ross was able to contribute to the hilarity as well with an opening dance number that became a running gag in the series.

Raye would open the sequence with a few verses of song and then would be joined by a troupe of male backup dancers who would continually startle her and jostle her about the stage, leading eventually to a sort of musical donny-brook. "Nat encouraged me and gave me more and more opportunities to do that sort of thing," Ross recalled, adding wryly, "because it also meant less writing for him, I guess." Ross, who later moved on to direct successful comedy films such as *Play It Again, Sam* and *The Goodbye Girl*, felt that his ability to handle comedy was enriched by his working with Hiken. "Simplicity," he cited as the first comedic virtue he learned from Nat, "and honesty, which is the essence of everything anyway. He was directing as though it were a play." [34]

At the center of it all, Raye endeared herself to the rest of the company with her cheerful trouper ways. She was a quick study, generous in helping fellow cast members and always ready to go full tilt even when rehearsing the most jarring pratfalls. And she was always on, eager to perform not only for audiences but for cast and crew between broadcasts as well. She was especially close to the show's dancers, or gypsies as they were called, frequently carousing with them after hours at parties or clubs where high spirits were elevated a notch higher by booze and grass. Her dealings with Nat were less flamboyant, governed by her respect for his talent and his supervision of her newfound stardom. As Ross put it, "She was a little, in my view, intimidated by him." [35]

Whenever Raye took issue with anything on the show, she did not have to break with her role as everyone's pal. Haggling on her behalf was a job she left to her husband and manager, Nick Condos. A former tap dancer, the hard-drinking Condos had a tumultuous private life with Raye, but in business he guarded her interests fiercely. Still, any issues that arose during the course of the show did not spoil his fondness for Nat. He and Raye would often try to include Nat and Ambur in their social forays through Manhattan nightspots. They succeeded more often than Nat would have liked. As a rule, he tried to minimize his socializing with his stars, preferring instead to maintain a certain friendly distance that would allow him to take a demanding stance when need be. "Martha was like a lot of people in the entertainment industry. They're very self-involved, they want to be loved, and they can be very seductive," Ambur said. [36]

Perhaps most seductive of Raye's traits was her talent, which could be at its most irresistible when unfurled in impromptu social situations. Ambur recalled a time returning with Raye to her hotel room one night after dinner.

> She was a little bit tipsy, but not much, and Nicky was with us too but he had passed out. There was a friend of hers there—she always had a "slave"—and this

slave talked her into doing this bit that she had apparently just dreamed up the night before, something to do with a very important debutante, dead drunk, entering a nightclub. I can only say it was brilliant. She was stumbling around, and with this *hauteur*—it was fabulous.[37]

When it came to the company he kept, Nat was much more at ease with Billy Friedberg, his trusted aide and by now a collaborator of long standing. Few people on the show had the chance to witness them at work; the twosome, both quiet men, kept to themselves a great deal, often at the office on West 48th Street, working at their own pace regardless of production demands. They remained a unit unto themselves when the show's broadcast was done. "I always remember when the show ended, it was invariably on a high note," said Lockwood, who worked closely with Nat on the series.

Everybody would say, "Martha, you're wonderful," and so forth; people were leaving the theater in droves, happy, talking, and out there standing on the corner, these two lonely little characters, Nat Hiken and Billy Friedberg, with two of the longest faces you'd ever see. The audience is going by them, laughing, giggling—it didn't mean a thing. They were just quietly standing out there, and after a while they'd cross Sixth Avenue and slowly go down the street . . . They weren't upset about anything, I'm sure. They knew it was good if it was good, they knew it was bad if it was bad, but they just were not up, the way show business people are when it's good.

What lay behind this seeming melancholy? After pondering the question, Lockwood considered that perhaps Hiken and Friedberg only paid attention to what did not work on the show, or they just felt let down once the month-long production process was over. But then he added, "I also think that's the way they took good news."[38]

◆   ◆   ◆

All Star Revue never approached the success of NBC's other variety wheel, *The Colgate Comedy Hour*, and the network decided finally to cancel the series at the end of the 1952–53 season. The Martha Raye installments, though, attracted enough of a following to warrant continuation in slightly modified form. The following fall, the beginning of Raye's third season, the show was expanded from sixty to ninety minutes and was rescheduled for the prime slot of Saturday nights at nine as a once-a-month replacement for *Your Show of*

Shows. In recognition of the program's rising popularity, major magazine editors began to pay more attention, assigning feature articles on both Raye and her series in *Life*, *Time*, *The New York Times Magazine*, and *Look*. The show had reached its peak of success. At the same time, behind the scenes, it began to unravel.

At the root of the problems may have been a simmering resentment on Raye's part. As Lockwood saw it, "The word was out that it's this guy behind those words and those ideas—she's a great performer but where would she be without Nat? She apparently couldn't handle it too well. It bugged her." The brittle undercurrent between Hiken and Raye often rose to the surface in disputes over the star's singing numbers. For all her antic buffoonery, Raye was capable of delivering a torch song with both musicality and passion, and the series always featured this talent to a certain extent, but the star, along with Condos, felt the program should do more to showcase this more serious side of her personality. Repeatedly during the third season, when the time came to make the final cuts before the broadcast, Condos would agitate for keeping a closing ballad at the expense of a sketch. Nat argued for cutting the song in favor of the comedy, and, as the final arbiter on the set, he would ultimately have his way. As the season wore on, the dispute became increasingly rancorous.[39]

Whatever the exact cause of Raye's discontent, the effect on the set was quite clear to Hiken, clear and inexcusable. As he put it, Raye was beginning "to play around." Not a sexual observation, this remark instead had a meaning of critical professional importance to Hiken. He meant that Raye was not taking the job as seriously as she should, that she was coming to rehearsal unprepared, not knowing all her lines. For him this was a mortal show business sin, one that he would not tolerate.[40]

Raye's personal life was probably another concern. Hiken professed not to care what performers did away from the show, but the turmoil in Raye's life was too closely entwined with the program and must have been a distraction. She divorced Condos, her fourth husband, in June 1953, charging that he had beaten her, but she continued to retain him as her manager. With Condos still on hand, still handling her professional affairs, she pursued a young dancer on the show, Ed Begley, and married him the following spring, as if flaunting her latest escapade in Condos's face.[41]

On a more professional level, Nat went through a squabble of his own, largely of his own making. The issue was the show's directing credit, a complicated question in those days. As was the custom on shows of this kind, the credit was split. Nat was billed as director, which meant that he handled the staging in terms of acting and comedic effect, and Grey Lockwood was credited as television director, signifying that he was in charge of the camerawork and lighting. Halfway through the third season, the Radio and Television Directors Guild intended to clear up this confusion by insisting that there be only one director to handle all duties, as had long been the case in the movies. Nat, anxious to elevate his position, followed the guild's lead and issued an ultimatum. As Lockwood remembered it, Nat's lawyer, Artie Hershkowitz, approached the executive producer one day, toward the end of rehearsal for the latest episode, and announced that he would not let Hiken's script go on the air unless his client was designated the sole director. "It was a great shock," Lockwood said of this move by Nat, "because I just worshiped him."[42]

Ultimately a compromise was reached that allowed the show to go on the air. But in the process, the guild muddied the waters even more with a nonsensical new arrangement. The apportioning of responsibilities would not change, but now Hiken's credit would read "Directed by Nat Hiken" and, in a rare feat of splitting hairs, Lockwood's credit became "Director: Grey Lockwood." The experience injected another sour note into what was now a less than harmonious company. In describing his relationship with Nat for the remainder of the season, Lockwood said, "We weren't unfriendly, but I didn't feel good. I can't live in that kind of situation."[43]

Even without the credit conflict, Raye's cavalier attitude toward the work may have been enough in itself to persuade Nat to leave the show. An attractive offer from another network then led him the rest of the way out the door. CBS made overtures to lure him away, and eventually Hiken signed with the rival broadcaster for five years, as a producer-writer-director, at a six-figure annual salary.[44]

The Martha Raye Show remained on the air at NBC, with the same variety-narrative approach and with Graziano still featured as Raye's on-screen boyfriend. Now written by Ed Simmons and Norman Lear, the series continued to build an audience, climbing from number seventeen to number nine among top-rated shows for the 1954–55 season, but it was riding the momentum originally propelled by Hiken's ideas—without, as critics noted, his ongoing guidance. Jack Gould of the *New York Times* pointed out that Raye's exasperating excesses were creeping back once again, and she was badly in need of bright material and discipline. "Miss Raye can be an immensely funny woman, and surely will again. But she should learn to keep her guard up against the false friends who sometimes may lack the fortitude to tell her 'no.' "[45]

Raye's aesthetic decline was accelerated by plunges in her personal life. It now became clear that the marital hijinks that had cropped up during her third season were an early indication that she was starting to spin out of control. Her marriage to Begley disintegrated, and in January 1955 she hospitalized herself for treatment of what appeared to be a nervous breakdown. Two years later she lurched into yet another marriage, which turned out to be just as disastrous.[46]

Her show left the air in May 1956. In the late 1950s, she staged a partial comeback when she joined *The Steve Allen Show* as a featured guest performer and managed to recapture some of the manic brilliance that she had displayed in her days with Hiken. But she would never again star in a series of her own.

Hiken, meanwhile, took stock of developments in the early-1950s TV industry and set his mind on a path that promised to lead him to both creative and financial satisfaction. The *I Love Lucy* phenomenon served as the model. Filmed live before an audience, the show combined both comedic spontaneity and huge monetary returns in the rerun market. Nat needed to devise a show concept, to be produced in the same manner, that could be sustained over several seasons, to accumulate enough half-hour films to sell as a profitable rerun package. But first, he needed the right performer, someone, preferably, who could combine the explosive energy of Raye with the discipline of Berle. That all this might overlay a lightning wit and unsurpassed verbal delivery would seem almost too much to ask for.

You'll Never Get Rich

Phil Silvers's fortunes at the beginning of 1954 were somewhat mixed. Although a success on Broadway—most recently in the hit comedy *Top Banana*—he did not enjoy nationwide stardom. He was known as a comedian's comedian, meaning he was not nearly as well known as other comics knew he should be.

The Brooklyn-born performer had been working on his craft for decades. He had gotten his start in show business as a child singer in vaudeville, a career that ended in adolescence when his voice changed—for the worse. He left music behind as a career, but he retained a quality of it throughout his life: his comedy would always be infused with an infectious rhythm.

His comedy roots were planted in burlesque. There, during the 1930s, he mastered what amounted to the American equivalent of *commedia dell'arte*. As he migrated from one theater to another along the burlesque circuit, he might not have known the partners he would have to work with, but there would be no question about the material. Leonard Stern remembered Silvers explaining this performer's craft: "He could go to any city and pick up a comedian or a straight man and work with him. They all knew the routines because they were so precise. So you could work with total strangers and do the 'Porkchops sketch' or 'Slowly I turn . . .' or whatever you were called upon to do." The characters and situations were set, but within that pattern an inventive comedian could weave in ad-libs and his own nuances. No other burlesque comedian was more inventive than Silvers. And few could match his discipline and verbal dexterity.[1]

Hollywood could not help noticing him. Unfortunately, the studios never devised a way to turn the bald, bespectacled comedian into a star. In a handful of bit parts, in such movies as *Tom, Dick and Harry* and *A Lady Takes a Chance*, he was able to flash some of his rare talent for playing fast-talking wise guys. But in the rest of his films, mostly musicals, he was confined to basically the same supporting role over and over again, a character he generically referred to as "Blinky," the energetic best friend to the leading man and brotherly confidante to the leading lady. His greatest Hollywood success occurred offscreen. The movie community raved over the off-the-cuff performances he gave at the town's most fashionable parties, and often he was invited for no other reason than to entertain.[2]

Ultimately, his rise to stardom stemmed from the weekly gin games at the Park Plaza Hotel where he had first gotten to know Hiken. Hiken, though, was not the one who set the crucial events in motion, but two other gin-game pals, Irving Mansfield and Sid Garfield. Without them, Sergeant Bilko might never have been born.

Early in 1954, Mansfield received a high-class assignment. Normally a broadcast producer, he took on the job of assembling a nonelectronic event when the Radio and Television Correspondents Association invited him to coordinate its annual gala dinner. The affair was to be held in Washington, D.C., and would offer entertainment not only to journalists and broadcasters but also to the highest echelons of the federal government, including the president himself. For the event, Mansfield put together a program that ran the gamut from Raymond Massey reciting an Abraham Lincoln address to comedian Sam Levenson and trick golfer Paul Hahn. But the lineup could use one more entertainer, as far as Garfield was concerned. He pressed Mansfield to include their mutual friend Silvers as well. The comedian had a routine known as "The Singing Lesson," and Garfield was convinced it would stop the show in the nation's capital, as it had done practically everywhere else it had been performed.[3]

Silvers had perfected the routine while he and Frank Sinatra entertained troops in World War II. Silvers would offer to give the man known as The Voice some pointers on putting over a song. To get things rolling, he would ask Sinatra to sing a few bars, but the second the crooner let out his first note Silver grabbed his face, pinched the singer's cheeks together, and rattled off a stream of spurious vocal critiques. Silvers repeated this every time Sinatra opened his mouth, unleashing a series of hilarious variations with devilishly precise timing.[4]

Mansfield agreed with Garfield's idea, provided that they found the right partner. There was no point to the routine unless the straight man was a celebrated singer who obviously knew more about his craft than Silvers ever would. Sinatra was not available, but Mansfield was able to substitute Julius LaRosa, at the time a rising young pop star.[5]

The appearance arranged by Mansfield and Garfield at Washington's Mayflower Hotel on February 6, 1954, seemed at first just like any other gig for Silvers. Two factors combined to make it something more than that. One was the presence in the audience of Hubbell Robinson, vice president in charge of programming at CBS. The other factor was the atmosphere of suspicion that the Secret Service imposed on the event. Even the telephones were disconnected in the hotel ballroom where the dinner was being held; the agents feared that a phone ring might activate specially rigged sound-sensitive bombs. The precautions put Silvers on edge, and when his nervous system accelerated he got even funnier.[6]

He performed his singing-lesson routine to cascades of laughter from an audience that included President Eisenhower, Vice President Nixon, and every major cabinet officer except Secretary of State John Foster Dulles, who was unable to attend because he was in Berlin attending the Foreign Ministers Council. Silvers made his biggest impression with impromptu remarks. At one point in the middle of his act, despite all the security precautions, a phone rang. A hush fell over the room as Secret Service agents pounced on the phone. A long moment passed. There was no explosion. Without missing a beat, Silvers turned to the side, cocking an ear as if receiving news relayed to him from the wings. "What? Oh yes," he said, then he turned to Eisenhower. "It's long distance. From Europe. Man named Dulles. Says he'll talk to *anybody*." The president, along with the rest of the audience, burst into laughter.[7]

Impressed with the comedian's energy and quick wit, CBS's Robinson considered what Silvers might be able to do for his network. After he returned to New York, he offered Silvers a contract to develop a situation comedy. Silvers was unsure whether he wanted to try television—Jack Benny had recently warned him that the medium could be a terrible grind—but Robinson succeeded in clinching his interest. He said that the producer, writer and director on the project would be Nat Hiken.[8]

Just casual friends at this point, Hiken and Silvers now found themselves suddenly paired together in close collaboration for brainstorming a series con-

cept. The pairing of these two men would turn out to be one of the most fortu-
itous partnerships in TV comedy.

At first no discernible sparks of brilliance flashed around them. They spent
several months casually tossing ideas at one another, mostly in Nat's 48th
Street hovel of an office, often while strolling along mid-Manhattan streets or
taking in games at Yankee Stadium. Nat's first idea was to cast the actor as a finagling army sergeant. Silvers did not think much of that. To him it smacked
of Abbott and Costello shenanigans already played out years earlier in such
service comedies as *Buck Privates* and *In the Navy*. He was sure they could do
better. Other ideas came, but all failed to inspire. When the time finally came
to meet with Robinson and other CBS executives, they had narrowed the list
of possibilities to eight, including Silvers as a minor league baseball manager,
a conniving stockbroker, and a manager of a gym. In the end Nat's initial instinct struck the right note for CBS. The network wanted the army show.[9]

Now that the network expected to see a pilot, Nat was called upon to exercise his two most celebrated talents, scripting and casting. As was his habit
when facing a deadline, he preferred bouncing ideas off a partner to help him
clarify his story and characters. Friedberg, then writing for Max Liebman on
Producers' Showcase, was not available, so Nat brought in Terry Ryan, one of
his junior writers from *The Fred Allen Show*. Ryan was flattered that he was
chosen to collaborate, but he soon discovered that Nat's fertile imagination
and cultivated skill left little room for anyone else's contributions. Mostly, he
was simply in attendance at the creation. "I remember on my first day he sent
me out to buy some toilet paper. I thought, 'Boy, this signifies the importance I
have in *this* operation.' "[10]

In naming his sitcom hero, Nat turned to his baseball-fan expertise, appro-
priating the surname of National League first baseman Steve Bilko. Especially
significant was the name's first syllable—"bilk." Ernest G. Bilko, stationed at
the fictional Fort Baxter in Roseville, Kansas, is nominally the master sergeant
in charge of the post's motor pool—a part-time job at best. Bilko's primary
duty, as he sees it, is the brazen fleecing and bamboozling of his platoon, his
commanding officers, his fellow master sergeants and virtually anyone else
who happens to cross his crooked path. Hiken was not breaking new ground
here for Silvers. Comical rascals were already his stock in trade, the sort of
character he had portrayed on Broadway in *Yokel Boy*, *High Button Shoes*, and
Top Banana. What Silvers's roles had always lacked were strong stories and situations. In a sense he was a victim of his own creativity. Too often directors

and writers relied on his ability to ad-lib, sometimes expecting him to invent entire sequences for himself. Hiken knew that he would have to support Silvers's talent with a rich premise and well-crafted plotlines if the series were to last more than one season.[11]

Nat's unorthodox military service during the war was one source for background when concocting Bilko's renegade exploits; some visits to New Jersey's Fort Dix also helped in fleshing out the setting. As for Bilko's con jobs, Hiken could draw upon the stories of outlandish press agentry that he had treasured for so many years. There was, for instance, the one about Eddie Jaffe's assignment to keep a rich playboy's name out of the newspapers. The *bon vivant* had, quite inconveniently, run over a woman, and he would just as soon not endure the added inconvenience of seeing his name plastered all over the tabloids. Jaffe's solution? He called every editor he knew and insisted that they run the sensational story. All the editors turned him down flat. Their journalistic integrity suddenly piqued, they were not about to get steamrollered by a pushy press agent.[12]

Jack Tirman, who sublet the 48th Street office to Nat, was another source of anecdotes. Once he had been saddled with the task of promoting a lackluster restaurant called the Kit Kat Club. Responding to pressure from the club's impatient owner, he came up with a scheme. He would get some ink for the dazzling dance team currently appearing at the club. The only problem was that there was no dance team. So Tirman invented one, the fabulous Gomez and Weinberg. A few mentions in the city's gossip columns emboldened him. He proceeded to plant a whole series of items about the nonexistent team: Gomez and Weinberg were held over. They went to Hollywood to appear in a movie, only to return to the Kit Kat owing to popular demand. Gomez and Weinberg got married. They had a baby. They lost the baby. They separated. They reunited. They returned to the Kit Kat yet again. Finally, when the hoax was uncovered, Walter Winchell, one of the dupes, confronted Tirman and lambasted him. Tirman, wilting under the Broadway titan's rage, groped for some way to appease him and grasped at a defense that only a lifelong flack would consider legitimate: he assured Winchell that if Gomez and Weinberg *had* existed, he would have given the columnist an exclusive.[13]

The actual scams that Nat had heard about over the years did not make their way into the Silvers show, but their inverted logic and sheer *chutzpah* were clearly mirrored in Bilko's wheeling and dealing.

In creating supporting characters, Nat's ideas were shaped by his casting choices. His handpicked assortment of faces and personalities turned out to be one of television's great comic menageries. At the core were his most reliable troupers: Billy Sands, a key player since the Berle-show days; Herbie Faye and Jimmy Little, bit performers on *The Martha Raye Show*; and John Gibson, another veteran of the Berle radio series. From other service comedies he recruited Harvey Lembeck and Allan Melvin, scrappy POWs from *Stalag 17* who now became Bilko's sidekick corporals; Harry Clark, the beleaguered noncom from *No Time for Sergeants*, who was transformed into Fort Baxter's mess sergeant, Stanley Sowici; and, in an especially grand coup, the basset hound faced Paul Ford, the bombastic officer from *The Teahouse of the August Moon*, who was cast as Bilko's Colonel Hall. From the Borscht Belt came the scrawny standup comic, Mickey Freeman; from Jaffe's place came the swarthy Bernie Fein; and from the fight game returned two of Hiken's standbys, Jack Healy and Walter Cartier. The most unforgettable find of all, though, came more or less from nowhere.

The dumpy, spectacularly ugly Maurice Gosfield ambled into an open casting call one day, brandishing an enormous list of credits. A handful of his bit parts on stage are easy enough to confirm; more difficult to pin down are his claims of two-thousand radio credits and one hundred TV appearances. Perhaps more to the point is the recollection of a producer who remembered Gosfield hanging around with other work-hungry actors on the third floor of the NBC building a few years earlier; he recalled that the slovenly performer was considered something of a joke. None of the man's background, though, really mattered to Hiken and Silvers once they got a good look at him. Nat had already picked someone to play the most woebegone member of Bilko's platoon, but immediately he knew that here was the man born for the part. Maurice Brenner, originally selected for the role, was recast as Private Fleischman, while Gosfield became Private Duane Doberman, the saddest of sad sacks and all-around human disaster area. The part, in Gosfield's case, required no acting ability—which was fortunate, because he had none to speak of.[14]

On the show's technical side, both Hiken and the network wanted to emulate the techniques pioneered on *I Love Lucy*. Lucy's misadventures were performed essentially like a live broadcast before a studio audience, with three film cameras trained simultaneously on the action to provide three angles that would later be pieced together in the editing room. The director halted production only for scene changes and technical mishaps. CBS dispatched director Al DeCaprio to the Desilu studios in Los Angeles to observe the technique firsthand and learn its fine points so that it could be adapted for use on the Silvers series. DeCaprio was then placed in charge of the Bilko show's camerawork and lighting, as Grey Lockwood had been on *The Martha Raye Show*. Hiken would handle the actors. To sidestep the thorny issue of directorial credits, DeCaprio was listed as director, while Hiken received the unusual "Staged by . . ." credit.[15]

In his first stint as a television producer, Nat ran into some problems right from the beginning. As he prepared for the pilot, he was not always able to assure that the production's details jibed with his intent. He explained to the set designer that this was a comedy show about the army, and the designer came away from the discussion assuming that the sets themselves should be humorous. Nat arrived on the set the first day to find the barracks room tricked up with supposedly funny details: doors that were slightly off center, for instance, or door knobs that would slip off when someone turned them. At considerable expense, the sets had to be redesigned and rebuilt. Another snafu occurred on the first day of dress rehearsal. The cast's fatigues arrived in perfect shape—immaculately laundered, crisply pressed—far too perfect for the ragtag platoon Nat had in mind. In an uncharacteristic explosion of temper, he railed against the stupidity of the wardrobe department, then barked at the cast to drop to the floor and roll around until the outfits were all sufficiently rumpled and soiled.[16]

When production obstacles were finally overcome and the pilot completed, the results satisfied both Robinson and his boss William Paley, who was supposed to have remarked, "This is money in the bank. Take it off the rack and go ahead." The network authorizied the filming of thirty-nine episodes and, as part of the finalized deal, agreed to apportion both Hiken and Silvers a percentage of the series.[17]

For the first few weeks of the production schedule, it was the potential for profit that kept Hiken and Silvers going as they soon began to feel like they were working in a vacuum. The network had so far failed to line up a sponsor, and without a sponsor no time slot could be assigned to the show. The company rehearsed in the Nola Studios above Lindy's and filmed half a dozen episodes at the Dumont soundstage on East 66th Street while a nagging uncertainty hovered over the set.[18]

Production problems exacerbated the situation. As producer, Nat had difficulty coordinating all the details of ushering a script through rehearsal, shooting, and editing, while at the same time writing and staging the program. Eventually, CBS asked Edward Montagne, an expert in TV-film production, to join the Bilko team. He took on the day-to-day producing duties, receiving credit as the show's production supervisor, thus freeing Nat to focus on the creative aspects of the series.[19]

Whatever difficulties the show experienced, there was also a growing feeling among the troupe that they were creating something special. For cast member Mickey Freeman, the realization began sometime during the second episode. As opposed to the usual sitcom procession of embarrassing predicaments, the episode was a wry trickster tale driven by the sort of logic that would have made Brer Rabbit proud. Early in the story Bilko vows to take revenge against his fellow master sergeants for fleecing one of his rookies in a shady poker game. He sets his plan in motion by leasing an empty store in nearby Roseville. The other sergeants, sure that the crafty noncom is up to something, want to know exactly what sort of scheme Bilko has in mind for the property. He assures them that he has no plans and that he has simply acquired a vacant storefront. The more he assures them, the more frantic the sergeants are to get in on the deal. In the end, their ringleader is so overcome by greed and curiosity that he is willing to crawl to Bilko on his hands and knees with a wad of cash clenched in his teeth to buy into the lease—only to learn that he has bought nothing but an empty store, after all. The deft unfolding of the story impressed Freeman. "That's when I began to see it," he said, adding in his Catskill-comic vernacular, "This is not just television-funny or radio-funny. It's funny-funny." Word of the clever new series filtered outside the studio and into the show business community; stars such as Jack Benny, Milton Berle, Myrna Loy, and Cary Grant began to join the crowds in the studio bleachers to witness the Friday filmings.[20]

Good news from the network's business people accompanied the growing interest in the show. CBS had signed up Camel cigarettes as a sponsor and soon added Amana refrigerators as cosponsor. For Hiken and Silvers, some of the fretfulness faded. Now they only needed to learn about the show's scheduling. When the news arrived, though, their anxieties returned in full. Their show would air Tuesday evenings at eight-thirty. They were slated to go up against an NBC comedy wheel that included Martha Raye, Bob Hope, and, most dismaying of all, Milton Berle, Mr. Television himself, a Tuesday-night institution for the past six years.[21]

Under the title You'll Never Get Rich, the show premiered September 20, 1955. The Nielsen ratings confirmed Hiken and Silvers's fears: 14.6 for their program and 23.6 for NBC's variety show featuring Hiken's previous star, Martha Raye. The gap widened the following week when Berle took his turn on the air. The situation did not improve over the next month, and CBS decided to modify its strategy, moving the Bilko show from eight-thirty, halfway through NBC's variety hour, to eight o'clock. Perhaps, the network reasoned, viewers had been reluctant to take a look at *You'll Never Get Rich* because they had already been immersed in the NBC competition by the time Silvers went on the air; perhaps they would be more willing to tune in at the top of the hour. Over the next few weeks, the program's fortunes began to change. The network's new scheduling tack might have been the cause, but another possibility, proposed by Freeman, was that an appearance by the Bilko platoon on *The Ed Sullivan Show* might have sparked the viewers' interest and encouraged them to tune in to the next episode in the series. Or, perhaps, after two months on the air, it was simply inevitable that the program would have found its audience. Whatever the reason, on November 29 the Bilko show nearly matched Berle's ratings. Later in December, *You'll Never Get Rich* bypassed the NBC competition and continued to dominate the time slot from then on.[22]

Although the number of viewers was an issue in the beginning, the reaction of those who saw the first Silvers episodes was immediately gratifying. "Every time you start to count out situation comedy as a dead duck, something comes along," wrote John Crosby of the *Herald Tribune*. "What has come along this time is the new Phil Silvers show, 'You'll Never Get Rich,' a wonderfully inspired bit of lunacy." In answering his own question—"What makes the adventures of Sergeant Bilko so funny?"—Jack Gould of the *New York Times* singled out the quality that Hiken had begun to develop several years earlier when creating *The Magnificent Montague*. "A set owner would have to search the channels far and wide for a more polished example of expert farce, which is quite possibly the most abused dramatic form in TV."[23]

The first thing viewers responded to, of course, was Silvers himself. Sergeant Bilko was the ultimate Silvers rogue, a character that allowed him to use every technique he had mastered in his twenty-five years of comedy experience: the machine gun spiels; the quicksilver turns from one character to another, from one idea to the next; the wonderfully agile takes; and, perhaps his greatest comic weapon of all, his brilliant, dimpled smile, dazzling with insincerity. And now there was one more addition to his repertoire: his ability to bark and growl a series of commands that brings a platoon to attention without the benefit of a single word of English. Thanks to Hiken, all of this was now enveloped in the sort of precise scriptwriting that had been so lacking in Silvers's stage shows.

Bilko's scams are fabulously and hilariously corrupt, from his perfunctory fleecing of his platoon—bedmaking contests, President Chester A. Arthur birthday bashes (five dollars a ticket)—to his most elaborate hornswoggles, for example, passing off Fort Baxter as a glorified tenement so that a congressional committee will award the post more money. As broad as the comedy got, though, it was always based on an understanding of human nature and revolved around sharply defined character quirks.

Bilko's schemes are so bald-faced, and his *modus operandi* so fearless and nimble, it is difficult not to root for him. Beyond that, Hiken layered in another attribute to endear Bilko to viewers. Ultimately, he is an underdog. No matter how larcenous his ambitions, Bilko can never quite cash in on the big payoff. And, in the end, he is not nearly as unscrupulous as he would like. Many times it is his conscience that sabotages what he considers his better, greedy instincts. In this series about a cynical but likeable con man, Hiken perfected a comedic approach that he had been developing ever since his days on *The Grouch Club* and *The Fred Allen Show*, an approach that managed to be both unsentimental and good-natured.

Helping make the show so consistently funny week after week was the density of the comedy. Silvers gives a virtuoso performance and dominates every scene he is in, but Hiken also surrounded his star with a wide array of characters to stir up the comedic brew and provide colorful foils that would drive Bilko to even more outlandish extremes. Many of these characters might have only one or two lines per episode, yet they were all distinctive and amusing in their own way, from Bilko's motley crew of a platoon to his rival poker-playing sergeants.

Some supporting actors, such as Sands and Faye, injected extra laughs by succeeding in keeping pace with Silvers's rapid-fire riffs. Others produced great hilarity by falling far behind. Paul Ford, for example, was an experienced actor when he joined the Bilko cast but he was no comedy machine. A late starter in the business, he began acting in 1940 at thirty-eight, after failing at a number of jobs, including proofreader, ad salesman, and gas station attendant. In the role of Bilko's Colonel Hall, he often groped for his lines on-screen, but this quality was ideally suited for a blustering and flustered officer struggling to maintain command of his post while Bilko verbally tap-danced around him.[24]

At first, Nat wrote the show entirely on his own. After the second episode, though, he realized that he would need help. *You'll Never Get Rich* was his first

weekly TV series, and he found the schedule taxing. Just as taxing was the type
of scripting involved. "It's difficult because all the humor stems from Bilko's
own character," Hiken explained in an interview at the time. "It's an awful ordeal for a writer because, since you don't write gags per se, you can finish a
whole script without knowing whether it's a prize or a bomb." At this early
stage—just a month into the show's first season—he was already hoping that
he would be able to divorce himself from writing altogether and just concentrate on directing. On past TV shows he had relied on a single partner but that
would not be sufficient for a season of thirty-nine episodes. For the first time in
his career, Nat assembled a full writing staff.[25]

Some writers recruited that first season were already well established in
broadcasting, including Tony Webster, who had written for *Your Show of
Shows*; Arnold Auerbach, a former Fred Allen scripter; and the team of Coleman Jacoby and Arnie Rosen, who had created many of Jackie Gleason's television characters. Others, like Barry Blitzer, were still relatively new to the
business. Blitzer, who had known Hiken only by reputation, was "in awe of the
legend." His first glimpse of the unprepossessing Nat proved to be less than inspiring. He thought, He's the accountant—where's the funny guy?[26]

To track all the scripts and the writers working on them, Nat kept a chart
that covered an entire wall in his office at CBS headquarters at 485 Madison
Avenue. This allowed him to make sure that he did not repeat situations or use
characters too often in the same way. Even more useful was his secretary,
Gertrude Black, a highly efficient woman who managed details better than
Nat and, as her husband put it, "knew what Nat wanted before he wanted it."
Nat's writers, unfortunately, did not possess this prescient ability. They would
have found it useful.[27]

Juggling ideas in his head was one of Nat's gifts. Verbalizing them was often
beyond him. In story conferences with his writers, his mind would take inventive turns and quantum leaps forward, but his mouth did not always keep up.
What often came out were strings of half sentences. As Blitzer remembered it,

Sometimes we'd say, "Nat, wait a minute, slow down a little." Because the ideas
were coming out so quickly and his mind was very fertile—some of those Bilko
premises were very unusual, off the wall. And sometimes every other sentence
out of him was, "You know . . . And Bilko says—you know." And we didn't
know. And you didn't always want to admit that. Sometimes he'd get a little impatient with you, and you didn't want to appear too dumb, so you didn't know,
and you'd have to figure out what he meant later on.[28]

While alternately bemused and impressed by Nat's flow of ideas, the writers were also intrigued by one of his nervous habits-cum-creative outlets. When he lapsed into silent thought, or sometimes when he spoke, he would take whatever piece of paper was handy and begin an elaborate, meticulous process of folding—his own form of origami. He might take a sheet from a pad of yellow lined paper and fold it over and over along sharp, straight lines until the entire sheet was so small that he could grasp it between two fingers. At other times, he might dissect a cigarette pack, extract the tinfoil inside, and fold it into animal shapes, then slit open the cigarettes, arrange the loose tobacco in tiny piles, and plant a tinfoil animal in each of them—all the while holding forth on a complex plotline, his hands working independently of his thoughts.[29]

Once the story was outlined, the writers would set off to begin the actual scripting. Typically, they would do this work in the West 48th Street office, where their first duty upon arrival was rousting out whatever freeloader happened to be using the place as a flophouse. When the writers turned in the script, Nat would read through it quickly, saying, "Good, this is good, this is very good." Then he would rewrite.[30]

"And, boy, would he rewrite it!" recalled Ryan.

A writer could slave over a script, from first draft to rewrite and polish, and in the end, feel quite proud of his work. Then he would visit the set and find that the script had been overhauled and—even more dismaying—significantly improved.[31]

For some writers, the greatest skill that Hiken brought to the scripts was his development of the story within the half-hour format. Rather than relying on one-liners or slapstick, he concocted inherently funny situations that could yield a series of even funnier complications. "Nat did something nobody else could do better and that was plotting," said Jacoby.

> The plots were layer upon layer. The average show of that era—*I Love Lucy*, for instance—Lucy would say, "Ricky's band is opening tonight, and one of the chorus girls fell out, and I can get the job if I just wear a wig . . . " And that was it. That was the whole plot. Nat would start with that and would go into several layers. There was a development of plot that was perfectly natural, and everything that happens seems almost inevitable without being predictable.[32]

One of the more memorable examples was the "Bivouac" episode. The story begins as Fort Baxter is about to stage its annual bivouac exercises, which means it is time for Bilko to pick a rare disease for himself so that he can dodge the maneuvers and goof off in the post hospital. His bamboozling of the medical officer, a tough troubleshooter brought in especially to thwart Bilko's scheme, is a little gem of comic chicanery in itself, but then Bilko manages to make it seem like the other master sergeants have been infected also, landing his poker pigeons in the hospital with him. From there Hiken and his writers turn the tale upside-down: when the medical officer discovers he has been tricked, he teaches Bilko a lesson by convincing him that he is suffering from a far more dangerous disease than the one he claims to have. Believing he is about to die, Bilko now sinks into an enfeebled, bedridden state. In one final farcical complication, Colonel Hall does not learn of this deception in time and makes a somber "deathbed visit," at which he divulges embarrassing secrets about himself to his supposedly doomed motor pool sergeant. In the end, when Bilko is told of the doctor's ruse, he has some information that he can hold over his commanding officer's head. The legacy of this sort of comedy scripting lived on years later, offering inspiration to some of TV's more astute creators. According to James Burrows, director of such shows as *Taxi*, *Cheers*, and *Friends*, "You call up a plot of *Bilko* occasionally, and you say, 'This is how they did it then. How can we change it a bit and make it different?'—still using Nat's ideas but kind of making it your own."[33]

Of the compliments paid to Nat's writing, perhaps the finest came in the form of spontaneous responses during the initial cast readings on Monday mornings. "I have to say in all honesty, this is the only show I ever worked on where you went in and read the script with the cast, without any ax to grind, and sat around and really laughed out loud at the writing," said Allan Melvin. "Usually, you create some humor out of what you have through the acting and the gimmicks and what-not. But this, it was all there to begin with."[34]

After the first reading, the cast would rehearse from Tuesday to Thursday before shooting the episode at the end of the week. In the rehearsal hall and in the film studio, the remarkable chemistry between Hiken and Silvers would crystallize. The introspective Nat had the Walter Mittyish ability to lose himself completely in Sergeant Bilko's aggressive antics, and when putting those escapades on paper he could capture Silvers's complicated patter in all its twists and turns. As for Silvers, the burlesque dynamo, he could bring an array of inflections and mannerisms that would often leave Nat marveling. While watching Silvers at work, Nat would sometimes say, "Did you see the take he just did? You see that little thing he did? You can't write that." More than a mutual appreciation and a respect for each other's craftsmanship, they seemed to be parts of a single whole. "I always felt that Ernie Bilko was equal parts Nat Hiken and Phil Silvers," said Stern. "Phil brought, from his burlesque days and from his nightclub act, the fast-talking man, with all that energy and a very distinctive style. Nat brought a literacy to it, an intelligence, that was in the subtext. Much of what Ernie says is witty. It's guised in this staccato tempo, but it's there."[35]

The two men also shared a serious-minded approach to comedy, rooted in authentic characterizations. For this reason Hiken avoided overt jokes in his scripts, emphasizing, instead, funny consequences to the characters' actions. Silvers would sometimes enforce this approach on the set. If he was rehearsing with a comedian who tried to throw some schtick into a scene, Silvers would bring him up short. "C'mon, make it real," he would snap.[36]

Silvers, the great improviser, naturally had ideas of his own to improve any given episode, but he would check with Nat before trying it on the soundstage. When there was an already established Silvers improvisation that Nat believed could enhance an episode, he would set aside time for it in his script. A favorite was the performer's "Freud-Spinoza debate." Silvers had come up with the routine during his *Top Banana* run. One night on stage, when he was supposed to deliver a line to one of the women in the cast, he mistakenly turned to one of the men instead and said, "Listen, honey. . . ." Silvers was in psychiatric therapy at the time, for treatment of panic attacks, and he immediately drew upon the jargon he had learned from this experience to cover his mistake. He explained that the blunder was a Freudian slip and, while remaining in character, launched into the story of the famous debate between Sigmund Freud and Baruch Spinoza (which, it seems, was the most vigorous debate ever conducted between great thinkers living two centuries apart). Nat included this trademark Silvers riff in two Bilko farces that involved psychological themes.[37]

Although he had the last word on everything that went on the air, Nat was also open to contributions from certain other cast members and had a special fondness for performers who could think quickly on their feet. Heywood Hale Broun discovered this when making a guest appearance on the program. Broun was the son of celebrated newspaperman Heywood Broun, and had been a sportswriter himself before taking up acting. In his big scene in this Bilko episode, he was playing a medical officer wooing the woman of his dreams. In the middle of his passionate speech, one of the other characters was supposed to interrupt him. "Like anybody who had appeared in summer stock," Broun recalled,

I prepared myself with a sentence in case I wasn't interrupted in time so I wouldn't be left there without anything to go on with. Well, suddenly I realized I was going on and on—"We will blow on the ashes of our passion and we will burst . . . " And I thought, *For Christ's sake, isn't anybody going to come in the door?* And I went on for about two minutes, desperately improvising, and finally I stopped and turned to Nat and said, "Isn't anybody going to interrupt me?" And he just grinned and said, "I wanted to see how you'd go." Which I felt was my acceptance into his company of improvisers.[38]

The best one at thinking on his feet may have been Hiken himself. For him, directing was an extension of writing, and the writing was not truly finished until the time came to call for action. Often he would come up with a line or a bit of business on the soundstage that would clinch a scene, sometimes feeding a new line to an actor even as he was about to take his place before the camera. Other, more conventional aspects of directing did not interest him as much. There would be times when camera-director DeCaprio would suggest a retake, to correct a technical flaw or a bungled line, but Nat would see no point in it, saying, "They came, they saw, they laughed. Leave it alone." Primarily, he still saw television as a vehicle for live performance.[39]

Occasionally, Silvers would ad-lib entirely on his own—when there was no other choice, when something unexpected occurred in the middle of a take. Few performers could react as quickly and aptly as he could. His most famous ad-lib came during one of the series' most celebrated episodes, entitled "The Court-Martial," but more popularly known as "Harry Speakup." The premise for the show concerned an efficiency-mad officer who has designed a procedure for inducting new recruits at unprecedented speed. One of the draftees is an animal-act performer, who is hiding his performing chimpanzee on the post. The chimp, wandering around unsupervised, steps into the induction line, which moves with such headlong abandon that the animal is processed into the U.S. Army. He is listed as Private Harry Speakup because one of the WACs in the induction line shouted, "Hurry, speak up" when the time came to type his name. To correct this gargantuan gaffe—without having to admit the mistake on the record—the Fort Baxter command decides to court-martial the chimp, with Bilko assigned as defense counsel. At one point while filming the trial scene, the chimp unexpectedly jumped up and picked up a telephone. Without a moment's hesitation, Silvers came up with a way to salvage the scene. "Just a minute, sir," he said to the presiding officer. "I think he's calling for another lawyer."[40]

"Harry Speakup," written by Hiken, Coleman Jacoby, and Arnie Rosen, is often singled out as the greatest Bilko installment and is usually included on any list of the best TV comedy episodes of all time. Certainly it is hilarious. But the Bilko series was so remarkable that it included many other episodes that were just as exceptional, among them the previously mentioned "Bivouac" episode, "The Eating Contest" (guest-starring the gaunt Fred Gwynne as "The Stomach," the army's all-time eating champion), "Boxer" (featuring a very funny performance by ex-middleweight Walter Cartier as a pugilist who prefers planting chrysanthemums to trading punches), "Bilko and the Beast" (in which Bilko reduces a vicious drill sergeant to a quivering, shuddering wreck), and "Where There's a Will" (concerning an elaborate con, based on a *Maltese Falcon* theme, to retrieve an inheritance swindled from one of Bilko's men). And then, of course, there were the series of uproarious episodes revolving around Maurice Gosfield as Private Duane Doberman, perhaps the most popular installments of all.

Beginning as just another member of the platoon, Gosfield quickly stepped forward as a key element in the show, capable of getting laughs merely by walking, or rather, crabbing, on stage. Once again, Hiken created a comedy phenomenon out of a nonperformer, the only term one could reasonably apply to Gosfield, for all his purported credits. But this time Nat might have done his job a bit too well, taking someone too low and raising him too high, up where the air was too thin for a little man's equilibrium.

◆   ◆   ◆

To say that Gosfield was a man with limitations would be a massive understatement. Fellow cast member Melvin pointed out that scenes involving Gosfield involved "certain technical difficulties, like getting him in front of the camera. Or getting him to say something." His trouble with dialogue became a subject of sporting interest to the rest of the cast. They would run a betting pool on how long it would take for Gosfield to flub his first line on any given day and, more often than not, whoever bet on the shortest amount of time would win the wager.[41]

Gosfield's difficulties extended to nonwork-related matters as well. As one member of the Bilko production team put it, he was "a warmhearted guy but kind of not all there." In rehearsals, those actors not on call would pass the time in an ongoing poker game, a nickel-and-dime affair more noteworthy for its exchange of quips than its transfer of money. Gosfield was eager to join the game, but the other players would not let him deal; he would only get the cards dirty. He would also try to jump into the snappy conversation that flew back and forth around the table but, as Edward Montagne put it, he was "always three steps behind." Eating was something else he had trouble mastering. Stuffing his mouth went smoothly enough (he was known to order a second main course while still halfway through his first), but then there was the issue of waste. Food would splatter this way and that, covering his clothes and the immediate vicinity, as he wolfed down his meal with both hands. "To eat with Doberman you need to get stunt pay," Melvin observed. Once, at lunch time, Hiken asked, "How is he with dry food?"[42]

When it came to the end product on film, none of this really mattered. Gosfield's utter hopelessness, as guided by Hiken, was the thing that appealed to people so much, especially when juxtaposed with wily-fox Bilko. He also brought out the motor pool sergeant's protective side. When a socialite snubs Doberman, Bilko launches an extravagant, and hilarious, campaign to convince her that Doberman is the most wildly desirable man in the world. When civilian grifters clean out Doberman in a rigged poker game, Bilko lays a trap to swindle the money back (the idea of anyone fleecing Doberman deeply offends Bilko; after all, that is *his* prerogative). When nobody in the platoon is willing to take out Doberman's sister on an upcoming visitors' day, Bilko convinces his men that an obscure genetic law dictates that a man as momentously ugly as Doberman must have an exceptionally beautiful sister (in the end, Bilko's flimflam is so convincing that even he falls under its spell; he wangles a date with Diane Doberman for himself).

Gosfield's unforgettably slobby presence and his cracked voice made him the surprise celebrity of the hit series. Wherever he went he was recognized. Fashionable Manhattanites invited him to cocktail parties. Broadway columnists frequently mentioned him in their ongoing accounts of the rich and famous. Beautiful women fawned over him and clung to his pudgy arms. Apparently, they were not so beguiled by fame that they actually lusted after him (only Bilko could have manufactured *that* intense a delusion) but they clamored around him just the same, as if he were an irresistible, living teddy bear.[43]

Doberman fan mail poured into the CBS offices, rivaling the number of letters received by Silvers. Most incredible of all, Gosfield, who could just barely get out a line on cue, was nominated for a best supporting actor Emmy for the 1958–59 season.[44]

A few years earlier, Rocky Graziano had gone through a similar experience and had taken it all in stride. Gosfield, though, let it all go to his head.

He came to believe that he was a great comedian and would tell people that, without him, the Bilko show would be nothing. He would show up on the set wearing lifts, a high-crowned hat, and a tailored vest sporting vertical stripes, all intended to lend an illusion of height to his stubby build. Or, as Silvers saw it, to cultivate an appearance that Gosfield felt reflected his true self. According to Silvers, "Dobie thought of himself as Cary Grant playing a short, plump man." Leonard Stern detected another dimension to Gosfield's feelings about himself. "Maurice saw himself as a Shakespearean actor, and his being on *Bilko* was an indulgence, which he tolerated, more or less. He never abandoned the ascot."[45]

Gosfield's fumbling on the set often infuriated Hiken. But his attitude toward the roly-poly cult figure was probably not as intense as Silvers's. At first, Gosfield's success baffled him. Seeing the fan mail pile up, he would shrug and say, "I guess they dig distortion." But as the Doberman mania continued to build, he began to resent Gosfield. He had worked too hard and too long to be upstaged by this virtual amateur, by this barely animate object. Later in the series, when the show was being filmed at a studio on West 26th Street in the fur district, Silvers would walk along Seventh Avenue at lunchtime and pass the furriers schmoozing on the corner. "Hey, Bilko! How's Doberman?" they would call. Silvers would mutter his reply: "Ah, fuck you."[46]

On the set, Silvers subjected Gosfield to some ribbing, the sarcasm of which Gosfield may or may not have recognized. Melvin recalled a time when the supporting actor's incompetence exasperated Nat more than usual. As part of one of Bilko's raffle scams, Doberman was supposed to deliver the contents of his piggy bank. All he had was one line, something to the effect that Bilko could have all the money saved inside, but he kept blowing it. "And Nat was really a stern guy at times," Melvin said. "I mean, he wanted the thing to *go on*. Money was being wasted as we kept reshooting. So he said, 'Jesus, Maurice, c'mon. If you can't say the line I'll give it to somebody else.' " Gosfield just stood there at a total loss, faintly sputtering but afraid to say a word. "We're all standing behind him, and Phil says to him, under his breath, 'Tell him "Nuts to you, Nat." Tell him where to go, Dobe. We're all behind you. You don't have to take that from him.' " The more Silvers egged him on, the more flustered Gosfield got.[47]

Once, Gosfield came close to standing up for himself, not to Hiken but to Silvers. Members of the platoon were taking part in one of Silvers's Las Vegas casino appearances and, as they were about to go on stage, Silvers made a crack about Gosfield's bathing habits, specifically the lack thereof. Gosfield, in high dudgeon, did not join the star on stage for a few moments. Drawing himself up to his full height, such as it was, he said, "Let him die out there by himself." [48]

At one point soon after his notoriety began, Gosfield considered acquiring the sort of training that might have substantiated his delusions of thespian grandeur. He asked Hiken if he could get some time off to study at the famous Actors Studio. Nat made it clear that he took a dim view of that. He warned Gosfield that if he improved his acting or diction in any way, he would get kicked off the show. He was trying to point out that Gosfield's value to the series had nothing to do with conventional concepts of talent. But Gosfield never could quite grasp the idea. [49]

◆   ◆   ◆

In its first season, the Bilko show emerged as one of television's most prominent prime-time hits. It enjoyed not only strong ratings and enthusiastic reviews but also industry honors. In 1955, the Academy of Television Arts and Sciences awarded five awards to *You'll Never Get Rich*, now redubbed *The Phil Silvers Show* (the more commonly known title of *Sergeant Bilko* would not be used until the program went into syndication a few years later). The series won the Emmy for best comedy series, best actor (Silvers), best comedian (Silvers again), best director for a film series (Hiken), and best comedy writing (Hiken once more, with his staff). On a less official level, the show also acquired one of the most prized emblems of status within the New York show business community. Lindy's Long Table, previously the domain of Milton Berle and his entourage, was now presided over by Hiken, Silvers, and their pals. [50]

The Bilko phenomenon claimed fans in the highest places. The day after one of the show's broadcasts, production supervisor Montagne received a phone call from White House secretary Jim Hagerty. "The Old Man missed last night's show," Hagerty said. "Can you get me a print?" Montagne immediately shipped off a copy of the latest episode so that Eisenhower, the former supreme allied commander, could keep abreast of Bilko's travesties on army life. [51]

Another distinction enjoyed by the show had to do with an aspect of Hiken's unorthodox casting. Besides his customary practice of hiring boxers and eccentrics, he now added African-American actors to his troupe and used them in a nonstereotypical manner. The racially integrated company at Fort Baxter included P. J. Sidney (later replaced by Terry Carter) as a member of Bilko's platoon, Billie Allen as one of the WACs, and Frederick O'Neal as a master sergeant. Seen today, these roles seem severely limited, involving no more than a few perfunctory lines per episode, but in 1955 the very idea of these characters was something new. Hiken was one of the first TV producers to present black characters as equals to their white counterparts, rather than relegating them to the roles of maids, porters, or Amos 'n' Andy buffoons. In fact, Hiken's inclusion of African-Americans was daring enough for its time that it offended certain Southern stations carrying the program. One of the advertising agencies sponsoring the show got jittery and requested that the black actors be removed. Hiken, Silvers, and Montagne refused. Nat had never been a political zealot, and he may have sidestepped a showdown with industry blacklisters a few years earlier, but he believed in certain progressive principles within his own personal dealings and was willing to stand by them.[52]

◆　　◆　　◆

Nineteen fifty-five was an impressive year not only for *The Phil Silvers Show* but also for New York television in general. Among the Emmy nominees that year were such New York productions as *Peter Pan*, *No Time for Sergeants*, and Rod Serling's *Patterns*. Competition was so stiff, in fact, that the academy could not include either Gore Vidal's *Visit to a Small Planet* or Paddy Chayefsky's *The Catered Affair*. As for comedy, this was the year Jackie Gleason turned his re-curring "Honeymooners" sketch into the classic half-hour filmed series, while Sid Caesar continued his extraordinary work on *Caesar's Hour* and the be-mused George Gobel offered a wry mix of monologues and skits on his new hit variety series. In terms of individual accomplishments, it appeared that New York's golden age was flourishing as much as ever. But, for those keeping a close watch, there were also less heartening developments.

The problems had begun in 1951. In that year, AT&T crews finished con-structing a series of coaxial cables and microwave relays that allowed televi-sion networks to transmit their shows from one city to another across the country. Since construction had begun in the East, New York broadcasters had extended their reach as each section was completed, but once the system reached California, New York no longer stood alone as a national broadcast center. On September 30, 1951, *The Colgate Comedy Hour* became the first commercial show to transmit its nationwide signal from Los Angeles. West Coast TV productions began to stake a greater claim on the prime-time schedule.[53]

Los Angeles clearly had its advantages. First, Hollywood performers were on hand to lend glamour to the network's programs, and second, the city was

already geared for motion picture production, with an abundance of technicians and ample studio facilities. New York's ad hoc array of converted theaters, radio studios, and rehearsal halls had managed to accommodate all the
city's programs, just barely, but there was no room for expansion. And New
York unions failed to make the producer's job any easier. They showed little
flexibility when imposing overtime regulations—in a business known for its
long, irregular hours—and could even, for example, invent complications for
the simplest tasks of moving equipment from one place to another. Montagne
recalled dealing with these arbitrary difficulties while shooting *The Phil Silvers
Show* at the Dumont Studios.

> The sets were built over on 57th Street, where CBS was, and they had to be
> trucked over to Dumont, and there Local 1 would unload the sets and bring
> them up to the stage. At the stage door Local 52 would take over. Now, if a prop
> had to be moved from the stage down to the prop room, 52 could take it to the
> door of the stage and Local 1 would take it down the hall to the room. It sounds
> complicated but this is what I was faced with when I came on the show.[54]

Some New York executives attempted to make the city a more agreeable
place for television production. At NBC, Pat Weaver planned to build a self-
contained studio, theater, and broadcast center, specifically tailored to video
producers' needs, but the network never constructed his proposed Television
City. Even if it had, it might not have made much difference, because it did
not address perhaps the biggest issue of all. More and more, television was relying on film rather than live broadcasts, and major show business players were
about to weigh in to tip the scales in California's favor.[55]

The burgeoning trend toward so-called telefilms did not employ the sort of
methods featured in the production of *The Phil Silvers Show* or *The Honeymooners*, both of which used celluloid to record virtually uninterrupted, the-
atrical-style performances. The new fashion involved, instead, a single
camera, studio back lots, and no audiences. Episodic dramas, such as *Gun-
smoke*, were essentially short, stripped-down Hollywood movies. Comedies,
such as *Father Knows Best*, were domestic B movie–style misadventures shored
up by canned laughter. The greatest expertise in this sort of production was
obviously concentrated within the major film studios. At first the studios
shunned television, their upstart competitor. But in 1955 that would change.
That year, Warner Bros. decided to break with industry practice.

Conceding that television would not go away, the studio planned to capitalize upon it as an outlet. Its first film series, *Cheyenne*, starring Clint Walker, premiered the same night that *You'll Never Get Rich* first aired. The program's success eventually persuaded other studios to move into television, establishing them as a new power in the medium. *Cheyenne* also helped promote the resurgence of the Western, a distinctly non–New York genre that would soon dominate the airwaves.[56]

Accompanying the gradual shift from New York to Los Angeles was a major personnel change. NBC president Weaver, despite his successes, had frequently been mired in disputes with his superior, RCA chief David Sarnoff. Sarnoff resolved the tense situation at the end of 1955 when he kicked Weaver upstairs. Weaver's new position as chairman of the board left him little power in programming, and soon he would resign from the company altogether. In his tenure as head of NBC television, he had managed to balance the cultural enrichment of live dramas and opera broadcasts with vigorous pop entertainment. His emphasis on quality comedy, in particular, had provided a platform for such talents as Hiken, Sid Caesar, Martha Raye, Carl Reiner, and Mel Brooks. When he left NBC, the Golden Age lost one of its principal guiding forces.[57]

◆　　◆　　◆

For Nat, meanwhile, work within his little Sergeant Bilko domain left him little time to ponder larger broadcast-industry changes. His workday would begin at six in the morning at his office at CBS headquarters. He wrote until it was time to assume his directing duties at the rehearsal hall or on the set, and when that was done he would head over to his West 48th Street office and write some more. By early evening, if no unexpected problems cropped up, he would return home to his apartment on Madison Avenue at 89th Street. After a brief nap, he would have dinner with the family and spend some time watching TV with Dana and Mia before going to bed.[58]

Occasionally, Silvers would visit the Hiken apartment, a nine-room affair, in a New York building that had once been part of the Astor estate. Nat's time with his family may have been hard-pressed by the show's demands, but for the recently divorced Silvers, accustomed to living in hotel rooms, the Hiken apartment seemed like a relaxed, homey place. The girls called him Uncle Phil and would run to hug him when he arrived. Dana learned one day exactly how important this greeting ritual was to the brash comic, who could sometimes display a sudden, brittle sensitivity. Silvers showed up that day and said hello to Dana, but she failed to come running right away because she was busy drawing a picture for him. "So later I went over and gave the drawing to him when I'd finished, and he didn't want it. He was sulking." She made sure to respond promptly from then on.[59]

The show's dramatic success brought no dramatic changes in Nat's lifestyle. After rubbing elbows with show business people during the day, he tended to keep his distance from celebrity hangouts. When he found time to go out to dinner with his family, he would take them to Chinese restaurants, or Luchow's—New York's answer to Milwaukee *gemütlichkeit*—or La Scala, a midtown Italian restaurant that was a particular favorite of his. Certainly, one thing his new success did not do was turn him all of a sudden into a slave of fashion. Before going out for the evening, Ambur would have to inspect Nat—"the tramper," as Fred Allen had once called him—to make sure that his clothes did not clash too raucously. Keen as his comic mind might have been, his sartorial standards could sometimes be so deficient that they could blind him even to sarcasm. A few years later, for his birthday, Dana bought what she thought would be a joke gift, an eyesore of a jumpsuit made out of yellow terry cloth. "I thought it was funny," she recalled, "but he opened it and he said, 'Oh, God, this is great.' He loved it, and I think he even wore it on the golf course, much to my mother's horror. Her dream was for him to be a good dresser, to have nice polo shirts and so on. Oh, he just couldn't have cared less."[60]

In one way Nat did alter his way of life. He and Ambur had tried vacationing in Westport, but they had no use for the fashion-conscious social set that congregated in that Connecticut shore town; instead, following Billy Friedberg's example, they began spending time in the more rustic Montauk, at the eastern tip of Long Island. Soon Nat bought a vacation house there, where he and his family spent their entire summers and some of their weekends in winter. Dana felt that, to a certain extent, her father remained lost in his thoughts while out there, but he was more at ease and better able to keep work at arm's length. (Reminding him of work would be occasional appearances by Gosfield, who would sometimes arrive uninvited. He would show up at the nearby golf club, to bask in the attention lavished upon him by the normally reserved country club women, and sometimes he set up a projector in the club barroom to show his favorite Bilko episodes—his idea of a command performance, which he himself probably commanded. Ambur remembered, "Somebody finally pointed out to him that he had to get his undershorts shorter so they didn't extend below his outer shorts.")[61]

While in Montauk, more than at any other times, Nat would unwind enough to play with his daughters. He bought them a croquet set and played the game with them on the front lawn; he taught them how to bat with a plastic whiffle-ball set; on the hottest days he would chase them around the house with the garden hose and water them down. "That was the only house he owned," said Dana. "He was loved in Montauk—people at the hardware store, everybody at the golf course. He just cherished his time out there."[62]

Nat found this getaway at a juncture when he needed it the most. As producer and part owner of *The Phil Silvers Show,* he felt his responsibilities preying upon him. He was ever-mindful of how much hinged on each episode. His cousin, Vivian Gill, noticed a change in him when he visited relatives in Milwaukee about this time. "There was an intensity about him, a nervousness that I had never seen before." She went with him to play golf one day and, while having lunch after the game, he confided in her. He said, "You know, sometimes I wake up in the middle of the night in a cold sweat, because if I don't come up with a new idea, everybody's going to sit without a job."[63]

Ambur could easily sense his unrelenting attention to the show. "Going to the theater at that time used to drive me crazy. He'd very surreptitiously tear a page out of the playbill, and his nervous tic was to fold it into tiny little pleats. He was trying to be very quiet about it, but that's what he did when he was thinking."[64]

His style of working exacerbated the situation. Together, his habit of procrastination and his innate perfectionism kept backing him into a nerveracking bind—he could not commit his ideas to paper until the last minute and he insisted on getting them exactly right, which meant that he had to come up with the finishing touches as the shooting was about to begin. He also lacked any ability to delegate authority, as much as he would have liked to have shed some of his responsibilities. If there was anything important to be done, he felt compelled to do it himself. No detail was too picayune for him to grapple with, as Aaron Ruben noticed one day while visiting the set.

Ruben arrived during a break in filming when the crew was setting up a scene that would involve bookies and racehorse betting. He was surprised to find that Nat was nowhere to be seen. He was even more surprised to learn that Hiken was in, of all places, the prop room. What, he wanted to know, would the producer-writer-director of a hit series be doing in the prop room? "He was in there writing down names of horses on a chalkboard to be put on the set," Ruben recalled. "He wouldn't trust anybody else to come up with all these imaginative names. All you have to say is, 'Get a bunch of names for horses.' But he had to be back there doing it himself." When a *New York Times* reporter visited the set on another occasion, Silvers summed up Hiken's approach in his own pointed way: "He thrives on strangulation."[65]

As the first season wore on, minor ailments kept Nat from completing some of the scripts and from showing up on the set. And when he was not available, the series would grind to a halt. In the end, Nat, Montagne, and CBS all agreed to cease production after thirty-four episodes, rather than the usual thirty-nine.[66]

According to Silvers's autobiography, all of Nat's anxieties and fatigue came into sharp, dramatic focus with the death of a friend during the first season. The friend was a young writer who died of a heart attack. "They're not going to kill me" was Nat's response. As Silvers remembered it, Nat then decided to relinquish his head-writing position as a first step toward leaving the show altogether.[67]

Nat did, in fact, decide to walk away from the series, as soon as he could find somebody to replace him, and Silvers's story offers a cogent account of how this decision came about. Yet, none of Hiken's surviving closest relatives or friends knew who this young heart-attack victim might have been. Montagne, though, offered an alternate version. He remembered that the death of Nat's father, from an edema, during the second season proved to be the turning point. Nat, so aligned with his father in outlook and temperament, left work for two weeks as he traveled to Milwaukee for the funeral and then allowed himself some time to grieve. "When Nat came back," Montagne said, "he didn't have the drive that he had once had. Finally, he said to me, 'Eddie, it killed my father—it's not going to kill me.' " By "it" he meant hard work.[68]

Contrary to this account, Ambur did not recall Max's death as the compelling factor in Nat's decision to leave the show. She pointed out that Max had been retired for some time and had not been burdened by work when he died. Still, it seems plausible that Max's death reordered Nat's thinking in some way. And there also may have been someone else's passing that was on Nat's mind.[69]

On March 17, 1956, as *The Phil Silvers Show* neared the end of its first season, Fred Allen died suddenly from a heart attack while out for a stroll on West 57th Street. Years of overwork and high blood pressure had finally taken their toll on the comedian, and Nat may have perceived this death as a warning about his own pressurized professional life.[70]

Allen, sixty-one at the time, had recently found a most suitable second career for himself. Always a lover of books, he had turned to writing one himself and had published a successful reminiscence of his radio days, which he had entitled, with typical dourness, *Treadmill to Oblivion*. A second memoir, about his vaudeville experiences, had already been scheduled for publication by the time of his death.

Allen had recently made some peace with the medium of television. He had found a niche for his barbed wit and impromptu quips as a panelist on *What's My Line?*. But he was not one to give up a pet grievance entirely. In his book he had still promoted radio as the superior vehicle for comedy, and had predicted that none of the current TV comedians would be performing on the tube twenty years hence. As for his own legacy, he was not much more optimistic: "Whether he knows it or not, the comedian is on a treadmill to oblivion. When a radio comedian's program is finally finished it slinks down Memory Lane into the limbo of yesteryear's happy hours. All that the comedian has to show for his years of work and aggravation is the echo of forgotten laughter."[71]

Burnout

Sometime before the end of the second season, Hiken had to establish the Bilko-show's line of succession, a line that ran on two tracks. When he left the series, as he hoped he would, somebody would have to take his place as head writer and somebody would have to assume his responsibilities as director. He grappled with the head-writer issue first. Without someone to oversee the intricate scripts, nothing else on the show would be possible.

He picked Leonard Stern as his heir apparent. Nat's gin-game acquaintance was not at all awed by the challenge that awaited him. He had been writing for Jackie Gleason for four years and had just left *The Honeymooners*, the other great sitcom to come out of New York during the 1955–56 season. He believed he was already an expert comedy craftsman who could tackle any task that came his way. Buoyed by Stern's credentials and confidence, Nat looked forward to the time, coming soon, when he could ease himself out of the series and move on to a less taxing project. Both men would be disappointed.[1]

Early on, confronted by Hiken's rewrites, Stern discovered that there was, after all, something for him to learn. Like others before him, he would see his scripts, the product of intensive effort, substantially recast—and noticeably improved, as much as 25 to 50 percent, he estimated. "Initially, I was chagrined," he remembered, "and I planned to be upset, but the writing was so good that I became humbled . . . Where you would have a line that would be satisfactory, he would find one that was perfect for the moment."[2]

As the weeks went by, some of Hiken's skill at etching distinctive characters rubbed off on him. Nat could inspire a writer, first by example, but also through deferential criticism, commenting on a script's virtues before discussing its deficiencies. Under Hiken's stewardship, Stern contributed, with other writers, to some of the series' best episodes, such as "Doberman's Sister" and "Where There's a Will." Soon, though, he realized that there was a limit to how much of the Hiken style he could absorb.[3]

"Nat was attuned to the show in a way you could never be, or never equal. It was an extension of himself and his fantasies and his writing skills and his lexicon. He was the most acute practitioner of timing and rhythms, and he had insights that had never occurred to me. I could emulate and attempt to duplicate but was never able to reach his inspired heights with those characters." When Stern received an offer to become head writer and comedy director for *The Steve Allen Show*, he decided it was time that he and Nat had a talk.[4]

Stern explained that he was flattered by the opportunity Nat was offering, but he felt that he could not quite tackle the job, that Nat was irreplaceable. After what Stern described as a soul-searching discussion, Nat agreed that his writer would be best off taking Steve Allen's offer, to work on a show where he would be able to create his own brand of comedy.[5]

Hiken must have found Stern's glowing assessment of his unique talent as disconcerting as it was gratifying. He was, after all, rather hoping that he *could* be replaced. With Stern moving on, he cast about for another possibility. He turned to an old standby. He had already brought in Billy Friedberg for the second season to help him meet the script deadlines. As a writer, Friedberg might not have enjoyed the same sort of rising reputation that Stern was acquiring at the time, but his experience working with Hiken qualified him in other ways. He knew Nat's work habits and thought patterns and had already absorbed much of his scene-building technique. In quiet moments, Stern observed, they seemed to share their own finely tuned wavelength: Nat at his desk, constructing his origami animals out of cigarette packs, Friedberg sitting nearby, tapping his foot, "much as if there was some music that no one else heard going on and he was keeping time with it. They were an interesting combination, the few times I saw them when they weren't talking or typing." Over the course of the season, Friedberg's growing familiarity with the Bilko sensibility established him as the front-runner among candidates for the next head writer.[6]

While fretting over the future of the series, Hiken also had to deal with a more immediate problem. In February 1956, Harry Clark, the actor who portrayed Stanley Sowici, died of a heart attack while playing handball at his local YMCA. Hiken had to invent a new character to take Sowici's place as the post's mess sergeant. As he often did, Nat put the finishing touches on the character only after finding the actor to play the part. And as was often the case, the term "actor" would have to be used loosely.

Hiken auditioned several performers but he was not particularly keen on any of them. Although they were competent, Nat did not see a potential in any of them to add a strong comedic element to an already hilarious series. Then he recalled someone he had met recently while he and Silvers were taking some time off in Miami, a comedian named Joe E. Ross. There was something about him, Nat now thought, that he might be able to put to good use. The qualities Nat had in mind had nothing to do with Ross' stand-up act.[7]

Brought up on New York's Lower East Side, Ross had started his show business career as a singing waiter in the Bronx, then moved on to burlesque at its most lowdown, where the comedians and singers were mere fillers between displays of female pulchritude. When Hiken had met him, Ross was making a living as a blue comic, the term in those days for raunchy comedians. He worked in strip joints and various buckets of blood around Miami. As fellow comic Hank Garrett put it, Ross worked in the sort of place where "if you see someone get up in the audience, you say, 'If you're looking for the toilet, sit down. You're in it.'" Ross's routines did nothing to uplift the tone of these places.[8]

What Hiken's memory tended to focus on was Ross's broad block of a face and his gravelly voice, a combination that was more likely to make him funny when he was not telling jokes and *trying* to be funny. On the basis of this impression—a hunch, really—Nat was willing to give him a chance, at least on a provisional basis. Even in the relatively unstructured world of early television, casting an obscure foulmouthed comic in an established network series was an offbeat proposition. Among those who considered the idea unlikely was Ross himself. Hiken's production coordinator, Kevin Pines, found the comic in Hawaii, where he was appearing at a club. "The call came through, and Joe was in the sack with a dame at the time," Montagne recalled. "Kevin said, 'This is Kevin Pines, casting director of *The Phil Silvers Show*.' And Joe thought it was a gag and he said, 'F you' and hung up the phone."[9]

A phone call later, Pines succeeded in convincing Ross that he was the real thing; once that hurdle was overcome, the comic did not need much persuading. He showed up in New York to join the cast, unperturbed that he had no long-term guarantee. He was accustomed to short gigs and, at forty-one, he was not expecting much of a change in his career path. On his first day of rehearsal, he arrived at Nola Studios wearing tuxedo pants and a full-dress shirt. Later, Nat took aside Mickey Freeman, an acquaintance of Ross's from the stand-up circuit. "Find out if he has any daytime clothes," he said.[10]

From the start, Ross's lack of acting experience was obvious. (Until then, the closest he had come to acquiring an acting credit was a pathetic stand-up appearance in a burlesque-style exploitation movie called *Teaserama*.) He had trouble remembering his lines, not as badly as Gosfield, but enough to require special coaching from Hiken. One day, while Ross was struggling with some dialogue, Nat suggested that he say "ooo-ooo," as a way to stall for time until the words came to him. Eventually, this verbal tic would become Ross's signature. Silvers also had to provide some tutoring. In their initial scenes together, Ross would infuriate the star because he was obviously not listening to Silvers's lines. When Silvers upbraided him for this, Ross's response was "why should I listen to you when I've read the script?" In time he began to grasp the concept of cooperating with his fellow performers.[11]

Nat's patience with the marginal comic proved worthwhile. Harry Clark had been a fine, blue-collar character actor and a welcome member of the Bilko-show menagerie, but his Sgt. Stanley Sowici was not as funny as Ross's Sgt. Rupert Ritzik. While filling the role that Hiken created for him, Ross's empty expression added an amusing dimension. It became an apparent sign of intense stupidity, as though every ounce of his concentration had to be mustered to interpret the simplest communications of those around him. His dim gaze was the perfect feature for a hopeless gambler, a pigeon for every Bilko scam. And surprisingly, considering his sleazy background, Ross projected a likeable childlike quality, making his Ritzik come across as a clumsy, overgrown kid. To clinch Ritzik's underdog appeal, Nat provided him with a remarkable shrew of a wife, played by Beatrice Pons, a stage actress with a voice sharp enough to cut glass, which she unleashed to full effect whenever she flung open a door or window to proclaim, "Do you hear me, everybody? My husband is a nut! Come to take him away!"

The earliest Ritzik episodes made it clear that the character could serve as the linchpin for some of the best Bilko stories. Every character at Fort Baxter was susceptible to Bilko's finagling to one extent or another, but few could succumb with such farcical helplessness. "A Mess Sergeant Can't Win" set the pattern. When Bilko learns that Ritzik is leaving the army, he offers, as an act of sincere goodwill, to pay back the $400 he has taken from the mess sergeant over the years through poker and various other disreputable means. But Ritzik refuses to accept, sure that this is just another Machiavellian con. Determined to make good on his offer by any means possible, Bilko concocts a sure-thing bet for Ritzik. He wagers that Colonel Hall and his wife will not celebrate their upcoming anniversary because they are about to split up—when everyone on the post knows they are the picture of marital bliss. All aquiver at the chance to beat Bilko, Ritzik manages to pluck defeat from the jaws of victory: to make certain that the Halls are still amicable, he badgers Colonel Hall with questions about his married life, which only makes the colonel suspect that something is going on behind his back. The Halls have a terrible fight, and the anniversary party is called off. Ritzik does not see his role in this disaster. As far as he is concerned, this latest escapade only proves that Bilko's power over human events has somehow grown greater than ever.

Bilko does not give up. He reaches for an even more can't-miss proposition: he bets that Ritzik was not born in Peoria, Illinois, as is generally accepted; he was born, instead, in Singapore, the son of a notorious dance-hall girl. Ritzik wavers. Can Bilko possibly be wrong? His wife does not help matters. "If Bilko says you were born in Singapore," she rails at him, "then you were born in Singapore!" At the last second, he decides to take the Singapore side of the bet and loses once again. Desperate to find some way to end his winning streak, Bilko now bets that the mess sergeant's name is not Rupert Ritzik. His real name, Bilko maintains, is Nathaniel Killman. Finally, Rupert wins (although even on this score he has his moments of doubt). In the end, Ritzik decides to stay in the army, after all. With a true compulsive gambler's logic, he announces that his luck has finally changed, and he plans to stay right where he is and clean Bilko out. A typical ending from Hiken, a devout believer in humanity's capacity for repeating the same mistakes over and over again.[12]

The Ritzik persona enabled Ross to acquire a new career as a performer. But unlike Gosfield—the show's other great beneficiary of Hiken's Pygmalionlike skill—Ross did not indulge in any delusions of grandeur. He appreciated his new windfall for what it was and remained highly respectful of Nat, whom he always addressed as "Mr. Hiken." Still, it was probably inevitable that Ross and Gosfield, the two unlikely Hiken creations, would be drawn together in some way. The two of them concocted a stand-up routine that they could perform as a team and, based on their Bilko notoriety, they were invited to appear on *The Ed Sullivan Show*. The act was a disaster. Ross, who had enough experience in nightclub comedy to know when he had dropped a bomb, shuffled sheepishly into the Bilko rehearsal hall the next morning, dreading the responses from the rest of the show's cast. Gosfield had not shown up yet. Instead, he phoned and asked to speak to his partner. "Baby, we're the talk of the town!" Gosfield enthused.[13]

◆   ◆   ◆

At the 1956 Emmy ceremonies, *The Phil Silvers Show* made another strong showing. The program won the award for best half-hour series, Hiken and his staff won the honors for best comedy writing, and Silvers and Ford were nominated for best comedian and best supporting actor, respectively. The continuing recognition confirmed the show's prominence and underscored Silvers's newfound stardom. After more than thirty years in show business, the forty-six-year-old comedian had finally arrived. As he had done for Martha Raye, Hiken had once again devised a vehicle that elevated an overlooked talent.[14]

Along with fame came more money, more than Silvers had ever earned before, but not quite enough, as it turned out. No amount could have been. As closely identified as Silvers was with Bilko, his sharpster alter ego, he was actually closer in one significant way to Ritzik: his ability to accumulate gambling losses was stunning.

"It was the classic case of the wish to lose, I guess," said Heywood Hale Broun, a close friend of Silvers. Most self-defeating of all, as far as Broun was concerned, was Silvers's habit of betting on baseball. "Betting on baseball is a mug's game. I had been a baseball writer, and in and out of dressing rooms and privy to secrets, and I didn't bet on the game. Every now and then the worst team beat the best team, and there's nothing like the point spread in basketball—it's too unpredictable. But Phil was a big baseball bettor and he was heavily in debt." Silvers's handling of poker games was especially un-Bilko-like. Mickey Freeman would occasionally perform on weekends at the Concord Hotel in the Catskills, where Silvers sat in on a big, table-stakes poker game. "They'd say to me, 'Tell Silvers to learn how to play poker.' "[15]

Boxing was another gambler's opportunity that tempted the comedian in the worst way. According to a perhaps apocryphal story Hiken liked to tell, Silvers once got a can't-miss tip on a Madison Square Garden boxing match from a fellow member of the Friars Club. The tipster was a Broadway producer named Joe Kipness, who had some inside information, and he was eager to help the debt-plagued comedian. Just bet on the kid in the black trunks, he kept insisting. Silvers borrowed the money for the bet and, sure enough, the fight went as planned. But when Kipness found his friend at the Friars, he could plainly see that Silvers did not project a winner's glow. By way of explanation, the comedian said, in a line worthy of Ritzik, "I liked the kid in the white trunks!"[16]

As Silvers's debts piled up, his erratic business sense took over to worsen the situation. According to Broun, the performer's grasp of business matters was so bad that he had trouble even finding advisers to handle his affairs for him. "At one point Phil asked *me* to be his business manager. 'This is insane,' I said. 'I'm an ex-newspaperman. I'm not a lawyer. I'm a friend of yours, that's about all I can say for it, but no thank you, I don't want the job.' "[17]

Eventually, Silvers owed so much money that he called on his agent, Freddie Fields, to arrange a new deal with CBS that could bail him out. The way Silvers saw it, he had one last chip to cash in: his partial ownership in the show. When Nat got wind of this plan, he tried to dissuade his star. He told him not to grab the cash now; better to hang onto the percentage and wait for the bigger returns likely to come further down the line. Silvers was not willing to wait. He authorized Fields to sell his piece of the show for money to pay his debts and to provide a financial cushion for the immediate future.[18]

Nat's plan to decrease *his* involvement in the show—in the creative sphere—was progressing too slowly to ease the increasing burden of his work. As he continued to handle most of the writing, signs of a burnout were becoming more apparent. By midseason, he found it more difficult to deliver scripts on Monday for the first scheduled reading. Eventually, the scripts would not arrive until Wednesday, just two days before filming; as a result, the cast and crew were under greater pressure to put the show on its feet and before the cameras on time. Silvers bore the brunt of it. The amount of dialogue he had to handle was enormous, and his ability to memorize continually awed the rest of the cast, but even he was overwhelmed by the new time constraints. The intensified production strain, along with a troublesome guest star, convinced Hiken and Montagne to alter their production methods.[19]

Mike Todd, the flamboyant movie mogul, was appearing as himself in an episode spun around the theme of his latest extravaganza, *Around the World in Eighty Days*. More concerned with his various movie deals than with his current acting assignment, he spent an inordinate amount of time on the phone and refused to take rehearsals seriously. Hiken was already under the gun because of his trouble finishing scripts, and now his guest star would not cooperate for an especially complex episode involving a host of scene changes. As if that were not vexing enough, Todd then announced he had to leave for California before Friday, filming day. Forced to improvise, Hiken shot Todd's sequences that night at Hy Brown's studio on West 26th Street (the series' soundstage from the second season on), without the usual studio audience. Todd finally performed as required, but only after Silvers read him the riot act and cursed him out in front of the cast, crew, and Todd's wife, Elizabeth Taylor.[20]

This nerve-racking experience demonstrated to Nat that a studio audience was not absolutely necessary to create a funny episode. He decided to dispense with spectators for the remainder of the series. Silvers was especially relieved. Now he could grapple and fiddle with all his high-speed dialogue under more relaxed circumstances, without three-hundred strangers watching his every move. According to broadcast practice, though, a comedy program needed some sort of laugh track; Nat had to find a substitute for the live response that had been accompanying the show. Canned laughter was out of the question. Nat would not tolerate such an obviously false device. Instead, he and Montagne relied upon another method, fairly common in the early 1950s but effectively extinct by the end of the decade, a technique that amounted to a live-audience response one step removed.[21]

A contingent of the Bilko company would take two episodes at a time to the army post on Governor's Island. A stand-up comic, either Mickey Freeman or Tige Andrews, would warm up the GI audience, then the projectionist would show the episodes while specially placed microphones would pick up the soldiers' responses. This recording would then be mixed onto the sound track, providing the show with a laugh track containing genuine laughs. At least, as much as possible. Sometimes there was so much laughter that canned material had to be substituted so that the dialogue would not be drowned out.[22]

Filming without an audience eased some of the tension on the set, but not enough for Nat. As part of his search for people to inherit his responsibilities, he hired a man named Charles Friedman to take his place as director. Friedman had compiled an impressive record in television comedy as director of *The Colgate Comedy Hour*. The Bilko cast, however, was not terribly impressed by his debut on their show, according to Mickey Freeman. "He got on the set and said, 'Gentlemen, now here's the story: Bilko is trying to take advantage of . . .' We've been doing the show for two years and he's going to tell it?" Hiken had his own differences with Friedman regarding the staging of the program. When he visited the set, he could not keep himself from kibbitzing. "Zimmerman, what're you doing over there? Stand at the *other* side of the bunk," he might suddenly interject. He would then recede into the background, making an attempt, at least, to stay out of the way, only to step forward again a few moments later. "Excuse me," he would say, deferring to Friedman's position as best he could, then: "Paparelli, who told you to be by the door?" After only a few episodes, he could no longer restrain himself; he ended the experiment and resumed directing once more.[23]

If the Friedman experience served any purpose, it underscored Nat's need to sever all connections to the Bilko show. He realized that any involvement, even as a consultant, would tempt him irresistibly to intervene in the day-to-day details; the all-consuming stress would overtake him once again. In the end Montagne, an executive producer for CBS's filmed shows, reached a decision regarding Nat's successors.

Friedberg was the obvious choice for head writer: he was already Nat's chief lieutenant on the writing staff. As for the new director, the cast was rooting for Al DeCaprio, the camera director, to take Nat's place on the set. But Montagne was looking elsewhere. Nat's style of directing had never been technical; his understanding of comedy and his ability to come up with material on the soundstage had always been his chief assets. His replacement, Montagne believed, should be another experienced comedy mind. His first choice, Carl Reiner, was unavailable; he was absorbed at the time in writing his play *Enter Laughing*. Eventually, following up on Friedberg's suggestion, Montagne hired Aaron Ruben, Nat's old friend, cousin by marriage, and *The Milton Berle Show* collaborator. His only directing experience until that point was an unaired comedy pilot starring Dick Van Dyke, but he had recently acquired some blue-chip comedy credentials as a writer for *Caesar's Hour* and, as a former Hiken writing partner, had some insight into the workings of Nat's mind. CBS executives were worried by Hiken's impending exit, and for the first time since giving the series its green light, they closely monitored the direction that the show was taking. Montagne managed to reassure them that the new team would be able to carry on.[24]

Nat made his departure official at the end of May 1957. As reported in the *New York Times*, he had "to take a rest for reasons of health."[25]

Just a year before, Hiken had been selected as the best writer in television in a poll conducted by *Time* magazine of TV comedy scripters.[26] At the height of the Golden Age, the competition for this honor was stiff, yet in one respect, at least, the selection of Hiken was a clear, sensible choice. There was a striking distinction between him and the other gifted comedy writers of his day. Most of the writers who would later acquire the most fame—Neil Simon, Larry Gelbart, Mel Brooks—were best known in the 1950s for working as part of a team on *Your Show of Shows* and *Caesar's Hour*. Hiken, on the other hand, was the principal writer on his show, as well as producer and director. He had become that great rarity, a television *auteur*, combining both a mastery of comic storytelling and a unique humorist's perspective.

Since *The Phil Silvers Show* first went on the air, he had accumulated seven Emmys, a raft of critical raves, and an extensive, faithful audience. Now, at the peak of his career, he was walking away from the show that had certified his prestige. As extraordinary as this move may seem, it was not unprecedented. At the end of the 1956–57 season, two successful comedy writers, besides Hiken, also took sabbaticals from television to get away from the relentless grind: Henry Taylor, who had written for Jack Carson and the Ritz Brothers, and Hal Kanter, who had been writing and directing the successful *The George Gobel Show*. According to a news report at the time, Kanter resigned from the hit series because "the business of thinking up something funny each week was wearing out his own sense of humor." But Nat was worrying about more than just his frayed nerves. He also fretted, in more general terms, about the industry as a whole. Ambur recalled, "When someone would run into him on an airplane in the early days of television and said, 'Why can't television be better than it is?' Nate said, 'This is the best it's ever going to be. It's going to go downhill, because it uses up talent too fast.' "[27]

The Phil Silvers Show continued for two more seasons without Hiken. His only involvement was the writing of the show's integrated commercials, a talent, honed since his first years in television, that the sponsors were eager to retain.[28] Hiken had dominated the creation of the show so completely that others had found it difficult at first to duplicate his expertise, but once the third season began, the new creative team proved it could maintain the quality remarkably well. Perhaps the show did not reach Hiken's hilarious heights as often, but it was still arguably the funniest show on the air.

The key to the series' continued success was the principal participants' familiarity with Hiken's approach. Friedberg, Ruben and Montagne had all worked closely with Nat and knew his techniques as well as anyone. Also helpful was the addition of a young Neil Simon to the writing staff. And Silvers himself had developed an instinct for what material would work best for him and his Bilko persona and was able to help sustain the quality of the show as well.[29]

Filling in for Nat in the critical position as head writer, Friedberg cleared the script premises proposed by the other writers, helped shape the story lines, and had the final say on the shooting scripts. "It was like talking to a second Nat," remembered Coleman Jacoby. "He was a student of Nat, he knew Nat's style very well, and he had a sense of humor of his own." Jacoby would tease Friedberg about Hiken's continuing influence over the show. "I used to infuriate Billy Friedberg by saying, 'Billy, every show we do, 50 percent of it is Nat.' Because the characters were so perfect that it made the comedy easy. They were intrinsically funny and they were so well cast."[30]

By the end of the third season, the workload was divided primarily between two writing teams, one composed of Jacoby and Rosen, and the other including Friedberg himself, working with Terry Ryan and Neil Simon. Even when involved in scriptwriting, Friedberg functioned primarily as an editor. He was the one at the typewriter, approving or rejecting ideas from his partners. Ryan sometimes found these sessions draining, as Friedberg continually egged him on to come up with more material to flesh out the half-hour story. At the same time, Ryan believed that Friedberg's approach, a sort of informed noodging, was helpful. Once, when another writer complained that Friedberg did no writing during their collaboration, Ryan replied, "But the script gets better, doesn't it?" Simon also valued his association with Friedberg, regarding him as an important teacher during his early TV-writing days.[31]

Some of the episodes overseen by Friedberg were truly exceptional. Among the best were two installments guest-starring Dick Van Dyke as a hillbilly recruit, and an Emmy-winning episode written by Jacoby and Rosen in which Bilko convinces Ritzik that he is a vampire, a ruse that fits into the finagler's plan to cash in on a Hollywood talent search for a new horror star. The series remained popular and soon acquired an additional following outside the United States. American comedies do not always find an appreciative audience in Great Britain, just as British comedies, conversely, sometimes do not travel well to the United States, but *The Phil Silvers Show* succeeded in bridging the cultural divide. The program began its British TV run in 1957, and before long Silvers found that 75 percent of his fan mail was coming from United Kingdom viewers.[32]

In America, the show's ratings began to slip somewhat during its fourth season but not to an alarming degree. Even so, CBS decided the time had come to cancel the program. One reason had to with a sponsorship problem. Schick, one of the two alternating sponsors during the fourth year, backed out of the show, leaving Camel as the sole advertiser. Camel was not willing to underwrite the show completely, and no other company was interested in buying airtime. The problem, according to Montagne, was Camel's entrenched position on the program in an era of broadcasting when sponsors and shows were closely coupled in the public's mind. "Because identification was so strong with Camel, others felt that the buy wasn't worth it," he explained.[33]

In his autobiography, Silvers cites another reason, one based solely on the concept of maximizing the difference between outgo and income. The size of the cast made *The Phil Silvers Show* a relatively expensive production. Most comedies of the day focused on a family of four or five and an odd neighbor or two. The Bilko show, with its central platoon, its master sergeants, WACs, and commanding officers, employed twenty-two actors on a regular basis. By putting an end to production payrolls and selling the show to the syndication market while it was still popular, CBS stood to make a huge profit.[34]

Something Silvers failed to mention in his book was the part he himself may have played in the Bilko demise. Early in 1959, he told a group of reporters that he was planning on leaving the show, saying that sponsors think nothing of dropping actors and it would be gratifying for an actor "to beat them to the punch once in a while." The comedian soon retracted the statement, but he might have already shaken the confidence of both the sponsor and the network regarding his commitment to the series.[35]

The last installment of *The Phil Silvers Show* aired on June 17, 1959, four years and 142 episodes after its premiere. By that time, Nat had been away from the program for two years and had moved on to other projects. Although he had announced that he needed rest when leaving the Bilko show, he had not necessarily meant that he would refrain from work altogether. He was determined to avert the fate suffered by Fred Allen, a victim of the weekly broadcasting treadmill, yet workaholic that he was, Nat intended to decompress from the Bilko experience by tackling a potentially less arduous series. He planned to traverse familiar, and favorite, territory.

Between Engagements

In 1958, Hiken planned on moving ahead by turning to the past. His idea was this: revive an eight-year-old radio show—unsuccessful then, forgotten now—and repackage it as a prime-time TV series. This excursion back to radio days hardly exuded a palpable aura of robust ratings potential. But, as a testimonial to Hiken's post-Bilko clout, he was able to sell his concept to CBS and landed a slot on the network's fall 1958 schedule.[1]

Nat had never accepted the failure of *The Magnificent Montague*. It was perhaps his favorite of all his comedic offspring, and he refused to give up on it no matter how much it stumbled commercially. Now he would have a chance to make a go of it in visual form. Aside from a personal attachment to the project and a certain nostalgia for its radio roots, *The Magnificent Montague* held a practical attraction for Nat as he sought an easier road to travel through his next television season. So much of the work was already done. The characters were all clearly defined, and there was an inventory of fifty radio scripts to draw upon when crafting plotlines. Unlike his experience on *The Phil Silvers Show*, he would not have to face a completely blank page every week. Instead, he could indulge in one of his favorite pastimes: retelling his stories and finding ways to make them better.

There was one crucial element he would not be able to transport from the show's radio incarnation. The program's flamboyant star, Monty Woolley, was no longer in good health and was not a practical choice for a weekly series. When considering who could replace him, Hiken hit upon an offbeat casting move.[2]

In 1958, few show business handicappers were likely to tout Sir Cedric Hardwicke as the next laugh-out-loud comedy sensation. For thirty years, on both stage and screen, Hardwicke had epitomized British dignity, reserve, and precision. True, he had acted on television since 1950, but his work had been almost exclusively confined to such lofty drama anthologies as *Studio One*, *Lux Video Theatre*, and *Producers' Showcase*, most notably in adaptations of his celebrated stage performances in *The Barretts of Wimpole Street* and *Caesar and Cleopatra*. But it was exactly this sort of distinguished background that Hiken planned to exploit for comedic effect. Like Edwin "The Magnificent" Montague, Hardwicke was a classically trained actor, well versed in the works of Shakespeare, Sophocles, and Shaw; the believability he could lend to the role appealed to Hiken, always a proponent of comedy that would "make it real," as Silvers would have put it. In fact, even if Woolley had been available, Hardwicke still might have been a wiser choice. In the close-up world of television, his restrained, nuanced style was preferable to Woolley's furniture-chewing theatrics.

As usual, Nat both wrote and staged the show, with Al DeCaprio coming on board to assist as camera director. Perhaps mindful of the difficulties he had encountered supervising the earliest Bilko episodes, Nat refrained from producing the series this time, although he took on the additional responsibility of ownership; the show was the property of Eupolis Productions, the company he had just formed with his lawyers, Arthur Hershkowitz and Howard Epstein.[3]

Besides Hardwicke, Hiken turned to the stage for other members of the cast as well. For the role of Montague's wife, Lily Boheme, Hiken hired Vivienne Segal, a former musical theater star, and for the part of Zinzer, the harried "Uncle Goodheart" director, he called on his cousin Gerald Hiken, a fine young character actor and an Obie Award winner, acclaimed for his performances in off-Broadway Chekhov revivals. To fill the role of Agnes the maid, his choice was fairly bold. Casting Pert Kelton, in creative terms, may have been the most obvious decision possible, for she had played the part on radio and personified the sort of wisecracking actress required by the role of Montague's working-class foil. Yet, she was still tarnished by the blacklist, and even though she had debuted the year before as Mrs. Paroo in the Broadway production of *The Music Man*, she continued to face restrictions on television.

The premiere episode was a video adaptation of the first *Montague* radio installment, based on one of Hiken's most outstanding half-hour scripts. Once again, the imperious, out-of-work Montague is forced to do the unthinkable— take the role of "Uncle Goodheart" on a radio soap opera (even though, in

1958, radio dramas of any kind had become a rarity). While retaining the structure and much of the dialogue of the radio original, Hiken tinkered with some aspects to keep the comedy fresh. In particular, he honed some of Montague's insults to a new sharpness. *The Phil Silvers Show* had generally steered away from one-liner laughs, but here Hiken seemed to relish the verbal parries, as when Montague prefaces his remarks to his radio director with "See here, you, your name escapes me and I hope I never overtake it.[4]

Hardwicke's reading of lines like these was offhand and enormously funny, projecting a devastating disdain. He proved to be equally effective at revealing Montague's shortcomings. As in the radio premiere, the proud Shakespearean was fond of spouting snatches of the Bard at the slightest pretext, and once again his wife was obliged continually to correct him. The sight of Sir Cedric Hardwicke, of all people, flubbing Shakespeare added an especially delightful wrinkle to the show.

After completing the excellent introductory episode, Nat went on to film two more installments. Then, in May, he received some painful news from CBS. The network would not be able to broadcast *The Magnificent Montague*, after all. The official explanation, reported in *Variety*, was rather convoluted. The show had been scheduled to air on Sunday nights at ten, and its sponsor was to be P. Lorillard, makers of Kent cigarettes. But, as the report explained, a change in the Tuesday schedule set a sequence of events in motion that sabotaged Lorillard's plans. CBS decided to air *The Garry Moore Show* Tuesday nights at ten, displacing *The $64,000 Question* from that time slot. To accommodate the successful quiz show, CBS moved it to Sundays at ten, which in turn displaced *Montague*. Hiken's program became the odd show out.[5]

Why CBS was not able to make room somewhere else on the schedule is not clear. The most plausible explanation is that the network had reasons, other than scheduling snafus, for leaving *Montague* out in the cold. One reason that comes to mind is the show's sophistication. The urbane repartee and the Shakespearean references did not fit into the usual mold of mass-appeal TV comedy in 1958.[6] Neither did the sharp-tongued, unsentimental approach. More than ever, television was relying on white-bread-family situations as the springboard for humor, most clearly evidenced in *The Donna Reed Show* and *Leave It to Beaver*, two successful series that were beginning their long broadcast runs at the time. Exactly how far Hiken was straying from this formula can be seen in the third *Montague* episode, "A Child in the House." Belying the innocent domesticity of the title, the episode is actually a takeoff on *The Bad Seed*, in which the Montagues baby-sit for their neighbors' child, a sweet-faced, pigtailed girl named Gwendolyn, who sings and skips around the apartment in between manufacturing evil-minded lies that plunge the household into chaos.[7]

Perhaps another factor weighing against the airing of *The Magnificent Montague* was the presence on the program of Pert Kelton. In casting the *Red Channels* listee at this point, Hiken qualified as a premature blacklist breaker. In Hollywood, for example, blacklisted screenwriters would not begin to receive screen credit under their own names until 1960, while the television blacklist would not be definitively broken until the John Henry Faulk libel trial in 1962. Nat's own small efforts in loosening the red-baiters' hold on his industry would not end here, but for the time being his actions had no effect.

With the premature cancellation of *Montague*, Nat found himself suddenly adrift. He was not without prospects, of course—his commanding reputation was still intact—but he was interested only in taking on a project of his own design, and developing a new show would take time.

Idleness had never sat well with Nat. "He must have wondered if he was just going to be a flash in the pan, if people were going to forget him," said his daughter Dana. "There was some sitting around and there was some anxiety, I'm sure."[8]

Nat had more than one reason to brood, not only his personal situation but also the general shape of the television industry. By 1958, the shift of television production from New York to California was practically a *fait accompli*. Illustrating this perhaps best of all was the direction taken by live drama shows, always the pride of New York programming. At one time, hour-long dramas were telecast from New York nearly every night of the week. Now only one major weekly anthology, *Kraft Television Theatre*, remained on the East Coast. The most acclaimed of all the live showcases, *Playhouse 90*, had premiered just two years before, in 1956, and had presented such classic TV plays as William Gibson's *The Miracle Worker* and Rod Serling's *Requiem for a Heavyweight*, but this series did nothing to promote the cause of east coast broadcasting. The show originated from Los Angeles, despite all the New York–bred talent that made the program such a success.

Profound changes in television production prompted some industry insiders to speak out in national publications and major newspapers, railing against the current trends in an impassioned, and futile, attempt to rally public opinion to their cause. In *Saturday Review*, CBS programming chief Hubbell Robinson decried the pat, formulaic nature of so many of the new shows, whether they be Westerns, private-eye melodramas, or family comedies. He exhorted producers to insist on creativity and intelligence and to desist from assuming that quality and sponsor support were incompatible. In the *New York Times Magazine*, Rod Serling held forth in particular on the issue of live versus filmed television as he lamented the precipitous decline in risk taking and spontaneity. Like Robinson, he denounced the imitative new programming, although Serling was quicker to single out the New York writer's great bête noire, TV Westerns, "each proudly flaunting the banner 'adult,' and each representing another mortal wound in the hide of live television drama." In what he himself conceded was wishful thinking, he proposed that New York inventiveness and West Coast film expertise could combine to produce a new wave of worthwhile programs.[9]

While some executives, such as Hubbell Robinson, believed that the campaign to improve programming could be waged in Hollywood, others felt that the shift from New York itself posed a problem. Ed Montagne was one of them.

> I remember talking to Hubbell when they were starting to move out to California. I said, "You're making a serious mistake. I'm a kid who grew up in Hollywood, and I know once you get out there, it's no longer going to be theater, it's going to be motion pictures, and the whole attitude will change." He said, "You're crazy." I was right. Everything changed. It became motion picture production, and those wonderful little stories that they used to do, the personal things that you could have done on the stage, were gone.[10]

In June, New York television people staged what amounted to a last-ditch effort to reverse the westward migration. Many of the city's most respected broadcast professionals, including Paddy Chayefsky, Carl Reiner, Sidney Lumet, Herbert Brodkin, and Fred Friendly, formed the Television Action Committee, with producer David Susskind as its chairman. Besides issuing the usual pronouncements about the medium's recent complacency, mediocrity, and infatuation with Westerns, the organization campaigned for the building of a "television city" production facility. The networks had already invested millions in Los Angeles–area studios. The committee hoped that a new, up-to-date facility in New York would lure programs back to the East Coast. The studio never materialized. And no other comparable projects would succeed where it had failed.[11]

Hiken joined in the public critiques of the business at this time. In an interview for *TV Guide*, he pointed out that there was no longer a training ground for young comedy writers, as there once had been in local radio when he had gotten his start on *The Grouch Club*. The increasing centralization of broadcasting made it more difficult for the new generation of writers to learn the fine points of comic storytelling. As for the exodus of talent to Los Angeles, he still showed no interest in following suit, even though many of his colleagues were already in California or would soon be on their way.[12]

The following year, a television scandal made national news and rattled the entire industry. In ways that insider critics such as Hiken and Serling could not foresee, it also instigated decisive changes in programming. The quiz show scandal first came to the public's attention in early 1959 when a New York grand jury investigated charges that producers were rigging the results of the show *Twenty-One*. A national congressional probe followed, climaxing that fall when Charles Van Doren, a Columbia University English instructor and a big winner on *Twenty-One*, admitted that producers had fed him answers before he appeared on the show's live broadcasts. Soon, investigators exposed similar frauds on other popular quiz programs.[13]

Foremost, of course, the scandal generated debate over television's ethical standards. Soon, though, the implications of that debate led to practical business decisions. The discredited contest shows had been independent productions, and so the networks, to prevent future embarrassment, started to regulate their programming more closely. And not just quiz shows. Using the crisis as a pretext, the networks began to exert more control over dramas, variety shows, and comedies as well.[14]

While this offscreen drama played itself out, independent producer Hiken was more concerned with finding ways to keep himself busy in the increasingly inactive New York production scene. Fortunately, he had something reliable to fall back on—his remarkable chemistry with Silvers. Beginning in 1959, after the Bilko show's cancellation, he and the comedian worked together on four CBS specials: *The Ballad of Louie the Louse*, *The Slowest Gun in the West*, *Summer in New York*, and *Just Polly and Me*. In certain respects, these shows were an ideal assignment for Nat at this point in his career. Not only was he collaborating with his most gifted star, he also had the luxury of creating without the pressure of a weekly deadline, with additional time to polish the material.

Summer in New York and *Just Polly and Me* (the latter costarring Polly Bergen, the wife of Silvers's agent, Freddie Fields) were variety hours that allowed Nat to return to sketch writing, the discipline that had first earned him recognition on *The Fred Allen Show* and in Broadway revues. The better of the two programs, *Summer in New York*, opened with a travesty re-creation of the birth of *Sergeant Bilko*, in which Silvers, portraying himself as an overbearing star, attempts to dissuade CBS executives from making an army comedy and pushes, instead, for his own pet project, a bathos-soaked tearjerker called "Leave It to Gramps." The skit is an amusing exercise in fast-talking comedy, as only Silvers could perform it, but clearly the highpoint of the show, and one of Hiken's gems, is the "Critic Sketch" that closes the program.

In this, Silvers plays *New York Times* theater critic Brooks Atkinson, who, accompanied by his wife, sets out to review the latest off-off-Broadway play (at a time when such productions were just starting to proliferate in the most unlikely little showcases in the lower regions of Manhattan). After finding the out-of-the-way building, he makes the mistake of walking up three flights instead of walking down three steps and winds up in the tenement apartment of a union-suited garment worker and his bedraggled wife (Jules Munshin and Carol Haney, in riotously funny performances). Munshin and Haney have no clue as to why the well-dressed, uptown Atkinsons have parked themselves on the frayed living-room couch. Not quite catching the name, they think perhaps the interlopers are the Epsteins, or perhaps the Openheims, of Openheim's Curtains. They march back and forth from the kitchen to the living room, trying to ascertain exactly what this is all about, while Atkinson interprets all the comings and goings and the harried remarks as the events in a boldly original new play. "Obviously by Paddy Chayefsky," he comments to his wife when he first glimpses the earthy "characters" in their squalid surroundings. He then revises his opinion at various junctures in the tenement-dwellers' "performance," detecting the hand of Arthur Miller and Eugene O'Neill in what he perceives to be some of the more compelling dramatic moments.[15]

The two other Silvers specials afforded Hiken the chance to work in a longer form as he scripted hour-length stories for his star. *The Ballad of Louie the Louse* was something that Nat literally dreamed up while vacationing in Montauk: he woke up one morning realizing he had come up with the basic framework of the story in his sleep. Shot on the still relatively new format of videotape, the program put a sardonic musical-comedy spin on the Runyonesque Broadway yarn, with lyrics as well as script by Hiken. In the title role, Silvers plays a rapacious loan shark who bleeds and harasses his clients without mercy, preying especially upon Times Square riffraff—horse players, beggars, clip-joint steerers, stumblebum drunks. Essentially, Louie is Bilko without any of the army finagler's endearing qualities. When Louie takes off for a Miami vacation, one of his debtors, a drunken newspaperman named Paul Barton, beseeches the heavens: let Louie's plane crash into the ocean and let everyone be saved but him. The next morning Barton learns that his wish has apparently come true. Racked with guilt, he decides to make amends by writing a glowing eulogy for Louie. Sodden with whiskey, he dispenses with all moderation and characterizes the Louse as a selfless humanitarian, a sort of Broadway Albert Schweitzer. A fantastic portrayal, to be sure, but one that still, nonetheless, includes an occasional, oblique glimpse of the truth, as when Barton states, "No man has ever died leaving so many people in his debt."

Barton's article takes on a life of its own and turns Louie into a national hero. It also turns Barton into an instant success, landing him a lucrative Hollywood contract to transform Louie's life into an inspirational, motion picture epic. The one thing that threatens to spoil all of this is the discovery that Louie did not die after all. If the world learns what Louie is really like, Barton's cottage industry of maudlin excess will immediately vanish.[16]

From this premise, Hiken unfolds a series of wry plot complications and character turns, on a par with the best of The Phil Silvers Show episodes, but now successfully sustained to an unprecedented length. The story ends with Louie becoming penniless and finding true happiness in poverty, only to be yanked back to his former miserable self by his old debtors, who discover they prefer living under his petty tyranny. The satiric view of human nature and the deft use of song to reveal character set the show apart from the usual star-driven specials of the time. The Ballad of Louie the Louse was really more like a musical comedy presented on the Broadway stage. Critics, though, were fairly mild in their praise of the program, as if, after four seasons of Sergeant Bilko, they had begun to take the Hiken/Silvers combination for granted.

The cast that Hiken brought together for the program was a cultural polyglot collection: from burlesque comic Silvers and former sportswriter Heywood Hale Broun to live TV drama actress Betsy Palmer and Chekhovian interpretor Gerald Hiken. Still, a seriousness in approach forged common ground between them, regardless of appearances. Silvers, on the surface at least, did not project much interest in the high-minded, dramatic side of New York theatrical life, as Gerald Hiken found out one day. Gerald was leaving rehearsal early so he could make it to his evening off-Broadway performance on time. Silvers asked someone where he was going, and when he was told that Gerald was headed downtown to appear in Three Sisters, he immediately turned and yelled, "Say hello to Patti, Laverne, and Maxine!" Gerald would later learn, though, that there was more to Silvers's attitude than the comic let on.[17]

As the *Louie the Louse* company was about to start taping the show, Gerald was still having trouble delivering his verses in the final musical number. Playing an incorrigible racetrack bettor, he was supposed to explain, musically, why there "Is nothing like two dollars/On a winning horse's nose." His cousin Nat felt there was something missing from Gerald's delivery but could not pinpoint what it was, which just left Gerald all the more frustrated. With only minutes left before taping, he stood alone, off to one side, when Silvers came over to ask how he was feeling. The downcast Gerald told him what the problem was, and Silvers asked, "What would Stan say?" Gerald had no idea what he was talking about. "Stan? Stan who?" "Stanislavski," Silvers answered. "Oh," Gerald said, "Stanislavski would say, 'Who are you singing the song for?' " And with that, he realized that his character was thinking of his wife and relatives, who all considered him a fool for betting on horses; the verses were his way of explaining what he loves about the racetrack life. "So, of course, when I started singing the song in the show, I had been inspired, I knew where the energy was going and it came out," Gerald recalled. "A woman I knew was standing next to Phil when I was singing, and he grabbed her and he said, 'He's got it. He's got it.' "[18]

In casting this show, Nat could take satisfaction in the inclusion of one performer in particular. He cast Pert Kelton in the prominent role of Concrete Mary, a Broadway panhandler. CBS had originally wanted Kay Medford for the part, but Nat insisted on Kelton; this time he was able to slip her past the blacklist cordon and, after the failed attempt in *The Magnificent Montague*, finally got her on the air. (Similarly, a year later he was able to hire his blacklisted friend Coby Ruskin to direct *Just Polly and Me*.)[19]

While *The Ballad of Louie the Louse* was theatrically oriented, Hiken's next long-form Silvers special amounted to a minimovie. With *The Slowest Gun in the West*, starring not only Silvers but also Jack Benny, Nat took aim at the genre that had been rankling New York writers so much in recent years. In the process he succeeded in tipping the Western on its ear with one of his most hilariously skewed concepts.

The setting is the toughest town in the West, Primrose, Arizona. Tougher than Tombstone, tougher than Dodge, Primrose is where all the most feared gunfighters congregated after those other, more notorious towns became too civilized to suit the tastes of any true diehard renegade. Outside gambling, drinking, and wenching, the favorite pastime in Primrose is gunning down the latest specimen of two-legged bullet fodder that the few upright Primrosians are injudicious enough to appoint sheriff. Into this hellhole one day comes Fletcher Bissell III (Silvers), aka the Silver Dollar Kid. He is quite notorious. He is regarded throughout the West as the most cowardly man alive, a spineless disgrace who has never once mustered up the nerve to go for his guns. And for this reason, as it turns out, he becomes the man who tames wild and woolly Primrose.

His rank cowardice is his protection. The Primrose gunmen would be all too happy to see the obnoxious Bissell dead, but no self-respecting gunslinger is willing to do the deed. Any gunman who did would instantly ruin his reputation forever; he would be laughed out of the territory as the man who drew on the yellowest man in the West. Seeing Bissell's invulnerability, the law-abiding citizens of Primrose appoint him sheriff.

Bissell runs roughshod over the local hardcases. He organizes them into glee clubs and beadwork classes, and there is nothing the gunslingers can do about it. The outlaws' only hope of exterminating the sheriff is to find somebody as cowardly as Bissell who has absolutely no reputation to protect. They find their man: the infamous Chicken Finsterwald (Benny), a man so craven that he once shot an eighty-four-year-old woman—in the back—then ran out of town when he found out the old lady had recovered and was out looking for him. He agrees to the Primrose outlaws' proposition, intrigued by the possibility of taking on a gunman that even he could best.[20]

Variety lauded the distinctive overturning of Western clichés. "Hiken is the master of the switch and the *schtick*, the piece of business that carries a comedy along. 'Slowest Gun' had a great switch; it also had plenty of funny business that kept buoying it into a fast-paced spoof with nary a lag."[21]

The setting of the show required Nat to arrange at least a temporary stay in California, the home of Western-film production. *The Slowest Gun in the West* was filmed on the Universal-Revue lot, where Nat acted as producer while also assisting, without credit, in the staging of the scenes.[22] Once again, his casting played a key role in heightening the comic situations. To provide a menacing foil for Silvers's cowardly machinations, he cast many of Hollywood's most leathery Western heavies as the Primrose outlaws, including Bruce Cabot, Jack Elam, Ted de Corsia, Robert J. Wilke and the incomparably imposing Lee Van Cleef.

On *Louie the Louse* and *Summer in New York*, Nat had worked with director Greg Garrison, a friend from the days in the early 1950s when they had both worked on NBC variety shows. Garrison had been orchestrating comedy on television for ten years—first on *Your Show of Shows* then on *The Milton Berle Show*—but he felt he did not truly begin to learn his craft until he worked with Hiken. "There isn't a major personality in the comedy writing field that I had not worked with," he said. "From Mel Tolkin and Lucille Kallen to Mel Brooks, Larry Gelbart and Goody Ace. Nobody but nobody had a more profound influence on my life than Nat Hiken. He was absolutely the best at what he did." Nat's instruction took an indirect path, more from osmosis than overt tutoring. He brought Garrison into the room with him as he wrote, reading the scenes to him and discussing them, until Garrison absorbed the material and was in command of the details that would make the show work when he went on the set. Sometimes, in his discussions with Nat, Garrison would offer alternate ways of handling a bit of stage business. "And Nat would say, 'You know, that's a really good idea, Greg. But why don't you try it your way and see how it works.' And I did. And I ended up doing it *his* way."[23]

Over the years of their friendship, Garrison had glimpsed the way Hiken's comedy mind operated even when away from the typewriter and the set; Nat could still find ways to set comic complications into motion. Garrison saw this one day at lunch. Often Garrison and Hiken ate at Lindy's, where Nat sometimes complained about the size of the corned beef sandwiches, which he considered grossly insufficient, at least compared with the grossly mountainous sandwiches at the Carnegie Deli. Once, when Nat invited Garrison to Lindy's, he took a detour down a side street to a nearby delicatessen and ordered a pound of corned beef, which he then carried with him in a paper bag to the famous Broadway restaurant. "He orders a corned beef sandwich, the waiter brings it to him, and Nat reaches into his little bag, takes out a half a pound of the corned beef, and puts it on each side of the sandwich," Garrison recalled. "Then he just sits there. I'm watching all this and I'm just fascinated by it because I'm just a dumb kid and I really don't know what's about to happen. And sure enough, Leo Linderman walks by, he looks at the sandwich, and he goes into the kitchen and starts screaming, threatening to fire the chef: 'You dumb sonofabitch . . .' And Nat looks at me and says, 'C'mon, let's get the hell out of here.' "[24]

While receiving an education on the Silvers specials, Garrison also witnessed the breakdown of one of television's most extraordinary partnerships. A hint of the troubles to come could be discerned on the *Louie the Louse* set. A visiting reporter had the chance to see the cast and crew unwinding during a lunch break, and at one point Silvers gestured to Hiken and said, "He'd be nothing without me, I tell you. Nothing. Spelled n-o-t-h-i-n-g. That's why he always comes crawling back!" He then added that he had made that remark so "that you're aware of the conviviality that exists between us." He was joking, but he may have also been drawing upon some real tension between himself and Hiken. Garrison became aware of a rift between the two while working on *Summer in New York*.[25]

The cause of the animosity, according to Garrison, was Silvers's premature sale of his *Sergeant Bilko* percentage. By hanging onto his piece of the show, Hiken had made a great deal of money from the series, and Silvers resented this discrepancy in their earnings. In an irrational quirk of thought, it seems that his bitterness clouded over the obvious fact that his loss was of his own doing. In turn, Nat was troubled by the comedian's resentment toward him. While working with the two men on *Summer in New York*, Garrison began to feel like the child who acts as intermediary between divorced parents. "Phil would say to me, 'See if you can get Nat to fix this.' In the past it would always be, 'Hey, Natty, maybe we should do this.' 'Yeah, let's try that, see if it works.' " Garrison added, "I found myself in rehearsals alone one on one with Phil a lot more than in the beginning. Now, that can be attributed to two things. It could be the fact that, after being with him over a couple of years, Nat trusted me a lot more, or the fact that he really didn't want to deal with Phil at that point." As much as Nat may have believed in Garrison's abilities, subsequent events support the second explanation. Once the series of specials was completed in 1960, years would pass before Hiken and Silvers would even consider working together again.[26]

Even though his ideas enjoyed a special affinity with Silvers's talent, Hiken continued to tinker with concepts that did not revolve around his Bilko star. These concepts tended to be ahead of their time. In 1958, after attending a Friars Roast of Rocky Graziano, he decided to bring the Friars' fine art of friendly insults to the TV screen, minus, of course, the raunchy jokes that usually distinguished these events. He went on to produce *The Friars Club Man of the Hour*, with Ed Sullivan as the guest of honor, verbally decimated by the likes of Jack Carter, Joey Bishop, Morey Amsterdam, Joe. E. Louis, and, most uproarious of all, insult comic Jack E. Leonard, a member of Nat's Lindy's Long Table crowd. The show, which aired in November, was an amusing platform for New York–style comedians, but CBS could not find a sponsor willing to take a chance on any follow-up broadcasts. Only years later did Hiken protégé Garrison revive the idea with *Dean Martin's Celebrity Roasts*, which, in 1973, succeeded in reviving Martin's then dwindling ratings.[27]

In 1960, Hiken created another ill-fated program that presaged an even greater television phenomenon. *Madhouse 60* was a fast-paced succession of sketches and blackouts, the latter usually composed of a single surreal gag (for example, a cuckolded husband finds his wife's lover hiding in the closet; the lover, feigning innocence, says that he thought the closet was the elevator; he presses a button on the husband's vest and the inside of the closet moves upward). In pacing and manic atmosphere, Nat borrowed somewhat from the Olsen and Johnson stage hit, *Hellzapoppin*, and in his use of bizarre blackouts, he was following the lead of Ernie Kovacs, but still the program was considered too adventurous to land a spot on the CBS schedule. Eight years later, time caught up to the idea: Dan Rowan and Dick Martin pulled in top ratings with a similar freewheeling, antic approach in *Laugh-In*, one of the pop-culture icons of its era.[28]

As the new decade began, Hiken was still without regular work. He had enough time on his hands in July 1960 that he could afford to substitute one week for *New York Herald Tribune* TV columnist John Crosby. He used the column to comment on the current state of the television business, although as a facetious, Robert Benchley–style essay. His article's purpose was to alert the public to a disturbing media trend. "This poison—permeating the TV press and eating at the vitals of what was once a fresh, exciting medium of entertainment—is Truth." The constant parade of meticulously reported behind-the-scenes stories, he warned, was robbing television of all the glamour and excitement that only artfully fabricated press agentry could provide. Concluding on an optimistic note, he predicted that television could still be saved: "But it's going to take a lot of lies to do it." The article demonstrated that Hiken, the former "Gripers' Club" columnist, had a knack for humorous prose, and suggested he might have had some future as a tongue-in-cheek commentator, but scriptwriting remained his favorite means of making people laugh, the form that came most naturally to him.[29]

When his five-year contract with CBS expired, Hiken turned to NBC as the home for his next project. After the experiments of *Man of the Hour* and *Madhouse 60*, he reverted to the more conventional sitcom format as the vehicle that stood the best chance of bringing him back to prime time. He was leery of the grueling weekly demands of this kind of show, but the potential rewards were great, provided that the deal was structured properly.

His cousin Peter Levin, who had remained in close contact with Nat over the years, was privy to Hiken's plans during this period. Their families visited often and spent time together at holidays—Christmas at the Levin home in

Connecticut, Passover at the Hiken apartment in Manhattan (although not religious, Nat was fond of family tradition and enjoyed presiding over the sedar). Often Peter and Nat would talk well into the night, sometimes reminiscing—"Nat very frequently had to rehearse our times together on Uncle Jake's farm."—sometimes discussing current business concerns. Nat revealed that he was intent upon creating a project that would support him and his family for years to come. "Nat was sort of soured by the Bilko experience," Levin recalled, "partly because of the work he had put into it, and then the fact that CBS really made out like a bandit on that show. Whatever he got from it in residuals was not as the creator but simply as the director and writer—and there's a whale of a difference."[30]

His next sitcom series would be the property of his own production company, and once the show had been on the air for four or five seasons, he would have a full package of reruns to sell, comparable to the highly profitable library of I Love Lucy films owned and syndicated by Desi Arnaz and Lucille Ball.[31] The work would be arduous—the type of work that had undermined his health on The Phil Silvers Show—but in the end he would create a veritable cash cow that could permanently free him from the weekly pressures that had dogged him in the past.

The Last Stand

Procter and Gamble wasted little time in latching onto the new Nat Hiken series. The project certainly seemed like a safe bet. Not only was Hiken returning to the half-hour sitcom, but he also was focusing his comedic talents once again on men in uniform. In late summer of 1960, with the *Sergeant Bilko* success in mind, Procter and Gamble agreed to sponsor the pilot for Nat's new police comedy after perusing nothing more than an eight-page outline.[1] Over the next three years, little else about *Car 54, Where Are You?* would come so easily.

For some time Hiken had been thinking of devising a series that would revolve around a pair of New York City patrolmen. As he told a newspaper reporter, he wanted to do a series that would be situated far away from the "chintz curtains and ranch-houses" that formed the backdrop for so many other sitcoms. He found the tone that he wanted when visiting several New York City precinct houses. What impressed him most of all was the matter-of-fact manner of the cops he found there. Unlike the hard-nosed characters populating TV crime shows, these police officers seemed no different from any other workingmen dealing with workaday problems. The criminal element did not stir up any great excitement; local petty crooks were received with a warm welcome, as if they were just old friends dropping by to say hello. "I'd never seen a policeman on TV talk or act like these guys," Hiken told an interviewer. "I began to think about the possibilities."[2]

In the little world Hiken created for *Car 54*—the fictional 53rd Precinct in the Bronx—law enforcement figures only incidentally into his policemen's lives. They are more concerned about finding low-rent apartments, helping the neighborhood drunk, and juggling seating arrangements at official police functions. When crooks intrude upon the scene, they do not seem to be bitter adversaries of the men in blue, more like neighbors, troublesome at times but not impossible. Besides, everyone in the show is at least a little bit peculiar, and both criminals and cops are part of the same pixilated community, a sort of *Chelm* of the Bronx, related in spirit to the town of fools of Yiddish folklore.

With his policemen protagonists, Nat found a refreshing antidote to the middle-class complacency of shows such as *The Adventures of Ozzie and Harriet* and *Leave It to Beaver*. As he explained at the time, "Policemen have the great dignity of the law and yet they are so underpaid that it's a struggle to maintain dignity and appearance. I believe more situations come out of people who have financial trouble." [3]

Nat's own financial concerns dictated the terms of the production. This series he would own, along with his Eupolis partners, Hershkowitz and Epstein. He would have to risk his own money in the venture, yet with the worries would also come the big payoff. He would, of course, write and direct, but also he hired himself as producer, despite his experiences producing the first episodes of *The Phil Silvers Show*. According to one friend, bad advice led Nat to this decision. Or, perhaps, he felt compelled to control the enterprise completely; since *Car 54* held such economic importance for him, and he was such a compulsive hands-on creator, he might not have been willing to leave the producing chores to anyone else. Either way, it was a decision that he would later regret. [4]

Casting the principals went smoothly enough, at least by Hiken's idiosyncratic standards. For the two central characters, patrolmen Gunther Toody and Francis Muldoon, he originally chose Jack Warden and Mickey Shaunessey respectively, but he and the actors' agents were not able to agree on salaries. Now that the money was partly his, Nat was more cautious than he might have been in the past. To replace Warden as Toody, he turned to a former member of his Bilko company. As mess sergeant Rupert Ritzik, Joe E. Ross had triumphed well beyond his limitations and had always proven to be a trouper, cooperative and hard working; his gravelly voice and dim demeanor, Nat believed, might go over once again in the part of a bumbling prowl-car cop. Selecting the actress to play Ross's wife was simply a matter of reuniting a successful pairing. Beatrice Pons, the former Mrs. Ritzik, the shrew ideal, became the somewhat less shrill, and more understandably cranky, Lucille Toody. The casting of Toody's partner took a less direct route. [5]

By 1960, Fred Gwynne was no longer sure that acting was a practical profession for him. A former advertising copywriter, the tall, gaunt young man
had appeared briefly as a union goon in *On the Waterfront,* had won small parts
on stage and had guest-starred on two memorable Bilko episodes, "The Eating
Contest" and "It's for the Birds." Less than carried away by his marginal acting
success, he had begun illustrating children's books and had started to dabble in
scriptwriting as well. He decided to make the most of his association with Nat
by getting his advice on an idea he was developing for a TV series. At Lindy's
Long Table, Nat listened to Gwynne's story and even offered some thoughts
on it, but his mind's eye was distracted. He was picturing the gangly Gwynne
alongside the short, stocky Ross—a Mutt and Jeff combination. As Gwynne
left that day, Nat mentioned that he might have something for him in an upcoming series. Only months later did he inform the actor that the part was the
lead role of Francis Muldoon.[6]

The contrast that pleased Nat went well beyond physical appearances and
into the sort of cultural disparity that Hiken loved to inject into his comedy.
Ross's parents owned a candy store. Gwynne's father was a successful stockbroker. Ross had learned most of what he knew in nightclubs and strip joints.
Gwynne had graduated from Harvard. Ross was a garrulous mug. Gwynne was
thoughtful, introspective. Not quite understanding why he had been chosen,
Gwynne decided while shooting the pilot that he should make himself sound
more like a typical New York cop. Hiken, who was directing the episode, apparently had his mind on other concerns because he failed to notice what the
actor was trying to accomplish. When the filming was done Gwynne went to
see Nat in his office and asked whether his accent had been all right. Nat,
Gwynne recalled, "looked quite horrified, quite suddenly, and he said, 'What
do you mean?' 'Well, I was putting on sort of a little bit through-the-nose tone,
a bit of a New York accent.' And Nat said, 'Good God, no.' He leapt up from
the table. 'No, no, no, no—I cast *you.* I want *you.*'"[7]

Reinforcing the connection between the new show and his previous hit series, Hiken filled the ranks of the 53rd Precinct with other Bilko veterans,
bringing in former platoon members Jack Healy and Maurice Brenner, and,
most notable of all, Bilko guest star Paul Reed, who now became the precinct's
commander, Captain Block. True to form, Hiken also kept his troupe racially
integrated—still an unusual practice in the early 1960s—with his inclusion of
such African-American performers as Nipsey Russell, Frederick O'Neal, and
Ossie Davis.

As for the show's production facilities, Hiken and his partners were fortunate enough to secure a studio in the midst of the program's actual setting. The Biograph Studios, on 175th Street in the east Bronx, had originally been built as a silent-film production center, the home of such early stars as Francis X. Bushman as well as motion picture pioneer D. W. Griffith. The five-story building languished for decades after the exodus of film production from the East Coast to California but was resuscitated in the early 1950s by the growth of New York television. Settling into the historic studio, *Car 54*'s cast and crew uncovered artifacts of the building's past—articles of old costuming like jodhpurs and pith helmets—from a time when Biograph filmmakers contrived far flung exotic adventures. By the early sixties, though, there was little about the studio that suggested movie industry glamour. More in keeping with the tone of its current project, the Biograph was now surrounded by mostly Jewish, working-class neighbors. Many of the show's company would commute to work on the subway, exiting at the 174th Street station, perhaps picking up a coffee and bagel at a corner candy store before walking to the studio entrance where neighborhood kids played on the sidewalk.[8]

While Nat filmed the first batch of episodes over the summer of 1961, reporters visited the set on a regular basis and generated a wave of glowing advance word about the show. In a typical assessment, Kay Gardella predicted, "When Hiken enters the TV swim, those who insist on sure things can bet it's time to put up the 'fasten your laugh belts' sign." Nat's responses to reporters' questions were usually not as ebullient. Others may have regarded his Bilko success as a guarantee of yet another hit, but he was not so sure. Proving that he was not one of the great self-promoters, he once harped on the one key element of *Sergeant Bilko* that was missing in his new project. Whatever personal difficulties he may have had with Silvers, he still hailed the comedian's ability: "Nobody can act with other people like Phil can. Nobody can bring a show to life like he does."[9]

Nat often focused on his pet peeves concerning the television industry. He lamented the lack of spontaneity of current programs, the new blandness spreading throughout the network lineups. At forty-seven, he was starting to look backward more often and wax nostalgic about a period only ten years past. "The wonderful time of TV was at the beginning," he said. "You could expect an actor to fluff his lines or some scenery to fall or a boom mike to come into camera range. But nothing happens anymore." He was also unhappy with the single-camera approach that he felt obliged to use on his new series. The three-camera method used on *The Phil Silvers Show* had already gone out of vogue in favor of Hollywood-style telefilm production. When shooting with one camera, the lighting could be perfected for each angle as the cameraman moved from long shot to closeup, giving the program a slick feature-film look. Although he understood the need to keep up with the times, Nat was still basically apathetic about technical expertise and, after shooting only a handful of Car 54 episodes, was already longing for the fresh interaction that he had been able to capture, flat lighting and all, on the Sergeant Bilko set.[10]

By this time, most of Nat's closest friends and associates were no longer trying, as he was, to stay competitive with West Coast techniques. They had already joined the exodus from New York. Coby Ruskin, beginning to emerge from the shadow of the blacklist, moved to the Hollywood production hub to improve his work opportunities. Aaron Ruben migrated west to produce The Andy Griffith Show (starring former New York TV actors Griffith and Don Knotts), and even Edward Montagne, despite his deep reservations about Hollywood-oriented television, switched coasts to produce a pilot for a Paul Ford comedy.[11]

Seen in retrospect, the 1961–62 season now takes on special importance in the story of East Coast broadcasting. Along with Hiken, New York diehard Herbert Brodkin, veteran of such anthologies as Studio One and Motorola TV Theatre, was beginning production of the courtroom series The Defenders, while Herb Leonard continued to turn out new episodes of the Gotham crime drama Naked City. The efforts of these three men, taken together, constituted a memorable last stand of New York's Golden Age, encompassing the spectrum of East Coast television at its best, from exuberant comedy to socially relevant drama to gritty police procedurals. New York boosters could derive some small measure of optimism: perhaps successful runs for these three programs might salvage, at least, a portion of the city's share in the TV business.

To get his series on the right track, Hiken had to overcome a bracing challenge: NBC scheduled Car 54 on Sunday nights at eight-thirty, during the second half of The Ed Sullivan Show, the ruler of its time slot for more than ten years. Nat made the curious decision to open his ratings battle against the variety-show institution with something less than his best work. The episode originally slated as the premiere, "Something Nice for Sol," was based on a script that he had crafted and refined over several months, but ultimately he chose instead to substitute a much more prosaic episode. Hiken's thinking, as he explained it to one of the cast members, was that the reviews of the first installment were not terribly important. Positive write-ups at that point would not pull in a significant number of viewers, and in any case, critics would be more inclined to take a wait-and-see attitude, curious to find out how the program would develop over the coming weeks. An appraisal of the series as a whole was more crucial.[12]

The response to the show went as expected. The premiere was generally panned, although reviewers also tended to point out that Hiken was capable of something better, implying that the series could improve. The second week's airing of "Something Nice for Sol" then lived up to the glowing advance word that had enveloped the program over the summer.[13]

In this warmhearted, nimbly constructed story, Toody and Muldoon search for the perfect gift to present to desk sergeant Sol Abrams for his twenty-fifth anniversary on the force. Sol is plagued by bad feet, so Toody and Muldoon decide to buy orthopedic shoes that will allow their beloved desk sergeant to walk without pain for the first time in years. The one catch: the gift must be a surprise. Somehow, the orthopedist has to observe Sol's walking pattern and take plaster casts of his feet without the desk sergeant suspecting what is going on. Toody and Muldoon's efforts to make Sol happy quickly plunge him instead into despair: he has concluded that the stranger coming into the precinct to watch him walk is an inspector from police headquarters looking for a medical reason to force him into early retirement. The complications eventually lead up to a hilarious sequence of Toody, Muldoon, and the orthopedist attempting to take foot casts while Sol sleeps.[14]

This and other episodes had a cumulative effect upon critics, as Nat had hoped, culminating in perhaps the ultimate payoff—a rave *TV Guide* review. In the December 23 issue, three months after the show went on the air, renowned cultural critic Gilbert Seldes wrote, "The hottest question in television right now is *Car 54, Where Are You?* and for once I've got the right answer. *Car 54* is in my living room every Sunday night. There are few other programs I stay home for—this is one I run home for."[15]

◆   ◆   ◆

During the early weeks of the show's production, a reporter had asked Hiken why he resisted current trends by remaining in New York. Among other reasons, Nat had cited the availability of unique performers, stressing that "there is a huge reservoir of talent here, and the faces are new to most of the country's TV viewers." This talent pool, which Hiken exploited especially for guest-starring roles, helped set the series apart from typically bland sitcoms churned out on the West Coast.[16]

First, naturally, Hiken indulged his partiality for colorful, Runyonesque characters. Special favorites were Gene Baylos and B. S. Pully.

The baby-faced, sad-eyed Baylos, like the young Phil Silvers, enjoyed the unfortunate distinction of being known as a comedian's comedian. Other comics clamored to watch him perform and howled at his jokes, but his career never ventured much beyond the Borscht Belt circuit. His eccentricities, which so endeared him to his fellow Broadway knockabouts, may have contributed to the modesty of his success. For one thing, he tended to perform some of his most memorable gags while on the streets of New York, away from the discerning eyes and beneficial clout of booking agents and syndicated columnists. According to the most widely circulated Baylos story, he once came upon a construction crew that had just razed a midtown block to make room for a new hotel. Grabbing a hard hat and a set of blueprints, he hurried over to the crew, jabbed a finger at the blueprints, and cried, "I told you *Forty-third* Street, not *Fifty*-third Street!" Another factor in his career—and a much more detrimental one—was his handling of the business side of comedy, which seems to have been less than shrewd, if the following Broadway tale can be trusted. A friend of Baylos was walking along a midtown Manhattan street one day alongside an important CBS executive, when he spotted Baylos hanging out in front of the Friars Club. Thinking he could do his friend some good, the man stepped over to the comic and said, "Gene, I want you to meet the head of CBS." Baylos replied, "Who the fuck needs him? I got four days up at Kutscher's."[17]

Although occasionally unwise about offers of help from some people, Baylos had no trouble accepting the assistance of Hiken, his Lindy's pal, who cast the comedian as a recurring *Car 54* character, alternately known as Backdoor Bennie and Bennie the Bookie, a doleful miscreant who yearns to escape the uncertainties of civilian life and return to his simpler existence in Sing Sing.

B. S. Pully, toadlike in appearance and with a bullfrog voice, enjoyed a special claim to fame: many considered him the filthiest comedian of his generation—no small accomplishment as long as Joe E. Ross was still alive. His act was so raunchy that the police would occasionally shut it down and drag him to court on charges of public lewdness. Among his fellow comics, Pully's irreverence was legendary. Hank Garrett, a stand-up comedian who played *Car 54*'s Officer Nicholson, remembered once going out of his way to see Pully in action at Murray Franklin's nightclub in Miami Beach.

I was working a hotel and I came over because someone said Pully's going to do a spot. Pully walks over to Murray Franklin and says, in his deep, raspy voice,

"Can I do a few minutes?" And Franklin said, "You say one dirty word, I will leadpipe you to death." Now, Pully gets on the stage and he's saying, "Good evening, ladies and gentlemen. I am here . . . " And the audience is screaming. They're falling on the floor. From where I'm standing, I can't see what's going on. Franklin is in the back of the room and all he sees is the back of Pully. Pully is peeing in his pants. The spot is getting bigger, there is pee all over the stage. Franklin wants to kill him. And after it's over, Pully said to him, "I kept my word. I didn't say nothin' bad."[18]

Pully was fond of telling reporters—apparently with a straight face—that the initials B. S. stood for Bernard Shaw (his real name, as it turned out, was Murray Lerman). By the time Hiken cast him on *Car 54*, the comedian had acquired some acting experience, mostly in 20th Century-Fox musicals of the 1940s, but far more important was his natural persona, his authentic Broadway quality that had caught the attention of George S. Kaufman when directing the original stage version of *Guys and Dolls*. Pully had arrived at the audition for the play to schmooze with one of his friends. As soon as he croaked out "Hello, pal," Kaufman immediately snapped to attention. He asked the comedian if he thought he could handle a role in which he would have to play dice. Pully's response: he pulled out a pair of dice from his pocket and said, "You're faded." On the strength of this first impression, he joined the *Guys and Dolls* company as Big Jule, first on stage, then on screen. Always a connoisseur of the genuine Times Square article, Nat was likewise impressed with Pully and hired him often for a variety of comical *Car 54* thugs.[19]

Although Baylos and Pully were amusing, distinctive additions to Hiken's troupe, they did not quite qualify as the greatest finds for the new series. That honor belonged instead to two other actors, Al Lewis and Charlotte Rae.

A veritable walking compendium of twentieth-century show business, Lewis had worked in circuses, medicine shows, vaudeville, burlesque, movies, Broadway, off-Broadway, live television, and telefilms. Along with his wide range of experience, he possessed that one quality that Nat prized perhaps more than any other—an unforgettable face, with its hawk-beak profile and its habit of creasing and folding, accordionlike, with every change of expression. An occasional bit player on *The Phil Silvers Show*, he appeared as supporting characters in two of the earliest *Car 54* episodes, attracting such an enthusiastic response from viewers that Nat invented a principal patrolman character for him—the ever-irascible Leo Schnauser.[20]

As Schnauser's popularity grew, Hiken broadened the scope of the character and began to work the patrolman's personal life into his stories. This, in turn, prompted him to provide Lewis with an on-screen wife. To play the character he called upon a relative, or, at least, someone he believed to be a relative.

Charlotte Rae first earned a reputation for offbeat, character-oriented comedy in the cabarets that flourished in New York after World War II. Nat met the plump, pudding-faced comedienne in the early 1950s when he went downtown to see her perform at the Bon Soir. He passed a note to her saying that he would like to speak to her, explaining that he believed they were cousins. The Milwaukee-born Rae, an admirer of Nat's brilliant work on *The Martha Raye Show*, was delighted to meet him, even if she had doubts about their alleged family connection. "I never thought I was related to him," Rae said. "I think one of my aunts on my father's side married a Hiken. Something like that. I could never figure it out." Even so, Nat continued to think of her as a cousin—his own, far more reasonable version of his mother's aggressive search for kinfolk wherever she roamed.[21]

Just as important, he appreciated the detail Rae brought to her work, the kind of precision in acting that could contribute to vivid comedic situations. He had featured her in two *Sergeant Bilko* episodes, then had cast her in a supporting role in an early *Car 54* story. Finally, he installed her as the flighty, hot-tempered Sylvia Schnauser. Before making this move, however, Nat needed some coaxing, courtesy of his secretary, Gertrude Black (now Gertrude Deems, after her marriage to *Car 54* actor Mickey Deems). As she had done on *The Phil Silvers Show*, Gertrude assumed wide-ranging managerial duties on *Car 54*. This sometimes included some artful maneuvering of Nat when he was unable to make what she knew was the right decision. Nat may have been devoted to family, but he could be reluctant to hire relatives such as Rae and Gerald Hiken; he was leery of the appearance of nepotism even if these particular relatives were clearly talented and deserving. Gertrude knew enough not to recommend an actor outright because Nat would inevitably find something wrong with the choice. According to Mickey Deems, "Nat'd be saying, 'We got to get a wife for Al.' And Gert would say, 'Well, you mentioned Charlotte Rae would be perfect.' Which, of course, he hadn't. And he'd say, 'Oh yes— Charlotte. Yes, she would be great.' "[22]

In the first episode devoted to the Schnausers, Rae and Lewis were supposed to go at each other hammer-and-tongs in a verbal brawl. Rae suggested that they prepare for the show by renting a studio and improvising scenes together.

"So we walked around this studio and he started insulting me—really big barbs—and I had to improvise on that. By the time we left we were really slinging it at each other. We were ready." The combustible chemistry they discovered that day would fuel many of the most memorable episodes in the series.[23]

Car 54 clearly had much going for it, in the typical Hiken manner, and so much of that was due to his choice of performers. At the same time, though, his unorthodox casting led to the first tremor of trouble to reverberate behind the scenes.

Deems pinpointed the beginning of the problem. The pivotal event occurred one day soon after the release of the show's initial ratings, which made it clear that the series would be giving *The Ed Sullivan Show* some feisty competition. "We were gathered around for a morning reading for what we were going to shoot that day," Deems recalled. "Joey Ross came to some line, and he turned to Nat and said, 'Nat . . . ' And at that we all jumped. He used to call him Mr. Hiken—he never called him Nat. He said, 'Nat, I don't think that's so funny.' And we all went, *Oh, my God, he's turned into a star.*"[24]

Like Maurice Gosfield before him, Ross let celebrity go to his head, leading him to believe that *Car 54* revolved around him, that the tail was actually wagging the dog. It did not take long for Nat to see how this development would transform the former strip joint comic. Stardom, as Ross understood it, meant not bothering to learn his lines. Not only did he neglect to read the script, he would often not bring it with him to cast readings, accentuating his self-importance by making it necessary for the script girl to run off and fetch him another copy. Even when he was at his most diligent, as he had been during *The Phil Silvers Show*, scripted dialogue could easily get the better of him; now he drew one blank after another.[25]

The idea of reprising the Gosfield experience was worrisome enough for Nat, but the Ross predicament turned out to be far more infuriating. Gosfield had fumbled his most perfunctory bits of business primarily because he simply had not been up to it. Ross, on the other hand, believed that preparing for a scene was beneath him. And, unlike Gosfield, Ross was one of the leads. Nat could not work around him. Every time Ross groped for a line and came up empty, he held up the production and cost money—Nat's money. Beyond that, Ross also differed from Gosfield in one other way, which incensed Nat further—Ross would often turn nasty. He was fond of lording it over extras and other people at the lowest rungs of the production. If his on-screen spouse, Beatrice Pons, spent an extra moment primping for a scene or asked for another take, he might cry, "Look, I'm the star of this show. You're wasting my time." He also saw no reason to rein in his crude language, as Deems recalled. "We had visitors on the set quite often and it was nothing for Joey to use four-letter words in front of children." [26]

Directing Ross became an ordeal for Hiken. "Nat took it for around four weeks, four weeks of having to reason with him," said Deems. "Reasoning with an idiot is a little difficult." [27]

Deems, obviously, was not one of Ross's fans, and was not inclined to be charitable, but his comments were consistent with other appraisals; some people, in fact, could be even harsher in their descriptions. An exception on the *Car 54* set was Lewis, who counted himself as Ross's friend (even though Ross had trouble remembering the actor's name; he kept referring to Lewis by his on-screen moniker of Leo). Others tried to be generous in their characterization, even if they were not much more complimentary than Deems. "Poor guy," Rae said of Ross, "he didn't seem to know what a bonanza he had fallen into." Gwynne, who nursemaided his costar and did his best to coax lines out of him, characterized Ross as "very childlike, a sweetheart, but very child-like to the extent that he had to be beaten every so often." [28]

With his sharp tongue, Nat could occasionally extract some revenge against Ross for all the trouble the actor caused him. Typically, he focused on Ross's remarkably sloppy habits, which rivaled those of Gosfield (and which were so at odds with Ross's suddenly lofty view of himself). Hank Garrett recalled a time when the cast was preparing for a masquerade party scene, costuming themselves as cowboys, strongmen, pirates, devils. "Someone asked, 'What is Joey going to be?' And Nat said, 'Well, if he changes his underwear no one will recognize him.' " Whatever satisfaction Nat found in his not-so-gentle ribbing, it was not enough to alleviate the ongoing exasperation that drove him from the set. [29]

After eleven episodes, Nat and his partners hired Al DeCaprio, Hiken's *Sergeant Bilko* collaborator, as the new director for *Car 54*. Ross's swollen ego alone did not force Nat to give up directing the series, but it dramatically exacerbated a situation already fraught with anxiety. [30]

◆   ◆   ◆

On *The Phil Silvers Show*, Nat had been able to concentrate on writing and directing because he had been spared the day-to-day responsibilities of producing the show; Edward Montagne had handled that for him. On *Car 54* there was no such buffer between him and the pressure cooker logistics of keeping a weekly series moving. And Nat, the perpetual procrastinator, remained ill suited for a job that required strict organization and adherence to deadlines. His Eupolis partners, Arthur Hershkowitz and Howard Epstein, shared the responsibilities with him, but they were lawyers by training and no more qualified than Nat for this kind of work. Actors who arrived at the studio as early as seven in the morning would find Hiken already at work in his office; he would not leave the studio until somewhere between eight and eleven that night. Overwhelmed by his producer's role, Nat gave up directing—except for an occasional episode—so that he could at least continue as head writer.[31]

Bringing in DeCaprio seemed like a simple solution, but Nat fretted that it was not good enough and tinkered with the situation some more. As confident as he was in DeCaprio's technical abilities, Nat did not believe his old camera director could handle the intricacies of comedy sufficiently well. He suddenly announced a new arrangement one day on his way home from work.

He often drove to and from the Biograph Studios with Mickey and Gertrude Deems, and on the way home one Friday he turned to Mickey and said, "Look, I better pick you up an hour earlier on Monday because you're going to start directing." Deems, a stand-up comic turned actor, had no directing experience outside a short comedy film. He was caught completely off guard. "What the hell are you talking about? Who's directing?" he said. "I don't know a camera from a hole in the wall." Hiken explained that DeCaprio would take care of the camera and lighting, and Deems would stage the comedy. DeCaprio would receive the director's credit on-screen, while Deems would work uncredited because he did not belong to the Directors Guild; in any case, there was no such thing as a comedy director credit. "Between the two of you, you'll work it out," Nat assured him.[32]

Two directors on the same set can lead to trouble, as Hiken himself should have known, based upon his dispute with Grey Lockwood, the camera director of *The Martha Raye Show*. Most likely he resorted to this alternative out of force of habit, continuing the dual director tradition that had been standard practice when he had first entered television. Perhaps he had also been lulled into a false sense of confidence by his harmonious relationship with DeCaprio on the set of the Bilko show. Of course, in that case, Hiken was the primary creative force behind the series and an acknowledged master of his craft; it was only natural that DeCaprio would defer to him. Now, however, DeCaprio would have to share power with a little-known comedian who had no significant directorial experience. Before long, the two codirectors began to lock horns.

An especially divisive dispute occurred while filming an episode entitled

"Get Well, Officer Schnauser." In this story, Schnauser, recovering in the hospital from a broken foot, looks forward to financial help from the precinct's Brotherhood Club Fund, only to discover that nearly all the money has been frittered away on misguided charities. A series of mix-ups eventually lands a satchel filled with $37,000 in Schnauser's lap, sending him into transports of ecstatic gratitude—until he learns that the money had been stolen from a bank. In his final scene, Schnauser, still in his hospital robe, sits dazed and crestfallen in Captain Block's office as the bank president counts the loot and repacks it into the satchel. Deems wanted to keep the camera far enough away to show both Schnauser and the bank president's handling of the money in the same frame, to heighten the comedy by showing the forlorn Schnauser's reaction in the context of the scene. DeCaprio, on the other hand, insisted on placing Schnauser and the bank president on opposite sides of the room and covering the action in a series of close-ups. When Hiken saw the rushes, he was not pleased. He ordered a reshoot, specifying that the scene be filmed along the lines that Deems had originally suggested. "I don't think Al ever quite forgave me for that," said Deems.[33]

The relationship between the two directors worsened, especially for De-Caprio who, after four years on *The Phil Silvers Show*, must have felt he had earned the right to command the set without interference. At the 1961–62 Emmy ceremony, Hiken received an award for "Outstanding Directorial Achievement in Comedy," in recognition of the initial *Car 54* episodes he had helmed; as he accepted the honor, he said, "I'd just like to mention that when the going got rough, a wonderful guy, Al DeCaprio, took over." This tip of the hat did little to appease DeCaprio. He left the show at the end of the first season.[34]

To replace him, Hiken hired Stanley Prager, a move that finally simplified matters. Prager had a strong background in comedy (among other things, he had appeared alongside Bert Lahr in Hiken's "Schneider's Miracle" sketch). He had also acquired experience as a director (after the blacklist had derailed his acting career). One person working alone could now take Nat's place on the set, and directorial squabbles could be eliminated. All that Hiken needed to do now was figure out how to juggle his responsibilities as both producer and head writer. At the end of the first season, to help him deal with this burden, he fell back on his usual solution. He called in Billy Friedberg, who became both coproducer and Nat's major domo in the script department. The solution failed to solve much. For one thing, Friedberg was really no more of a producer than Hiken was. And for another, Nat remained incapable of delegating authority, no matter how many partners and assistants he collected, whether the job entailed rewriting a script or drawing a pencil sketch that would appear in a precinct scene. As the project continued to overwhelm him, his nervous eccentricities, always a part of the way he worked, often became more pronounced.

"Nat was mad as a hatter," said Car 54 casting director Edith Hamlin. This assessment was delivered with a great deal of affection and was overstated for effect. It was also understandable when viewed from Hamlin's unique perspective.[35]

Through the 1950s, Hamlin had worked extensively on serious-minded drama anthologies, with such broadcast impresarios as Herbert Brodkin and Fred Coe, and such acclaimed playwrights as Paddy Chayefsky, Horton Foote, and Rod Serling. She had never worked on a comedy series. "There were a lot of people pushing me, saying, 'You have to get sitcom experience,' " she recalled. "I had such a disdain for sitcoms—that's like daytime drama. But they said—and they were quite right—'Work with Nat. He's the best, and it's a whole other thing.' "[36]

Car 54 was a whole other thing not only in terms of Hiken's talent. Hamlin was unprepared for dealing with Nat's work habits, a whole other experience compared to the relatively methodical practices of TV drama. The first thing that puzzled her was the ritual that Nat had to perform each day before facing the work that lay before him. Coming into Nat's office for a meeting, she found him carefully arranging three piles on his desk. Two of the piles, composed of small, shriveled objects, caught her eye in particular. "I looked at Billy Friedberg, because Billy was a buddy, and I said, 'Billy, those look like dried ears. What are they?' Nat had a stack of dried apricots, a stack of toasted almonds, and a stack of dried figs, and he couldn't start until all three were in place. He was very compulsive about it."[37]

She found Nat's idiosyncrasies at their most peculiar and frustrating when the two of them met to discuss casting, Hiken's renowned specialty. Hamlin was familiar with many actors in New York theater who were struggling, talented, and eager to work. Nat, though, did not want to know about them. According to Hamlin, he was so racked by anxieties that "he wanted to work with the same five people all the time," standbys such as B. S. Pully, Gene Baylos, Larry Storch, Jake LaMotta, Heywood Hale Broun. The idea of trying anyone new terrified him.[38]

Hamlin referred to the handful of favorite performers as Nat's security blanket. Relying on certain actors had always been a quirk of Hiken's—he had, for instance, regarded Rocky Graziano as his good luck charm—but on *Car 54*, with so much riding on the show's success or failure, he leaned on his stock company more than ever. Broun found that he would sometimes be hired even when good casting sense would seem to disqualify him. Once he received a call to appear on the show when he had played a supporting role in an episode just two weeks before. He pointed this out to the casting person making the call and was told, "But you have the wire glasses." Even though he could use the job, he thought "that was about as unimaginative as you can be. Yes, I had a pair of wire glasses, which I wore for that kind of part, the prissy, prissy man. That was the reason I was hired again, because I had a pair of glasses."[39]

If Hamlin had only minimal success injecting fresh blood into the cast, it was not for lack of trying. "We would discuss a part endlessly," she recalled. "We would go through fifty names, and finally I would say about one of them, 'Nat, trust me. You'll love him. He'll be marvelous.' And he would say, 'Edith, you know what? Get me Pully.' " She once imagined taking this process to its ultimate conclusion. "If I said to him, 'Olivier, Nat—okay? This small part— Olivier? What do you think?' He would say, 'Edith, I don't know. Can he do takes?' I'd want to pull my hair out." Once she managed, against great resistance, to cast a young Hal Linden, the future star of *Barney Miller*, in a small role. "I got my head handed to me," she said. Hiken came looking for her, and Friedberg warned that she was in big trouble. She recalled, "I said to Nat, 'What's the problem?' He said, 'Edith, darling, he doesn't have a funny bone.' I said, 'But he does, Nat.' He said, 'No. Next week we use Pully.' "[40]

Hamlin found that Nat needed not only security blankets but also handlers. As she put it, "The name of the game was Get Nat to Write." Hiken had shown on the Phil Silvers specials that he was still capable of turning out excellent scripts on time, on his own, but the agonies he went through feeding the weekly Bilko pipeline were now magnified to new extremes on *Car 54*. Exempting himself from directing the show did not help. As if unable to restrain himself, he kept drifting back to the set, to observe and to kibbitz. Gertrude Deems would sometimes have to reel him back. "At one point Gertie ran after him," Garrett recalled, "and she said, 'Nat?' And he said, 'What, Gertie?' She said, 'Next week's script?' And he said, 'Do we have a script for next week?' She said, 'Not *yet* we don't.' "[41]

Most often the job of keeping Nat on track fell to Friedberg. Nat was known to head to the set as early as eight o'clock in the morning, eventually prompting director Prager, at his wit's end, to head in the opposite direction back to the offices. "Why are we both directing? What am I doing here?" he would say. Friedberg would then have to try dragging Nat back to the typewriter and channel him back to his task. From a distance, Friedberg's constant scrambling after the wandering Nat could seem comical, like something out of one of Hiken's own shows, but the experience, always played out against a looming deadline, took its toll on Friedberg. He had already begun to suffer from a heart condition before joining *Car 54*. Handling Nat's erratic habits could not have helped.[42]

"Nat was driving Billy crazy," said Hamlin. "He was driving himself crazy. But everybody loved Nat. He didn't have a mean bone in his body."[43]

The actors, removed somewhat from the scriptwriting tug-of-war, were especially appreciative of Hiken. The initial script readings were still uproarious, and the performers prized the stories and dialogue that could make it so easy for them to be funny. As for Hiken's unscheduled visits to the set, which caused Friedberg and others so much aggravation, the actors were witness to how well Nat could contribute on the spot. "He would walk over to a corner," Garrett recalled, "and kind of mutter to himself, smoking nonstop, and instead of laughing he would kind of hiss through his teeth, à la Teddy Roosevelt, and come up with this brilliant idea." Al Lewis expressed his admiration in no uncertain terms: "I worked for three geniuses in comedy writing—George S. Kaufman, S. J. Perelman, and Nat Hiken."[44]

Getting Nat to put the hilarity on paper, though, involved constant coaxing and coaching from Friedberg. Typically, Friedberg would put the scriptwriting process into gear by initiating the discussion of the story. At times Nat would stop dead in his tracks, frozen by doubts about his ideas. Friedberg would reassure him, telling him that the material was terrific, not simply to boost Nat's ego but because he could discern the value of the germinal story concept and knew that Nat could bring out its comedic qualities once he started developing it. Hamlin was intrigued by this process, so different from the methods of writers she had observed while working on anthologies. Serling, Chayefsky and other dramatists would simply head to their home or office, and come back some time later with the finished script. Comedy writers such as Hiken and Friedberg, on the other hand, worked out loud, batting the script around between them. As Hamlin described the process, "Nat and Billy would talk it, or Nat would talk it and Billy would fix it. Or he would get stuck and Billy would push him along. He hit a bump and Billy would get him over it. It was almost like a dance team." Keeping the dance going was the key. Nat and Billy might get started in the morning, bounce ideas for an hour, then Nat would cut the session off for lunch—at ten-thirty. "You couldn't hate him," Hamlin said, "but you wanted to shake him."[45]

Hiken overtaxed himself with so many responsibilities that he could not keep track of what he had done and what he had not done. Often he would think of some task for his director, then assume it had been accomplished, as if his thinking it meant others were aware of it as well. When he showed up on the set asking why his orders had not been carried out, the director would have to explain that the orders had never even been issued. This sort of problem Nat brought upon himself, but other difficulties originated outside the *Car 54* company. The most nettlesome had to do with the show's laugh track.[46]

As he had done on *The Phil Silvers Show*, Hiken used the laughs lifted from preview screenings, recorded this time at the Johnny Victor Theater at Rockefeller Center, with Hank Garrett priming the audiences with a stand-up routine. (Ross had delivered some of the early warm-ups but, seeing no reason to alter his strip joint act, he had offended audiences with off-color material.) NBC did not care for the technique Hiken was using. Like the three-camera shooting method, and the live-broadcast approach before that, the preview track had gone out of favor. NBC wanted *Car 54* to use canned laughter, as was heard on the sound tracks of other comedies at the time. Hiken refused.[47]

To be precise, the *Car 54* laugh tracks were not themselves 100 percent genuine. Sometimes the sound engineer would have to supplement the recordings with canned responses because of a technical flaw in the process. When previewing the episodes, the projectionist would have to keep the volume down so that the film's dialogue would not interfere with the recording of the audience. This, in turn, meant that the viewers were not always able to hear the actors' lines and would not respond as much as they should have. Still, Hiken made it clear that the canned supplements should be within reason; he did not want uproarious responses to gags that were only mildly amusing at best. The track had to be at least based on a real audience reaction. Nat, a product of live broadcasting, would not stand for the totally synthetic hilarity heard on *The Donna Reed Show* or *Leave It to Beaver*.[48]

During the second season, Nat battled constantly with the network over this issue. The longer the struggle lasted, the more acrimonious it got. Like Fred Allen, Hiken had no patience for network interference and, left to his own devices, would not have bothered much with diplomacy in his dealings with executives. Friedberg often had to step in for Hiken's own good, either fielding calls from NBC himself or calming Nat down enough so that Nat could handle the calls without inflicting too much damage upon his relation-ship with the network.[49]

Always a purist, Hiken even resisted NBC's request that the show be filmed in color. To his mind, all that mattered were the programs' situations and in-teractions between characters. Color, he felt, would only distract the audience from the comedy.[50]

Dealing with all his other difficulties might have been more tolerable if Nat could at least extract the thorn that continued to dig into his side every time the cast assembled to shoot a new episode. But Joe E. Ross still did not learn his lines and still played the prima donna. If anything, he was getting worse. Before the first season was completed, Deems had to resort to drastic measures just to keep Ross from sabotaging the filming altogether. He instructed actors doing a scene with Ross that they should wait a beat after every line that Ross flubbed, then continue with their own dialogue. When the take was done, Deems would move the camera in to shoot Ross's lines in close-up so that they could be cut into the larger scene. Getting the lines out of Ross was torturous, Deems recalled. "I would stand by the camera with the script, and I would read him the lines, one line at a time, and he'd repeat it. Which can be pretty dev-astating to a professional actor. But Joey—it didn't faze him at all."[51]

Even though Nat was no longer directing on a regular basis, and usually did not have to deal with Ross first-hand, he was increasingly enraged by each needless delay caused by his star's arrogance and neglect. Lewis, when he passed Hiken's office, would sometimes hear Nat read the riot act to Ross. "He just tore the skin off of him . . . He'd be screaming, 'And I found you in the gutter, I work my ass off and I write until midnight and you don't remember a line. I'm going to throw you out.' Oh, it went on and on."[52]

The diatribes had little effect. Finally, Nat decided to follow through on his threats and replace Ross. He planned on cutting out the Toody character and promoting Schnauser to ride alongside Muldoon in Car 54. According to Gwynne, when Nat called in Ross and told him he was fired, Ross broke down and cried. Although furious with Ross, Nat could not withstand this pathetic reaction. He relented and let Ross stay on. By doing so, he might have lost his chance at continuing the show with at least some peace of mind.[53]

At one point during the second season, NBC executives visited the Car 54 set and were given a tour by Nat. He began to talk about some of the difficulties in producing the show and, as if tapping into a stream of thought that he could not hold back, he told the executives he was not sure how he could continue another season.[54] Most likely he regretted having said that, but just as likely he was already looking for a way out of the series. Two years of *The Phil Silvers Show* had worn him down and undermined his health, compelling him to leave before the series had run its course. Now *Car 54* was beginning to fit the same pattern. This time, however, the pressures were even more intense, combining the burdens of producing on his own, dealing with a destructive star and grappling with the network. And hovering above it all was the specter of past success, as Ambur observed. The standard Hiken had to live up to loomed higher than the standard most comedy creators set for themselves. "I asked him once if it wasn't kind of tough following Bilko. He said, 'It's murder.' " [55]

The problems behind the scenes were bound to have an effect on what appeared on-screen. Ross's lack of preparation disrupted the interaction between performers, and perhaps just as detrimental was Hiken's absence as full-time director. This made it difficult for him to contribute last-minute bits of business that could have enhanced many of the episodes. The series was not as consistently funny as *The Phil Silvers Show*—as Nat had feared—but it hit many a high note with episodes that were both ingenious and hilarious.

Car 54 had no virtuoso star like Silvers to carry the series from one week to the next. To compensate, Hiken relied more on guest stars and a parade of flamboyant supporting characters, such as Larry Storch as Charley the drunk, who disintegrates from stone-cold sobriety to reeling, cross-eyed inebriation just by reminiscing about the gin mills he used to frequent; Rocky Graziano as Antoine the beautician, a sweet-natured, bird-watching imp of a man who turns into a human tiger the second he steps into the boxing ring; and Bernie West as Haberdashery Harry, a clothes thief who fusses over his swag like a Lower East Side men's apparel merchant ("Look at the way a man carries a garment," he moans as a detective hauls off his "merchandise" to the evidence room). [56]

Along with the array of characters came a variety of story lines and comedy styles. Hiken orchestrated a skillful little bedroom farce in "One Sleepy People," in which Muldoon mistakenly believes he has become an irresistible love object for Lucille Toody, while Lucille reaches the opposite and equally erroneous conclusion about Muldoon. With "Pretzel Mary," Hiken parodied the Runyon-inspired sentimentality of *Pocketful of Miracles* in a story about a "dear, old" pretzel vendor, one of Toody's long-standing charity cases, who is, in fact, an unconscionable harridan. Turning to his favorite culture-clash theme in "How Smart Can You Get?" Hiken, cowriting with Tony Webster, placed a Harvard-educated rookie in the car with Toody and Muldoon. Toody is left out in the cold, struggling to get in a word here and there about Spike

Jones or the nonchalance of Mickey Mantle, as the rookie and the highbrow Muldoon absorb themselves in esoteric discussions of fine art, music, and philosophy. As Toody later explains it to his wife, Muldoon "said more in French in one day than he said in English in nine years." Although Hiken, the self-styled Broadway character, avoided concerts and museum tours whenever he could, he could be quite conversant in cultural matters when the need arose; it is probably safe to say that, with "How Smart Can You Get?" he presented the only sitcom episode of the 1961–62 season to include references to Matisse, the Budapest String Quartet, rococo nineteenth-century architecture, and Voltaire's philosophical debt to Michel de Montaigne.[57]

Perhaps distinguishing *Car 54* most of all from other comedies of the period was its New York ethnic flavor. At a time when sitcoms were dominated by white-bread, vaguely Protestant families, Hiken's 53rd Precinct was populated by a pungent assortment of Italians, Greeks, Latinos, Germans and Poles. Standing out most prominently was Hiken's own ethnic identity.

Jewish humor had always been a part of Hiken's shows to one extent or another. It was evident in many of Silvers's inflections, for instance, and was personified by such Jewish characters as Mrs. Storecheese of *The Martha Raye Show* or Privates Fender and Zimmerman of Bilko's platoon. Now, on *Car 54*, Nat reached back more than ever to his Yiddish roots. Distinctly Jewish characters were showcased in nearly every *Car 54* episode: the Schnausers, desk sergeant Sol Abrams, Haberdashery Harry, Sam Katz the butcher (played with low-key, comedic precision by Gerald Hiken). The most outstanding examples—perhaps the best three episodes in the series—were the installments guest-starring Molly Picon, the darling of the Yiddish stage.

Picon's Mrs. Bronson is the definitive Bronx Jewish grandma—warm-hearted, generous, and just slightly meddlesome—who, in her own loveable way, is a woman not to be trifled with. The character was originally created by Gary Belkin in a script he wrote on spec, or at least started on spec. He sent the first half to Hiken, who commissioned Belkin to complete it and revise it; Hiken then added some revisions of his own. The story, which manages to combine Yiddish sentimentality with social satire, began for Belkin with the recent pubic outcry against the razing of old neighborhoods to make room for new housing projects. Picon's first *Car 54* episode takes place in a leveled section of the Bronx that surrounds one lone apartment building (fortuitously, across the street from the Biograph Studios there was just such a building, where the exteriors for the episode could be filmed). Everyone in the building except Mrs. Bronson has moved. As long as she remains there, and stalls the wrecking ball, construction crews cannot start work on a new entrance to the George Washington Bridge. One city official after another—from Toody and Muldoon to the police commissioner—goes to her apartment with the intention of evicting her. She greets them all with open arms, and they all end up sitting at her kitchen table for tea and cake; most of them wind up doing minor repairs—fixing the leaky sink, reconnecting the doorbell. Nobody can resist her grandmotherly charm. She agrees to move only after Toody and Muldoon find the pet dog that she has been expecting to return home.[58]

In the second, even more amusing episode, the police face the reverse problem. This time Mrs. Bronson has moved into her new apartment in the new housing project too early. Her lease stipulates that occupancy begins August 1 and so she moves in on August 1, ignoring one of the basic facts of city life, namely that no construction project is completed on time. Her new home at this point is nothing more than an architectural skeleton of girders and floorboards. Once again she plies city officials with tea and cake; Toody and Muldoon accomplish nothing more than spooling Mrs. Bronson's knitting yarn and joining her in choruses of the bittersweet Yiddish song "Oif'n Pripetshok." Ultimately, she says she will leave and make way for the structure's completion—provided she can make a few changes in the building's design. The project is supposed to be the picture of streamlined modernity. Where, Mrs. Bronson wants to know, is the radiator going to be? How else is she going to call for the janitor than by knocking on the radiator? "Where will be the fire escape?" she wants to know. Not that they have any function in this fireproof building but where else will people sit in the summer and get to see their neighbors? By the time Mrs. Bronson is done, the new building has been transformed into a vintage tenement.[59]

Broun, who appeared as one of the ineffectual officials trooping through Mrs. Bronson's shell of an apartment, was impressed with the episode's undercurrent of wry commentary. "It was so full of sociological knowledge," he said.

> She wouldn't leave the apartment because they were going to build a huge soulless project. She was saying where's the front stoop where the kids can gather? "Where's going to be the gas meter?" "Well, we don't need a gas meter." "But old ladies need a man to come read the meter so she can talk to him." The whole pointless loneliness of the projects is in that show . . . It was all the kind of thing that Jane Jacobs, the great writer about city life, might have written, and it was in a *Car 54* sketch."[60]

The third Mrs. Bronson installment was less satirical and more farcical, but just as funny. This time, with her housing problems finally solved, Mrs. Bronson opens a marriage broker business, one that attracts the attention of the police and the bunco squad. It seems she is setting up matches between ordinary people from the Bronx and glamorous celebrities. Who better to bring a little stability into the lives of the flighty glitterati, she reasons, than down-to-earth Bronx citizenry? She matches Mrs. Harrigan the old cleaning lady with Charles Boyer, Mr. Feigenbaum the iceman with Kim Novak, and Mr. Eisenberg the delicatessen owner with Joan Crawford ("You see," Mr. Eisenberg explains quite reasonably, "we're going to live six months in Beverly Hills and the other six months in the back of my store.") City officials bent upon closing down Mrs. Bronson cannot resist her cockeyed logic any better than Feigenbaum the iceman. Soon they are waiting with bated breath for their own possible matches, with Ava Gardner, Eddie Fisher, Brigitte Bardot. As in so many of Hiken's shows, people's dignity and sense of purpose are fragile things; even the most high-minded are no match for their own vanity.[61]

◆　　　◆　　　◆

In working with Hiken, Belkin came to the same conclusion reached by other writers before him. "He rewrote your script and, unlike other shows, he usually made them better." Despite this sort of appreciation, the Writers Guild began to look askance at Hiken's name appearing so often among the writing credits for the series, suspecting that he was simply attaching his name to scripts that he had little to do with—not an unheard of practice. In one case, the guild tried to take away Hiken's credits on two scripts coauthored by Terry Ryan, one of the busiest writers on the series. Ryan felt compelled to write a letter, objecting to the guild's efforts on his behalf. He explained that working with Hiken was a unique experience: "He is truly prolific and original and I must reluctantly admit that in most of my cases, in one way or another, he has contributed 50% or more to the script. I've worked with no other show that could make that statement . . . I know I sound as if I'm brainwashed, but I'm just impressed."[62]

Similarly impressed was the show's music composer, John Strauss. Strauss had originally met Nat through Charlotte Rae, his wife, and had first worked with him on *The Phil Silvers Show*. As, respectively, composer and lyricist, he and Nat collaborated closely on *Car 54*'s theme song. A serious-minded composer and a student of the neoclassicist Paul Hindemith, Strauss had his own ideas for the musical portion of the song, ideas with which Hiken took issue. "It was an opportunity for me to learn something I've always suspected I would have difficulty with, and that's simplicity," said Strauss.

> He came up with the lyric, and the lyric presented a way to go, and it was something that was already in his head. I kept coming in with things and he'd say, "No, no, no, it's too complicated." He kept singing something, and I said, "I don't want it to be like that. I want it to be me." It's this whole idea that, as a composer, you're special and you have a style and personality. And I gave up all that and I wrote the thing that worked. So I've saved the complication for things I write that are intended for audiences who like complication. Nat was very direct. His genius was in terms of his sense for comedy and keeping the attention of the audience.

The success of the memorable little *Car 54* ditty, one of the most anthologized of all TV themes, bore out Nat's judgment.[63]

Not all writers appreciated Nat's input. As always, it could be difficult to divine what he wanted, and it could be exasperating dealing with all the changes he made. As *Car 54* writer Tony Webster put it, sometimes Nat would even change the house number in an episode's fictional address. These minor irritants, for an experienced comedy writer like Webster, could build into an ongoing tension. "Nate was very tough to work for on *Car 54*," Ambur observed. But this sort of tension was relatively trivial, compared to the impasse that emerged during the second season between Hiken and Friedberg.[64]

The writing staff became aware of the trouble in December 1962, after the situation had already come to a head. On Christmas day, Terry Ryan received a phone call at home from Nat. At first he thought the call was a gag. Their relationship was much more professional than personal, and he could not imagine Hiken calling him on a holiday. Once Nat made it clear that he was no impersonator, Ryan must have suspected that something important had happened. Nat soon explained what it was. "I fired Billy," he said. He said that recently he had gone to the soundstage to direct, leaving a section of a script undone, and had told Friedberg to finish the scene for him. When he had returned, he found that Friedberg had written nothing. Soon after that, he had some other writing for Friedberg to do, and once again nothing had been put on paper. Ryan pointed out that, when he had collaborated with Friedberg on *The Phil Silvers Show*, Friedberg had not done any of the actual writing then, either. Nat was surprised to hear this. "Nat was so god-damned prolific," Ryan said, "that he didn't realize, when he was working with Billy, that he was giving all the ideas."[65]

According to this story, Nat fired Friedberg because he was shocked and disappointed at his collaborator's inability to write on his own. By itself, this does not seem to explain how such a close, long-standing partnership could suddenly come to end. On and off for eleven years, Hiken had managed to function without Friedberg's unassisted writing; surely he could have adjusted to this revelation about his old friend's limitations and continued working with him as he had done before. What is more likely is that, when Nat confronted Friedberg about the unfinished scripts, an argument erupted that inflamed an already strained situation. Beset by so many responsibilities, Nat could easily have made something more out of the issue than it deserved. And Friedberg, already dealing with a heart problem, was beleaguered enough to feel that this was the final straw. Hamlin could see that Billy was reaching the end of his patience after months of stroking and shepherding Nat, and that his health was becoming increasingly shaky. To be told now that he was not doing his share must have enraged him. According to Hamlin, "Nat didn't mean to, but he took Billy's insides out . . . He didn't know what he was doing."[66] It says something about Nat's preoccupation with his own problems that he was not truly aware of how much his old friend was suffering.

As it turned out, Hiken would not be able to take much more of the Car 54 experience himself.

The series had finished its first season with a rating of 23.2, just three-tenths of a point behind its formidable rival, The Ed Sullivan Show. In its second year, Car 54 remained competitive, and in January 1963, NBC announced that it was confident that the program would be picked up for another season.[67] Nat did not share that confidence. His original plan had been to keep the show on the air for five seasons and then reap the rerun rewards, but in the end Car 54 lasted only two years. Canceling the program was Hiken's idea.

Some of those who worked on the series pointed to network meddling as the chief reason Hiken decided to terminate the series. According to this theory, NBC's lobbying for a canned laugh track initiated the troubles, then another, more distressing conflict forced Hiken's hand. Hiken was never happy with the show's positioning opposite The Ed Sullivan Show, and he repeatedly tried to persuade NBC to move the show to a less competitive time slot. Finally, by the end of the second season, NBC agreed to reschedule the program, but only if Hiken agreed to new terms: he had to give the network a piece of the show. Hiken refused. He would pull the plug on the series before he would even consider doing that. He still had one more option, though. Procter and Gamble, the show's sponsor, was interested in taking *Car 54* to CBS, and the network's executives in New York made plans to pick up the program for the fall of 1963. Unbeknownst to them, however, CBS executives on the West Coast had just scheduled *Glynis*, a sitcom starring Glynis Johns, for its last remaining time slot. *Car 54* was shut out.[68]

Mort Werner, NBC's programming chief at the time, would have been the one NBC executive most qualified to confirm this version of events. He died in 1990. Lower-ranking executives from the early 1960s, who were not privy to the *Car 54* decisions, have differing views. Grant Tinker was an NBC West Coast program executive during this period, and he believed that a network attempt to acquire part ownership of the series sounded plausible. Herb Schlosser, an NBC business affairs executive at the time, maintained that the program's scheduling would not have been an issue between Hiken and the network because, according to him, it was most likely that Procter and Gamble chose the Sunday time slot. "I thought there was a lot of enthusiasm for this show. That I can remember," he said. "I liked it, and everybody hummed that theme song, and Sunday was a good place for it."[69]

Whatever role NBC played in *Car 54*'s demise, Hiken was apparently planning on moving on to another project before the second season ended. His choice for his next pilot was predictable—yet another version of *The Magnificent Montague*—which he shot at the Biograph Studios during a break in the *Car 54* schedule. Even without network interference, he may have had reason enough to close down the series. Some members of the show's company place the blame for *Car 54*'s cancellation on Joe E. Ross's antics.[70] Without a doubt, Ross certainly qualified as an albatross around Nat's neck, but he was just part of the problem. The demands of producing while also creating were just as unsettling.

Ultimately, the pressures affected his ability to write, the core talent that had formed the basis for his entire career. "I think he was getting too tired to summon it all the time," Hamlin said. "It's like rubbing the lamp and the genie comes, but the genie wasn't coming that easily anymore. And Nat was getting tired of rubbing the lamp."[71]

For most of his career, Hiken had succeeded in keeping business woes from overrunning his life at home. He may have been preoccupied with work while with relatives or his immediate family, but he had kept his concerns to himself. Now the barriers began to erode. Peter Levin noticed that whenever the subject of *Car 54* came up, Nat would just shake his head. His visits to the Levin home were less frequent during this period, and when he showed up, Nat rarely held forth anymore with his humorous renditions of events of the day. Sometimes he would simply fall asleep while sitting in the living room. As Levin put it, "He didn't have the time to tell or retell his stories."[72]

One day, when he dropped any pretense of putting up a good front, Dana saw her father's desperation emerge into sharp focus. Dana, a high school student at the time, was having her own troubles struggling through her teen years, and one evening, when she was feeling especially low, she sought out her parents in their bedroom. Her father had just returned from work and, as was his custom, had stretched out on the bed with Ambur beside him. Dana recalled, "I said, 'Sometimes I feel like killing myself.' Dad said, something to the effect, 'Yes, Dana, I know what you mean. Sometimes I feel that way myself.' Mom got very upset at that."[73]

At the studio, Nat tried, with decreasing success, to rely on his security blankets, as Hamlin called them. "Anybody who could lighten the atmosphere around Nat, or make him feel loved, was cherished," she said. "That was one of the reasons, of course, that Billy was so important, one of the reasons he loved Nipsey and Molly. One of the reasons he loved Pully. They made it easier for him. I can't think of many people I worked with for whom it was as hard as it was for Nat." Now that Friedberg, one of his most cherished sidekicks, was gone, the final weeks of the second season were especially onerous for Nat. Not quite ready to quit, he grasped at one last familiar thread: he called Ed Montagne in California and asked him to come back east and produce *Car 54*. With Montagne working beside him, tackling all the logistics as he had done on *The Phil Silvers Show*, Nat thought he might be able to continue. But Montagne was now under contract with Universal Pictures and had to turn down Hiken's offer. Nat had no other ideas for keeping the series going. He shut down the production after the April 14, 1963, episode.[74]

With only two seasons of film in the can, Hiken's hoped-for meal ticket fell well short of its mark. Once again, he had burned himself out.

He had tried to play the TV game by the old rules at a time when the rules were changing. Unwittingly, he had contributed to the tension on the set by at first insisting on the old dual-director system, when any self-respecting director, such as Al DeCaprio, had come to expect full authority over both cameras and actors. Hiken had also maintained, quite rightly, his complete independence as a TV creator, even though that meant flying in the face of increasing network control over programming. Looking back at the *Phil Silvers Show* experience, Montagne recalled that he had talked to CBS's Hubbell Robinson no more than three or four times during the entire four years that the show had been on the air.[75] On *Car 54*, Hiken had to grapple with NBC on a regular basis over the laugh track issue and, according to some, over the question of ownership. He had already spread himself thin enough as the show's triple-hyphenate overseer; the distraction of haggling with the network compounded matters.

The show's troubles had not only sabotaged his financial plans, but had also cost him his friendship with Friedberg, perhaps the closest one in his career. According to Ambur, the unrelenting stress also made inroads into his health.[76]

Car 54 was not the only New York show to vanish from the airwaves in the spring of 1963. ABC canceled *Naked City* at the same time, leaving Herbert Brodkin's *The Defenders* as the sole survivor of the New York trio that had staked a last defiant claim on the prime-time schedule just two years earlier. *The Defenders'* end was also not very far off; the series lasted only until 1965.

By the time *Car 54* ended, no reasonable person believed that New York was about to recapture its Golden Age glory any time soon, and certainly Hiken understood this. He demonstrated, though, that he was not only one of television's most talented practitioners, but also one of its most stubborn. Despite advice from friends who had already made the switch, he still did not consider Los Angeles an option. As he explained to Fred Gwynne one day, "You know, if I went out to Hollywood, I'd just play golf. I'd write a little in the morning and play golf and drop dead."[77]

11

Content Is Out

The 1963–64 season opened without a Hiken show on its schedule. After the two-year forced march of *Car 54*, Nat was thankful for a respite. Still, the broadcast landscape that took shape along the airwaves that autumn must have been a dismaying sight for someone who had scaled the comedic heights of the Golden Age. The prime-time schedule was dotted with dim-witted yokels, a jokey extraterrestrial, and a talking horse, along with the usual assortment of freshly scrubbed families fussing with their tidy little problems. True, there was a welcome exception—the sharply written *Dick Van Dyke Show*, created by transplanted New Yorker Carl Reiner, earning both high ratings and critical acclaim—but not much else would remind viewers of 1950s comedy at its best. Certainly not *The Beverly Hillbillies*, *My Favorite Martian*, or *Mr. Ed*. As Leonard Stern put it, the networks were opting for "a kind of comedy where, at best, you'd never use a laugh track, you'd have to use a smile track." The room for excellence was getting mighty cramped.[1]

To concoct a vehicle that would carve a niche for him in this new order, Hiken brainstormed in his West 48th Street office, across from Jaffe's motley meeting ground, or at Lindy's and other Broadway haunts, not quite as bustling these days with show business friends; so many of them, after all, had already left for Hollywood. His first instincts led him down a well-worn path. His latest version of *The Magnificent Montague* starred Dennis King as the titular Shakespearean blowhard, and Myrna Loy, receiving top billing, as his remarkably patient wife, Lily Boheme (Hiken changed the show's title to *The Magnificent Montagues* to accommodate Loy's importance in this edition). In his one concession to changing times, Hiken updated Montague's hated new role from Uncle Goodheart, star of a treacly radio soap opera, to Uncle Sunshine, host of an equally nauseating kiddie TV show. Otherwise, Hiken simply dusted off his memorable radio pilot script once more, tweaking the dialogue here and there with a new, even more caustic line (as when Montague turns to his nemesis, the maid, and snaps, "Agnes, when you throw out the garbage this morning, don't let go").[2]

As he filmed the pilot at the Biograph Studios, Hiken suspected that he may have made a grave mistake in casting one of his leads. Throughout rehearsals, Loy glided from one line to the next without the slightest change in expression. Her blank-faced performance worried Nat, but rather than question the respected Hollywood star's approach, he moved onto the soundstage for the first day of filming, hoping that something would change once the camera started to roll. Nothing did. Once again, Loy seemed to sleepwalk through her scenes. Hiken's distress grew—until he watched the rushes. Although apparently apathetic on the set, she glowed on screen, a true master of the understated movie actor's craft. "That's one thing that Nat really didn't know a hell of a lot about—movie technique," said Mickey Deems. "Most New York people at that point didn't."[3]

While Nat fretted over Loy's performance, something else about the production qualified as a more legitimate worry. How would The Magnificent Montagues fit into current network plans? CBS had backed off from the show's first TV incarnation in 1958, most likely because of the program's offbeat, sophisticated approach. What sort of welcome would the series find now, five years later, when the television business was seeking even blander forms of entertainment?

Hiken first peddled the pilot to Desilu Productions and stirred up some initial interest, but he and the Hollywood TV powerhouse could not come to terms. Negotiations collapsed in September 1963. Next, he approached NBC—with just as little success. Finally, he turned to CBS, and for the second time in five years, the tiffany network made a deal with Hiken to bring Montague to television. The initial commitment to the series did not last long. The network reconsidered, became less enthusiastic, and kept the pilot on the shelf for months before eventually dumping it into the 1964 summer replacement schedule as a one-shot filler. Yet again, Nat had managed to bring his favorite creation back to life only to see it slip into broadcast limbo.[4]

Hiken's other TV projects got no further. For a while he developed a sitcom concept that featured Al Lewis as a self-made business tycoon who returns to his old working-class neighborhood, and another that would have reunited Lewis and Charlotte Rae as a husband and wife who work as a marriage-counseling team, while going at each other with Schnauserlike ferocity in their personal lives. Neither show went into production.[5] The closest Hiken came to getting a series on the air was the filming of another pilot, this one developed in partnership with rising young comedian Alan King.

The Alan King Show, subtitled "Speak Out," was one of several projects on which Hiken and King collaborated at this time. A throwback to Nat's earliest days in broadcasting, the program amounted to a variation on the *Grouch Club* theme. King, known as an angry young commentator on everyday annoyances, began the show with a stand-up spiel on one of his pet peeves, then went on to interview noncelebrity guests, giving them a chance to speak out about their most irksome gripes. Unlike *The Grouch Club,* all of these gripes were genuine, not concocted by Hiken himself. Serving as both announcer and straightman was the austere Frank Gallop, veteran of Hiken's Milton Berle series on radio. Significantly, Hiken chose a project that did not entail intensive writing. To prepare for the pilot, he discussed each guest with King and cued him in to certain funny facts that the comedian could solicit when he met the guests for the first time during the videotaping. If Nat could get the series on the air, he would not have to slave over a new sitcom story-line each week.[6]

The pilot, produced for CBS, was an amusing exercise in conversational humor. The network, though, had no interest in placing the program in its lineup. *The Alan King Show,* like the latest *The Magnificent Montague,* did not fit into the game plan of James Aubrey, the autocratic new president of CBS television.

Aubrey came to typify the new television broadcasting regime at its worst. For many of those who entered the TV industry in the 1950s, he was a veritable big bad wolf of the networks, huffing and puffing and blowing down the already weakened structure of Golden Age standards. Lupine allusions, though, did not figure into the way people described Aubrey when he was at the height of his power in the early 1960s. Instead, many of those who dealt with Aubrey preferred to evoke the image of another creature, one that was more insidious—they called him the Smiling Cobra.

In many ways, Aubrey was the industry's golden boy. He came from a wealthy Midwestern family, graduated from Princeton, and served as an Army test pilot during World War II. He was handsome, polished, bright, well read, athletic, and, when he wanted to be, irresistibly charming. His television career began in the early 1950s at CBS where he apprenticed as a junior executive, then blossomed after 1956 when he moved on to become vice president of programming at ABC, by far the weakest of the three networks. While there, his emphasis on filmed action shows made the network competitive for the first time in its history. Soon, CBS wanted him back. The network appointed him vice president for creative services in 1958, and by the end of the next year promoted him to television president. Aubrey's sudden rise to power at CBS coincided with the exit of Hubbell Robinson, the programming chief who had instigated the development of The Phil Silvers Show and had served as a standard-bearer for quality at the network. He had met Aubrey years before and was not interested in working as the ambitious young executive's underling. This changing of the guard altered the course of CBS programming.[7]

Aubrey's success was extraordinary. The network's profits nearly doubled between 1959 and 1964, and at the end of the 1963–64 season, fourteen of the fifteen top-rated shows were CBS properties. Just as extraordinary were the outer reaches of inanity explored by Aubrey's prime-time lineup.[8]

Many of the most notoriously insipid shows of the era were his handiwork: My Favorite Martian, Dennis the Menace, Mr. Ed, Petticoat Junction, The Beverly Hillbillies. The latter three targeted Aubrey's favorite market, rural America, which was, in itself, a reasonable objective, but only the most undiscriminating sectors of that audience seemed to interest the CBS president. (A deviation from the rule was CBS's The Andy Griffith Show, a rural sitcom that did not sacrifice quality or insult its viewers' intelligence.)

In his quest for the lowest common denominator, Aubrey did his best to weed out remaining vestiges of high-road programming. In 1960, soon after becoming president, he canceled Playhouse 90, the most renowned of the drama anthologies and one of Hubbell Robinson's most prized projects. The following year, another series greenlighted by Robinson also came under attack, though less directly. Rod Serling's The Twilight Zone clearly did not conform to Aubrey's programming strategy. It was too offbeat, and it incurred the extra expense of assembling a new collection of characters and settings each week. Still, Aubrey could not prevent it from going on the air—Serling may have commanded too much prestige at the network to be shunted aside so easily. What Aubrey did instead was wage a war of attrition by making unreasonable cuts in the program's budget. At the same time, he attempted to squelch The Defenders, keeping it on the shelf for a year, and then only putting it on the air under pressure from CBS chairman William Paley. Similarly, The Dick Van Dyke Show managed to survive Aubrey, without the CBS president's blessings. In fact, he succeeded in temporarily eliminating the one season-old series from the 1962–63 schedule. This time it was the show's producer, Sheldon Leonard, who overcame Aubrey's will by rallying support from the sponsors.[9]

Aubrey was very blunt about his intentions. When the fate of *The Defenders* was in question in 1965, Edith Hamlin accompanied the show's producer, Herbert Brodkin, and his agent, Ted Ashley, to a meeting with the CBS president. Aubrey announced that he was canceling the show. "Herb wasn't about to argue," Hamlin said, "anymore than Nat would argue—he wouldn't put himself on the line. Agents usually would. So Ted Ashley said to the Smiling Cobra, 'Why is *The Defenders* canceled?' Jim Aubrey said, 'Because content is out.' We left the office, and Herb and I both said it at once: we both turned on Ted Ashley and we said, 'If content is out, what's in?'"[10]

One thing that clearly was not in was Hiken-style comedy. The rural audience that Aubrey focused on was precisely the sort of market that Hiken had been unable to penetrate to any great degree when making *The Phil Silvers Show*.[11] His comedic bailiwick remained both ethnic and urban, and his chances were dim at best for coming up with a program concept that would appeal to Aubrey's low-slung vision of Americana. *The Magnificent Montagues* missed this audience by a huge margin. And although *The Alan King Show* may not have been diametrically opposed to Aubrey's plans, there was little chance that Hiken would ever tolerate the network president's way of dealing with people.

Aubrey's cynically mediocre programming accounted for part of his notoriety. But it was his steely, high-handed manner, coupled with his deceptively affable demeanor, that earned him the Smiling Cobra moniker. He was at his worst when dealing with Hubbell Robinson. After leaving CBS and venturing into independent production, Robinson returned to the network in 1962—at Paley's behest, not Aubrey's. Given his impatience with Robinson's content-conscious approach, it was only a matter of time until Aubrey devised a way to force him out. As described in Lewis J. Paper's biography of William Paley, Aubrey dropped the hammer, in his patented manner, while the network prepared for the 1963–64 season. In a meeting with the CBS president, Robinson presented his ideas for the fall schedule. Suddenly, Aubrey interrupted him. "You're through, Hub," he said. When Robinson said that his presentation was not, in fact, quite finished, Aubrey said, "No, I mean *you're* through." Flustered, Robinson replied that he wanted to speak to Paley, but Aubrey cut him down again: "I've already talked to Paley. I accept your resignation. *He* accepts your resignation." The final grain of salt was rubbed into the wound when Robinson announced his leaving the network to fellow executives over closed-circuit television. While Robinson spoke, Aubrey could be clearly seen sitting to the rear, smiling triumphantly.[12]

Hiken had his own run-in with the CBS president during a meeting about *The Alan King Show*. The confrontation was less dramatic than the Robinson episode, but it was typical of the Aubrey approach. By this point, Nat had already taped the King pilot twice and was eager to move on and begin the series. Based upon Hiken's track record, other executives a few years earlier might have given the go-ahead. But when Nat, accompanied by King, walked into Aubrey's office, he learned exactly how little his industry honors now meant. Aubrey demanded that Hiken and King tape yet another version of the pilot; he also announced that the show was going to be scheduled as a summer replacement. Nat did not care for the executive's tone. He listened to Aubrey's marching orders for a while, but not for long. In the middle of the meeting he got up, said "That's it," and walked out. King followed. "Hiken had such a background, such a reputation," King said, "and he was being talked to like he was some kid off the street."

Even if Hiken had held his indignation in check, another clash would have been inevitable. Aubrey made a habit of combing through scripts for every one of his shows and instructing writers on how to correct them. Hiken, accustomed to exercising complete and ultimate control over the writing of his programs, would never have permitted that sort of second-guessing.[13]

Although Aubrey has often been singled out as the chief culprit, he was no aberration—more like a vanguard for television's new way of doing business. Paley, for one, sponsored Aubrey's rise to power and approved of the profits that his TV network president generated, no matter how much he may have clucked his tongue in private over the undignified buffoonery of *The Beverly Hillbillies*. Eventually, in February 1965, he fired Aubrey, but the issue was the CBS president's arrogance, not his abandonment of quality.[14] As for the other two networks, they did little to buck the trend that Aubrey spearheaded. They were merely less successful at it.

Aubrey-style condescension and arrogance were not the only problems faced by Hiken and other Golden Age comedy writers trying to set up work for themselves in the early 1960s. When dealing with executives not quite up to speed on the comedy craft, they sometimes were stymied simply by head-scratching obtuseness. "I came out to Los Angeles after four years of *The Honeymooners*, a year with Bilko and four years with Steve Allen," Leonard Stern remembered.

I felt eminently qualified, and I was asked to work on a pilot for Screen Gems. They said, "But we don't want any jokes in it." I said, "It *is* a comedy." And they said, "Yes." I said, "Well, you want it to be funny." They said, "Not necessarily." I said, "It's a comedy?" They said, "Yes." I said, "Are you maybe saying to me you don't want any *bad* jokes, obvious jokes?" They said, "No. We don't want jokes." I said, "It's a comedy?" They said, "Yes." I said, "Please explain it to me." They said, "We don't have anybody who's funny." "[15]

In the venerable comedy tradition of oneupmanship, Al Lewis offered this other experience that occurred just a few years later.

I go into the producer's office, the guy was about twenty-six. Somebody introduces me, we sit down. The guy looks up: "Mr. Lewis, have you ever played comedy?" I swear this on my kids. I said, "Well, I can tell you a little about my background. I did *The Munsters, Car 54,* about a half dozen Bilkos, worked in the circus, worked vaudeville, burlesque, had my own medicine show a couple of years." "No, no, no," he says, "what I mean is *real* comedy." I'm looking at this guy—I can't insult him—I don't know what to make of that. First he says, "Have you ever played comedy?" and I tell him very nicely—I figure, maybe he didn't read the résumé. I don't know where he came from, Mesopotamia? And he says, "No, no, I mean *real* comedy." I'm stuck. I said, "Well, I don't think I've played *fake* comedy. I'm sure it is that I don't understand. What you're saying is very clear in *your* mind—could you explain to me what you mean by real comedy?" And the guy said, "I want to thank you for coming in but it's obvious, Mr. Lewis, that you just don't understand." I got up and walked out. How? Why? When? I don't know. Imagine Nat working for someone like that, who happens to be the executive producer, his father is the executive vice president. What do you do?[16]

In 1964, Hiken turned fifty. At a time in his life when he might have expected comfort and stability, he found growing disruption and uncertainty. The premiere of *The Munsters* that fall marked yet another desertion from the ranks of his New York circle: to star in this latest sitcom manufactured in the Aubrey factory, Al Lewis and his former *Car 54* costar Fred Gwynne joined the procession to Los Angeles. Early on, Lewis grew disenchanted with the scripts he had to perform. In desperation he fired off a telegram to Hiken. He kept his message brief. "Help!" the wire read. Hiken playfully scolded him for abandoning the East Coast by wiring back an equally pithy reply: "Suffer." Around this time, Nat's cousin Gerald also made the California move, but for different reasons. Rather than take advantage of Hollywood opportunities, he chose to leave the commercial theater rat race behind and start a small repertory company in Stanford. "Nat was very disappointed," he recalled. "He just couldn't understand how I could give up the bright lights, because that's where his heart was. Mine wasn't." [17]

Some friends, such as King, made only brief trips to California to appear on single installments of a show. Reports on their experiences probably discouraged Nat even more from joining the westward trend. "Whenever I came back from the Coast," King said, "I'd have lunch with Nat, and he'd say to me, 'What went on?' I'd say, 'You're not going to believe this, some of the most talented people, the most prolific, intelligent people from New York, they get out there, and I call them on the phone and they say, "How about this weather out here?" That's where their conversations have gone.'" [18]

Two television seasons came and went, and still Hiken's name did not appear on any new programs. During this period of inactivity, he had some reason to feel flattered, provided that he regarded imitation as flattery's sincerest form. In 1961, a thinly disguised Sergeant Bilko format supplied the basis for the cartoon series *Top Cat*, substituting a wise-guy feline for Bilko and a pack of scruffy tomcats for his platoon, and featuring Maurice Gosfield as the voice of the Dobermanlike Benny the Ball. In the following year came two shows that were not overtly imitative but which clearly tapped into a similar service comedy vein: *Ensign O'Toole*, starring Dean Jones as a glib-tongued naval officer and including, in the supporting cast, Bilko veteran Harvey Lembeck as one of the sailors; and Edward Montagne's *McHale's Navy*, revolving around finaglers at sea, with Billy Sands, the former Private Papparelli, on hand, evoking a connection with the earlier Hiken series. The most calculated attempt to recapture the appeal of *The Phil Silvers Show* came from Silvers himself.

The New Phil Silvers Show, premiering in the fall of 1963, transplanted the Bilko premise to a civilian factory. Silvers starred as a janitorial supervisor named Harry Grafton, who, with the aid of his goldbricking staff, runs a series of scams at the expense of his superiors. At last, after a four-year absence, Silvers, the motor-mouthed sharpster, had returned to the airwaves. But not for long. All Silvers's energy, talent, and skill could not sustain what amounted to a pedestrian retread. Watching this forced attempt to recapture an uproarious success, Nat felt that CBS had tried to make the show on the cheap, as Ambur recalled. "Nate said they just weren't spending the money on talent. There just weren't funny people on the show other than Phil. Every single person on

Bilko was a *character.*" *The New Phil Silvers Show* limped through one season before folding up. It would be the last series that Silvers would headline.[19]

This professional disappointment for Silvers was followed by other difficulties. Soon after his series failed, he developed cataracts and, before long, suffered even more crippling psychological problems. The condition had been simmering for years. His inner demons had first shown themselves in the early 1950s, before *The Phil Silvers Show,* when anxiety attacks had made it difficult for him to take the stage and perform *Top Banana* on Broadway. Now, as his career turned erratic, full-scale chronic depression began to engulf him. Years would pass before he would be able to emerge from this enervating illness.[20]

In 1964, another key member of the *Sergeant Bilko* troupe went into a decline. But this one did not survive. On October 19, Maurice Gosfield died, after battling the long-term, devastating effects of diabetes.[21] His grand vision of himself had taken a beating in the five years since he had last played Duane Doberman, as producers barely noticed him, let alone cast him. In 1961, two years after *The Phil Silvers Show* was canceled, he managed to land a bit part in an obscure low-budget movie entitled *Teen-Age Millionaire.* Two years later he made an even briefer appearance in the Doris Day comedy *The Thrill of It All.* His *Top Cat* voice-over turned out to be his most important post-Bilko gig. Whether he ever realized the true nature of his brief fling with fame is not clear. More likely, he attributed his sudden fade to bad breaks and the fickleness of the public's tastes.

While performing his *Thrill of It All* bit on the Universal Pictures lot, he ran into an old Bilko acquaintance for what turned out to be a rather pathetic reunion. Edward Montagne was having lunch in the studio cafeteria that day with Tim Conway, one of the leads in his series *McHale's Navy.* Gosfield stepped over to the table to say hello and was introduced to Conway. Meeting the young comedian triggered an association in Gosfield's mind, between Conway's experience in *McHale's Navy* and his own stint on the Bilko show. Like Gosfield, Conway had debuted as an unknown supporting player on a TV service comedy and had quickly attracted a following. But, of course, there was a huge difference. Unlike Gosfield, Conway was a skilled comedian whose popularity was based upon an inspired slapstick performance. The distinction seemed to be lost on Gosfield. He regarded Conway thoughtfully for a moment, then said, "You know, one time I was a star like you."[22]

In their quotes for Gosfield's *New York Times* obituary, Hiken and Silvers did their best to uphold the dumpy actor's perception of himself as a man of taste and distinction. Nat mentioned that Gosfield had once sent Ambur an etching that bore a French inscription, and characterized the actor as a meticulous practitioner of his craft. Silvers, perhaps laughing up his sleeve, stated, "Maurice Gosfield's bedraggled appearance on television belied the articulate, knowledgeable, witty man he really was."[23] Gosfield could not have said it better himself, assuming he could have remembered the lines.

Just six months later, the Bilko company suffered another loss. This death struck much closer to Nat, even though the friendship had been disrupted in recent years.

Billy Friedberg's health had already worsened by the time he left *Car 54*. Edith Hamlin observed this when she and her husband would go out for an evening with Friedberg, who occasionally would turn an alarming, sickly pale yellow and would ask to be driven home early. Soon after his split-up with Hiken, he moved to California where he found work as producer and script supervisor for the sitcom series *Camp Runamuck*; the change in climate failed to improve his cardiovascular condition. Neither did his smoking habit, which was as entrenched as Nat's. Plaguing him even further were problems in his marriage. After separating from his wife, he moved into the Beverly Hills home of his cousin, the actor Teddy Hart, and he died there of a heart attack, at forty-nine, on April 7, 1965. Nat, saddened by both his friend's death and the rift that had separated them, eulogized his estranged partner at a memorial service held in a Manhattan synagogue. He focused especially upon Friedberg's passionate love of show business. He was barely able to contain his tears as he spoke.[24]

While haggling with CBS over series proposals, Nat tried to continue his old Broadway life, even though the quirky distractions, always a stimulus for his comedic thinking, were not quite as abundant these days. Sometimes he would have to import them into his 48th Street office. During his writing sessions with King, he would insist on ordering in lunch from a local coffee shop specializing in lousy food just so he could watch the restaurant's amusingly tottering old delivery man walk through the door. He also hired Mel Brooks, ostensibly as a writer, although his real purpose was to come in for an hour or so at lunchtime and convulse Hiken and King with his hilarious stories.[25]

The opposite pole of Nat's lifestyle—the house in Montauk—remained as rewarding as it had ever been, with no effort required by him. The seaside town was still his escape from business, a place to relax, play golf, lounge around the house with his family, and, lately, a place to contemplate his future. Between the revenues from *The Phil Silvers Show* and *Car 54, Where Are You?*,

Nat had money to live on for the time being, but his frustrations were mounting, even if he usually did not let it show. "He really was in an awfully good disposition," Ambur remembered.[26]

As far as King was concerned, Nat's keen comedic sense and skewed perspective were still there, along with the ability to invent droll, incongruous situations, both at the typewriter and away from the office. King remembered a time in the early 1960s when he had just finished an engagement at a hotel in Florida, where Nat and Ambur were also staying. King had come up with the extravagant idea of hosting a party on a chartered city bus, equipped with a small band and a bar. "We're driving this bus around to various restaurants and nightclubs, with these elegant, quite affluent people, having this great time," King recalled,

and Nat says to me, "You want to have some fun? Tell the driver to pull up at the next bus stop." And a woman got on, a nurse, and the bus started to move. She looked around—she didn't know what the hell was going on. She saw me and said, "What's going on, Alan King?" I said, "Well, you see, they're trying to improve the bus service so they have these, what they call, party buses." And this woman, very seriously, said, "It's about time." That's where Nat's brain was. He'd say, "Let's see how they react."[27]

Where Hiken would next apply his talent remained an unanswered question as another television season opened in the fall of 1965. One program on the new schedule provided some hope for the current state of TV comedy. Although produced in Los Angeles, NBC's spy spoof, *Get Smart*, became a sort of New York–writer sanctuary—employing such people as Mel Brooks, Buck Henry, Arne Sultan, and Leonard Stern—while supplying a platform for the kind of audacious, freewheeling gag writing that had been missing from television for some time. Even if the airwaves continued to be cluttered with the likes of *Gilligan's Island*, at least one network had left some opening for genuine laughs. Hiken may have taken heart upon glimpsing this chink in the armor of the new regime, but he did not actively try to capitalize on the situation. By 1965, after two years of spinning his wheels with his own TV projects, he had already begun to explore another avenue for his talents.

The best way to survive the crushing pressure of weekly television, Hiken decided, was to step away from it altogether. He now intended to write movies, following the example of such New York TV scripters as Carl Reiner, Norman Lear, and Larry Gelbart. His first project was a sex farce that, as he envisioned it, would have paired the unlikely duo of Al Lewis and Sophia Loren, with Lewis portraying a widower garment manufacturer who marries Loren, an Italian actress with a strong appetite for other men. When this script failed to go into production, Nat threw himself into another project, a satire that he was quite enthusiastic about. The story first took shape after he began ruminating about the 1964 presidential election.[28]

When Nat had been producing *Car 54*, his verbal improvisations on current events had started to fade, a casualty of his growing exhaustion, but now he absorbed himself in a story that allowed him to unleash this kind of thinking in script form. Lyndon Johnson's landslide victory over Barry Goldwater— 486 electoral votes to 52—raised questions about the Republican Party's future. Some observers wondered how the GOP could resurrect itself after such an overwhelming defeat. Hiken, however, wondered not *how* the party would rise again but rather *if* it would. His script *Hail to the Chief* takes place in the future, in the year 2021. The Democrats have laid exclusive claim to the presidency for fifty-five years and look forward to another runaway victory in November. They are so confident, in fact, that their new nominee will not even bother to announce his plan to end the war in Vietnam until his *second* term. The Republicans, meanwhile, are reduced to holding their national committee meeting in a seedy, midtown Manhattan hotel room (which is only paid for until six o'clock). Their problem is not finding a winning candidate, it is finding *any* candidate. The party is so destitute that no one is willing to run on its behalf. In desperation the national committee latches onto an obscure presidential scholar in Maine, Professor Lester Spooner. The Republican officers soon learn that the professor is a bit squirrelly, peculiar enough to hide away during the entire campaign so that he can finish writing his fiftieth book on the American presidency. This turns out, quite inadvertently, to be a strategic masterstroke. With nobody really to run against, the Democratic nominee begins to run against himself—and starts losing. By election day he has managed to sabotage his campaign so badly that the unseen Spooner wins in a historic upset.

The Republicans learn exactly how extensive their man's eccentricities are when Spooner takes the oath of office stark naked. It seems he regards this as a show of openness and complete honesty. And this is only the beginning. As president, Spooner plans to remove the stars from the American flag and trade Arkansas to France. He also urges the South to recommence the Civil War (they should never, he says, have relinquished their glorious right to own other human beings), and, just moments later, tries to incite blacks to take the country by force (they are, after all, Spooner points out, biologically superior to whites). At first, the Republicans are eager to devise some way to ease this looney out of office but, as is usually true in Hiken's world, actions produce unexpected consequences, and the Republican leadership discovers that Spooner's crazed antics accidentally achieve benign results.[29]

Hiken revised and polished *Hail to the Chief* over several drafts. An early 204-page treatment reveals that the initial conception of the script contained a great deal of extraneous material, which he subsequently pared away, leaving a clever, unique premise and many funny scenes, which incorporated both broad strokes and oblique satiric jabs. The script had two problems: it was highly topical, making it liable to become dated quite quickly, and it was, obviously, extremely political, at a time when politics were considered box office poison. Hiken was well aware of the difficulties he faced. "Nobody's ever going to do it," he told Ambur. "I just have to write it."[30]

Predictably, *Hail to the Chief* attracted the interest of producers with a taste for bracing comedy—it was optioned several times—but commercial considerations prevented any studio from putting the script before the cameras. Before long it became clear: if Nat was going to get a screenplay of his into production, he would have to come up with another story to tell.[31]

At the end of 1965, something came along to help him bide his time while continuing to formulate movie plans. Carol Burnett wanted him to write her next comedy special for CBS.

Burnett had long been an admirer of Hiken's work and, while in New York during the 1950s, had performed sketches of his both on stage and on television, most notably his "Jealousy" skit, which she enacted on *The Garry Moore Show*. She and her producers had wanted to work with Nat before. Now that Hiken was at liberty—more at liberty than he would have liked—they were able to strike a deal.[32]

Carol + 2 was one of a series of specials that Burnett made for CBS before embarking on her award-winning weekly program. The "2" in the title referred to her costars, Lucille Ball and Zero Mostel. For Nat, the show was an agreeable assignment that fit his current needs. The production would take place in California, but he would only have to write a single variety program, with no ongoing deadlines involved, and he would be working with three highly talented performers. He was also comfortable with the special's format. As opposed to the single-camera telefilm approach, *Carol + 2* was to be recorded on videotape before an audience, with no breaks in the performances except for scene and costume changes—reminiscent of Hiken's early days on

All Star Revue. Burnett, who had just relocated from New York, still preferred to use this modified live method.[33]

Credited as both producer and writer, Nat created a series of sketches for *Carol + 2*, some new, some adapted from his inventory of short pieces. His most memorable work for the show included a skit that takes place at the William Morris Agency. Through an office doorway we hear Burnett and Ball arguing about the merits of casting Cary Grant and absorbing his exorbitant salary into an upcoming film's already bloated budget. Burnett and Ball then step through the door, into the office—two frumpy, slouching charwomen cleaning up at the end of the day. Their insider show-biz haggling continues, all their privileged information culled from memos they have collected from executives' wastepaper baskets. Soon their discussion takes a more personal turn as they talk about Burnett's fiancé, Ralph the doorman from the Paramount Theater. Ball, older and wiser, shakes her head. These show business marriages never work: "Just don't come crying to me when your careers clash."[34]

A particular favorite of Burnett's was the "Goodbye, Baby" sketch, which Hiken had written earlier with Charles Sherman. The comedienne felt it epitomized Hiken's craft at its best. Burnett, with baby carriage in tow, waits at a bus stop with her visiting sister, Ball, who is about to board a bus on her way to the airport for a trip to Miami, the first vacation she has ever taken. But before Ball can get on the bus, Burnett insists that her sister stay long enough to hear her baby say good-bye, something the infant seems reluctant to do. "Nothing complicated about the premise at all," Burnett said. "I'm just trying to get my sister to hear my baby say good-bye. As simple as that. And it just went to the most ridiculous complications—at the end we're just screaming and she's lying down on the sidewalk—and it all evolved very naturally. His premises were always very truthful and they came from very simple things."[35]

Carol + 2 aired on March 22, 1966. It was Hiken's first new show in nearly three years. Back in New York, he found that his prospects for any future work had not improved. If the trip to California enlightened him in any way, it underscored exactly how deeply rooted show business had become on the West Coast. His friend Coby Ruskin was urging him to make the move, and Nat was finding it harder to resist his arguments, especially now that he was planning to enter the film industry; the movie business was even more entrenched in California than the TV industry was. Nat's obstinacy, as impenetrable as it might have seemed, had its limits, after all.

Hollywood Bound

The inevitability of the decision did not make it any less agonizing. Over and over again, Nat and Ambur reviewed the reasons for staying or leaving. Ambur tried reassuring him, telling him she was willing to relocate if the dictates of business left him no choice. Like Fred Allen, neither Nat nor Ambur had any taste for the insular Hollywood life, revolving almost solely around show business, but Ambur suggested that they could live their life apart from Los Angeles peccadilloes, spending their time instead with relatives such as the Rubens, or old friends such as the Ruskins or Billy and Marsha Sands.[1]

For all the sound business reasons, and despite Ambur's counsel, Nat was slow to commit himself to the change. Not only was he reluctant to uproot and relinquish his New York ways, there was the disruption in the family to consider. Dana was already away at college and would not be terribly affected by the move, but Mia, with another year of high school ahead of her, faced an awkward adjustment. Nat continued to waver. In the end, it was a housing problem that tipped the scales and made the choice somewhat easier.

A real estate developer with ambitious plans bought the Hikens' apartment house. The old New York charm of the building held no allure for the new owner, who viewed it simply as an inconvenience occupying a valuable parcel of land on the city's Upper East Side. The residents he considered even more inconvenient: their presence was the one thing preventing the immediate razing of the structure to make way for a huge high-rise. The new landlord began pressuring people into leaving by letting living conditions deteriorate. He left an especially emphatic hint by shuttering the street-level windows with thick metal plates, making the less than subtle point that the building would no longer be an accommodating place. Like it or not, the Hikens were going to have to move somewhere. They looked over an apartment at the Beresford that appealed to them, but Nat decided that if they were going to move at this point they might as well follow the work.[2]

In the summer of 1966, Ambur went to Los Angeles and stayed with the Ruskins as she began her search for a house. Nat, meanwhile, spent some time in his beloved Montauk. Dana remembered getting a call from her father while he was there waiting out his last weeks on the East Coast. He spoke wistfully to her about the clear, beautiful day and the Montauk sky's brilliant tone of blue. "He just felt terrible about having to leave." Departure time came when Ambur found a house in the affluent community of Brentwood, bordering on Beverly Hills and strategically located for business purposes within an easy ride of the movie studios. Unwilling to eliminate all their East Coast connections, the Hikens kept their Montauk home as well. Before going, Nat attended one last New York affair, a farewell dinner thrown for him by his friends at La Scala restaurant. Those Lindy's pals remaining in New York were all there, including Jack E. Leonard, Gene Baylos, and Alan King, and they all took turns standing up and telling their favorite Nat Hiken stories in what amounted to a friendly roast. The choice anecdotes and the Broadway camaraderie only partially lifted his spirits. They also served as reminder of what he was about to leave behind.[3]

In the fall, Nat left the invigorating congestion of Manhattan for Los Angeles's loose confederation of towns connected by sun-washed boulevards and interweaving freeways. A route Hiken often took wove through the Santa Monica Mountains, down into the San Fernando Valley, and through the gates of the Universal Studios lot. Ed Montagne, Nat's best contact in the movie business, was producing movies there, having moved on from the McHale's Navy TV series to a string of successful theatrical films starring Don Knotts. Hiken and Montagne often met for lunch and discussed the prospects for striking a deal at the studio. As the weeks went by, it became clear that Nat's move was not going to produce immediate results.[4]

Montagne was able to arrange a lunch meeting between Nat and Universal head Lew Wasserman. The talk was cordial, and Wasserman was interested in making use of Hiken's talent, but no definite plans emerged from the conversation. "We never found something that Nat wanted to do, or that Wasserman would approve," Montagne recalled. As eager as he was to enter the movie business, Hiken was not about to leap at the first offer. He had little interest in working as a writer-for-hire, preferring to initiate his own project or, at the very least, accept an assignment only if it met certain demanding standards. "Nat was not the easiest man in the world to please," Montagne said. For someone with no feature-film credits, Hiken's attitude was probably a hindrance, no matter what his television reputation might have been. As for the project he wanted to do most—*Hail to the Chief*—his chances were not any better than they had been while he had been headquartered in New York. "It was so far out that everyone was afraid of it," Montagne said of executives' reactions to the script.[5]

As his state of limbo dragged on, Nat found he had plenty of time on his hands to absorb a social climate that did not agree with him. During a period when he needed to produce script ideas, he was thousands of miles removed from the setting that had always stimulated his imagination. In the dispersed world of Los Angeles, there was no substitute for Lindy's or Stillman's Gym or Jaffe's place. In a city where a person could not get anywhere without getting behind the wheel of a car, he sorely missed the long, leisurely strolls down Manhattan streets, the chance to clear the head and take in the motley pedestrian procession. What he encountered in the place of these New York things were show business parties where people tended to discuss their latest deals and how much money they were making. He may not have qualified as one of the most vehement anti-Angelinos, but he would have at least appreciated the sentiment of his old Bilko writer Coleman Jacoby, who once said of his new Hollywood experience, "I spend the first four hours of every day being appalled."[6]

One consolation was the chance to play golf year-round, even if Nat was deprived the pleasure of witnessing Rocky Graziano bluffing his way into the most restricted clubs. Often he played with Coby Ruskin, with whom a jaunt on the links was often punctuated by arguments about golf technique. Future TV director James Burrows, then in his mid-twenties, was a friend of the Ruskins and had the chance to see this occasionally testy friendship in action; he also saw how Nat managed the disputes. Burrows was playing golf with Hiken and Ruskin at Rancho Park on a day when the two older men had just concluded a bitter fight; Burrows did not know whether the argument had to do with Nat's infamously slow backswing or with something completely unrelated to golf and not quite so important. Coby continued to play the game with Nat but the rancor still festered. This did not surprise Burrows; he knew Ruskin as a sweet-natured but quite irascible man. "We got to the fifth hole,"

Burrows recalled, "and Nat and Coby were walking ahead, and then they were kind of walking together and all of a sudden Coby started laughing." When Nat stepped away, Burrows caught up to Ruskin and asked if Hiken had said something. "Yes, he did," Ruskin replied, "and I'm not mad at him anymore." Burrows asked what he had said, and Ruskin answered, "He came over to me and said, 'Did you ever notice how Arthur Murray looks like a guy who survived a hanging?' " And with that, recalled Burrows, the fight was over.[7]

At times, when with family and friends, Nat seemed able to take advantage of the extra hours of leisure that went with his professional inactivity. Aaron Ruben noticed that Nat relaxed more during visits. He was more likely to swap jokes and stories over an after-dinner drink, projecting a lighter mood than he had in the past when he had been immersed in his hit television shows.[8]

Much of his free time Nat spent catching up with old broadcast associates. A producer contacted him to clear the rights to one of the *Martha Raye Show* sketches that Raye herself wanted to reprise on the next installment of the new variety show *Hollywood Palace*. When Nat learned that Grey Lockwood, the Raye show's television director, was working on the program, he stopped by to visit. The dispute between the two men over directing credits was now long forgotten. Nat gave Lockwood a big buss and happily reminisced about the book shows they had created for Raye. "Grey, we made movies," he said. "We made movies." At a time when show business did not seem to appreciate him as much as it should, Nat found that these nostalgic encounters could provide a boost to the ego. During a lunch at the Universal commissary with Montagne, Milton Berle spotted Hiken and announced to those around him, "Here's the funniest comedy writer in the business." Another time, Nat visited Greg Garrison, now directing and producing the popular *The Dean Martin Show*; Garrison introduced Nat to his star, and Martin immediately began raving about *The Phil Silvers Show* and *Car 54, Where Are You?* "Nat would beam a bit," Garrison recalled.[9]

Garrison invited Nat to the soundstage several times, a fact that did not escape the notice of the show's head writer, Harry Crane. "Whenever Nat would come to the show," Garrison said, "it used to drive Harry crazy. He'd say, 'I know he's a friend of yours, isn't he, Greg?' I said, 'He taught me everything I know, for crissakes.' And he said, 'Well—but he's not, uh, he's not, uh, uh . . .' I said, 'Harry, no, he's not going to do the show.' And every time I'd say that, I'd stop for an instant, and I'd say to myself, 'God, wouldn't that be just great. God-damn, Nat writing for Dean!' "[10]

Garrison knew, though, that this was not a possibility. He could sense that

Hiken was no longer up to the task of writing a weekly show. He could see that a pervasive tiredness was slowing his friend down.[11]

Garrison was not the only one to discern this change.

At the same time that he was pleased to find Nat easing up somewhat, Aaron Ruben also noticed that he looked pale. Alan King, when visiting in California, sensed that Nat was not physically well, although he had trouble identifying exactly what appeared wrong. "I felt Nat was running out of steam, creatively and physically," King recalled. He thought Nat might have felt set aside, overlooked by the entertainment business, adding, "I get the feeling he almost bordered on depression. But Nat was always so quiet you never knew." One physical symptom was quite pronounced—his harsh smoker's cough. Despite this, he did nothing, or was unable to do anything, about cutting back on his cigarette smoking. And, as always, his diet continued to embrace the rich and the artery-clogging.[12]

One of his old friends, and his most kindred creative spirit, was having problems of his own at this time, difficulties that were much plainer to see. One night, while the Hikens and Rubens were at a party at Sid Caesar's house, Nat noticed Silvers sitting by himself, unresponsive, clearly beset by an over-whelming depression. Unable to rouse the comedian himself, Nat took his cousin Sandy aside and told her, "Talk to Phil," hoping she might cheer him up. She did not have much success. Like any case of clinical depression, Silvers's condition was caused by a complex web of factors. The rift with Nat might have been one factor among many. Throughout the 1960s, Silvers had trouble finding a role suited to his unique talent. According to Sandy and the comedian's agent Freddie Fields, an element in Silvers's desperation may have been the hope—a hope unfulfilled—that Hiken would create another success-ful vehicle for him.[13]

Nat's professional doldrums continued into 1967. That year, he and Ambur returned to Montauk for the summer and enjoyed a respite from their Los Angeles lives. Yet, when they came back west in the fall, Nat's prospects were still uncertain. His finances, though far from desperate, were growing worrisome. According to Peter Levin, who acted as a financial confidante, Nat, like many other creative people, had little aptitude for money matters and had made only minimal investments over the years. He was no spendthrift, certainly—he was quite frugal and had always lived well within his means—but he had never devoted much thought to making his earnings grow. "He was really going into what capital he had while out there, because he was writing on spec mostly," Levin recalled.[14]

Even if Hiken had had the inclination and energy to reenter weekly television at this point, the direction being taken by TV comedy remained discouraging, despite some welcome, recent additions to the prime-time schedule. Dean Martin's off-the-cuff clowning provided some engaging spontaneity, and Carol Burnett reintroduced well-crafted sketch comedy to the airwaves with her new weekly variety show, but otherwise, labored shenanigans, canned laughter, and the lowest common denominator still held sway. Eventually, TV comedy would bounce back, but that revival was still several years away.

In the meantime, in early 1968, an intriguing possibility arose for Hiken. To his surprise, it did not emerge in feature films. His old gin-game pal, Jule Styne, approached him with a proposition. Besides his celebrated work as a composer, Styne had also produced for the stage, and he was now interested in turning *The Ballad of Louie the Louse* into a Broadway musical.[15]

The script and lyrics for this Phil Silvers special were well suited to theatrical treatment, and Styne's proposition offered Nat an alternative that he might have previously overlooked. A detour to the stage at this point could give his career a shot in the arm. Other New York comedy writers, such as Carl Reiner and Larry Gelbart, had written successful plays—*Enter Laughing* and *A Funny Thing Happened on the Way to the Forum*, respectively—that had helped them bridge the transition from television to films. Perhaps *Louie the Louse* could do the same for Hiken. If nothing else, the experience could be satisfying from a creative standpoint. The theater has always been a writer's medium, and Nat would be able to adapt his script according to his own inclinations— in contrast to working in the movie industry and the revamped television business, where writers were often subjected to executive interference.

Although Hiken regarded the theater as relatively unprofitable, the stage could be as appropriate an outlet for him as early television had been. In his storytelling craft, he had always been theatrically oriented, as evidenced by his success in writing Broadway revue sketches and in producing essentially live-performance playlets for *The Phil Silvers Show*. Further, it is tempting to speculate that his enduring pet project, *The Magnificent Montague*, would have been better suited to, and better received in, the theater than it had ever been in broadcasting; if Hiken had taken the best of his *Montague* situations and fashioned a full-length story, he could have produced a bright stage farce, for an audience that would have been receptive to the comedy's classical references.

Hiken and Styne discussed the *Louie the Louse* project. Without other lucrative possibilities, Nat might very well have pursued the venture. But another offer, in the more financially rewarding field of movies, finally came Nat's way. The Styne proposal fell by the wayside.[16]

The film deal involved Don Knotts, who was having difficulty developing the story for his next film. The concept was originated by Jim Fritzell, who, with Everett Greenbaum, had written other Knotts movies for Universal, lightweight, popular comedies such as *The Ghost and Mr. Chicken* and *The Reluctant Astronaut*. The new idea involved Knotts, the jittery little man, portraying a parody version of *Playboy*-empire mogul Hugh Hefner. The basic comic incongruity appealed to Knotts, but he and Fritzell had not been able to come up with a workable story line. Greenbaum pitched in as well and still the shape of the story proved elusive. Knotts decided he needed to talk to somebody who might have a fresh perspective.[17]

While performing in New York television during the 1950s, Knotts had been well aware of Hiken's reputation, and now he asked Montagne, his Universal producer, if he might arrange a meeting with Nat. Hiken met the actor for lunch, listened to the story concept and began turning it over in his mind. Even as they talked, his ideas began to click. He called up Montagne after the meeting and said, "Eddie, I think I got a bead on this." After Nat's long, indecisive, floundering year and a half in Los Angeles, this movie deal now came together very quickly. He discussed his slant on the story with Montagne; Montagne met with Wasserman; the arrangements were finalized.[18]

Knotts's earlier films, though amiable family comedies, did not measure up to the standards usually associated with Hiken, and the idea of his taking part in this series of movies would previously have seemed unlikely. But he was genuinely intrigued by the farcical, satiric possibilities of Knotts and Fritzell's idea, now entitled *The Love God?* As outlined by Hiken, the story begins in a small town where the unworldly Abner Peacock (Knotts) devotes himself to bird watching and publishing an ornithological magazine. *The Peacock*, as the journal is called, faces bankruptcy, only to be rescued by an unlikely savior, Osborn Tremain, a smut peddler who acquires the magazine and allows Abner to stay on as nominal publisher. In fact, Tremain is only interested in the publication's fourth-class mailing privilege (Tremain has just had his revoked). When Tremain turns *The Peacock* into a porno magazine without Abner's knowledge, and Abner lands in court on obscenity charges, First Amendment activists elevate the magazine into a symbol of free speech and, consequently, a newsstand smash. Abner finds he has accidentally become the standard-bearer for the sexual revolution.[19]

After polishing the story over the course of several drafts, Hiken delivered a screenplay that seemed to confirm his original judgment of the concept's potential. According to Montagne, the script was "hilariously funny." Others at the studio felt the same way. After Wasserman read *The Love God?* he stepped over to Montagne's table in the Universal commissary and said, "Eddie, this is the first script I've laughed at in years." He invited Montagne up to his office to discuss the project further. Wasserman told him that *The Love God?* might be a bigger picture than they had anticipated. "He wanted to drop Don and put Dick Van Dyke in it," Montagne recalled. Van Dyke was not only a performer with greater range but was also, in those days, at the height of his movie career. Montagne objected, pointing out that Knotts had brought the idea to Universal and had pitched the story to Hiken. Cutting the actor out at this point would have been unfair, he told Wasserman, but he then went on to suggest an alternate plan: keep Knotts as the lead but surround him with a prestigious supporting cast, including Jane Fonda as Liza LaMonica, the glamorous editor who transforms *The Peacock* from a sleazy rag into a sophisticated swinger's magazine, and Walter Matthau as J. Charles Twilight, the gangster who bankrolls the venture. "Then it's not a Don Knotts picture," Montagne reasoned, "it's a bigger picture, an A-picture." He left the meeting believing that Wasserman was at least willing to consider the idea.[20]

The next day Montagne recruited an ally for his proposal. He described his casting scheme to Ed Muhl, Universal's production chief, who liked the plan, and together Montagne and Muhl arranged to meet Wasserman in the hope of getting a firm commitment. But Wasserman had already backtracked. He decided that *The Love God?* would be simply another Don Knotts movie, without the added expense of a blue-chip supporting cast.[21]

This was the first indication that the film would not live up to expectations. Instead of Jane Fonda, the editor would be played by Anne Francis, a competent, likable actress but without the star quality of the young, charismatic Fonda. In place of Walter Matthau, the gangster would be portrayed—as Edith Hamlin might have predicted—by B. S. Pully, a Hiken trouper who could deliver amusing performances when playing certain specially tailored roles, but who was not remotely the consummate comic actor that Matthau was.

Another casting notion promised to regain some of the ground lost by the rejection of Montagne's plan. It should have been the most natural bit of casting for Hiken, but it was one that did not occur to him, not consciously anyway. The idea came to Montagne while looking over the scenes involving Osborn Tremain, the porno peddler. He told Nat, "You've written Phil into this thing." Nat had no idea what he was talking about. "You're crazy," he said. When Montagne got him to read one of the Tremain scenes, Nat suddenly realized what must have been going through his head when writing these sequences. When formulating Tremain's underhanded schemes, he had reflexively shaped them in the Silvers manner. Hiken and Montagne invited the comedian and his agent Freddie Fields for a meeting.[22]

Silvers did not share their enthusiasm at first. Fields, though, could see this was an excellent opportunity for his client, who had been struggling the last few years. He urged him to take the role, pointing out that here was a chance to work again with two old, good friends, who had obviously done well by him in the past. Finally, Silvers agreed. But once again the *Love God?* partners faced an imminent reversal. The next day, Montagne got a call from Wasserman. The deal had fallen through. Silvers had insisted on equal billing with Knotts, and Wasserman turned him down, preferring to market the movie as the latest in a series of successful Don Knotts pictures.[23]

Montagne did not believe that billing was the real issue. He felt that Silvers, in his fragile psychological condition, had gotten cold feet at the prospect of tackling a major project at this point in his life. "I always suspected that Phil had a change of heart after he left us . . . That's a guess on my part. Nat felt the same way."[24]

Hiken was furious. Dana, on a break from college, was visiting her family at this time and happened to be in Montagne's office soon after her father and his producer had gotten the bad news. She witnessed Nat's railing against the unreliability of Silvers. No doubt he felt betrayed; he also must have been bitterly disappointed at the lost chance to reunite with his comedic alter ego and to recapture some of the Bilko magic. Embarking on a new venture in a new medium, he would have welcomed that kind of insurance.[25]

Instead of Silvers, Hiken and Montagne ended up settling on Edmond O'Brien, a strange choice, indeed. O'Brien, though a respected character actor for some thirty years, was hardly known for his delivery of flippant, nimble-tongued comedy. Nat could not have been encouraged by the way things were going. Eager to include at least some elements from past successes, he contacted his cousin Gerald and asked him to play one of the supporting characters. He was disappointed once more. Gerald's commitment to his repertory theater made it impossible for him to do any films. Nat did manage, however, to acquire some additional moral support when Billy Sands, interested in moving behind the camera at this point in his career, signed on as associate producer.[26]

Determined to make this project work despite the reverses, Hiken insisted upon directing the movie himself. Universal executives were opposed to the idea, unwilling to hand over the production to someone with no experience directing feature films. Montagne had his doubts as well. He thought Nat might be taking on too much in his first foray into Hollywood moviemaking, but, seeing how important it was to Hiken, he lobbied on his friend's behalf and won the studio's approval.[27]

To fill the supporting roles, Hiken returned to New York and availed himself of the East Coast talent pool. The quality of New York acting was yet another thing he missed about his former home. "He said actors in New York had more body to the voice," Ambur recalled. "In other words, they were not just mouthing the lines, they really had more on it." Ambur accompanied him, and they turned the casting trip into a brief getaway. After a day of auditions, Nat met Ambur for an evening out and greeted her by saying, "Find an apartment. We're moving back." He was only joking, even if the sentiment was genuine.[28]

Once the film's production got under way back in Los Angeles, Nat himself may have regretted his insistence on directing. At home, he complained of a succession of snafus, including problems with the second unit, which failed to supply the kind of footage he wanted; consequently, the sequences had to be reshot, adding expense to the budget and creating havoc with the schedule. How much Hiken may have contributed to these difficulties is unclear, but Montagne concluded that his old friend had problems handling the production because he was venturing into unfamiliar territory. "When we were doing TV, it was a small group of people, with practically no supervision whatsoever," he said. "A movie company is so much larger and the moves are not as fast as they would be in television." He added, "It was almost too big for Nat—directing it. Not writing it. Jesus Christ, he could outwrite anybody."[29]

Perhaps most distressing for Nat was the task of extracting a performance from Edmond O'Brien. "Poor Eddie was starting to slip at that point," said Montagne. "He wasn't the great actor he had been." In a role that might have been played by Silvers, the quickest comedian of his generation, Hiken had the sad duty of coaxing a portrayal out of someone whose memory was starting to fail and who was having difficulty remembering his lines.[30]

Knotts found Hiken to be businesslike on the set and full of enthusiasm, and Montagne, too, believed Nat was pleased with the film overall. At home, Nat was far more candid in his appraisal of *The Love God?* "One of the great bombs of all time, and he knew it was going to be," recalled Mia. The realization that his motion picture debut had gone awry was a devastating blow for the compulsive, perfectionist Hiken. "I think that he must have been very hard on himself about that. It must have been terrible," Dana believed. Still, Nat continued to put up a good front as he moved from the soundstage to the editing room late in 1968 and tried to salvage something from the footage he had shot. Giving himself something to look forward to, he made plans to vacation with his family in Yucatan once the movie was completed.[31]

At first, he seemed to be in good spirits and good health. Each day, after lunch, he and Montagne would go for long walks across the expansive studio grounds, sometimes covering as much as a mile or a mile and a half. The therapeutic value of these excursions, though, may have been undermined somewhat by the hefty servings of ice cream that Nat devoured while out strolling. What he did not mention to his partner was that he was suffering "a pain here and there," as Sandy Ruben put it. If he was worried about these ill-defined symptoms, he was more worried about getting the film done, finding ways to fine-tune the project in the editing room, perhaps make something worthwhile out of it, after all. According to Sandy, "He'd have an appointment with the doctor and call home and say, 'Ambur, call the doctor and tell him I just can't do it because we're just overloaded here, working late.' "[32]

By the first week of December, Nat revealed to Montagne how run-down he had become. As Montagne remembered it, Carol Burnett had called at the end of the prior week, asking Hiken for help. She was performing one of his sketches on her show and did not feel that the scene was coming together the way it should. After completing his editing stint at Universal on Friday, Nat worked with Burnett and her company over the weekend, revising the sketch and offering suggestions on how it should be staged. He returned to the editing room Monday morning, unmistakably exhausted. "I'll never do this again," he said of his weekend sketch-doctoring house call.[33]

As he continued editing that week, he managed to find the opportunity to tend to some personal business, something that had been nagging at his conscience. For some time, the Rubens' marriage had been deteriorating, and now it had become clear that Sandy and Aaron would be divorcing. While burdened with his film, Nat had been so preoccupied that he had not been able to find the time to speak to his cousin about her troubles and now, finally, on Thursday, he made a special point of calling to express his sympathies and to apologize for not staying in touch during her distress. As a way to make up for lost time, he proposed that they meet for dinner the next night. But Sandy had to decline. She and Aaron had already been invited to the twenty-fifth anniversary of Carl and Estelle Reiner, to be held at the Beverly Hills Hotel to-morrow night, and, despite their marital breakdown, they planned on showing up together to help the Reiners celebrate their marital longevity. Feigning in-dignation, Nat joked, "Ask Carl why he didn't invite me," then he made plans with Sandy to get together sometime soon.[34]

At one point during the Reiners' party that Friday, Sandy was talking to producer Sheldon Leonard and comedy writer Joe Stein, when someone brought up the fact that the *Variety* obituary section that week had reported the deaths of two writers. Sandy told Leonard and Stein that Fred Allen used to tremble when he noticed two writers on the same obituary page; he held to the superstitious belief that these things came in threes.[35]

◆   ◆   ◆

Ambur had tickets for the opera Saturday evening. As was his custom, Nat stayed home, while Ambur went to see *The Tales of Hoffman* with Lucy Ruskin. Coby Ruskin, as diligent an opera-avoider as Hiken, was at home with his wife's godson, preparing to grill steaks on the barbecue. He gave Nat a call and invited him over for the boys' night in, but Nat turned down the offer. After a tiring week of work, he preferred simply to stay at home. He ordered in Chinese food and settled down to watch the six o'clock broadcast of the UCLA–Notre Dame basketball game.[36]

Twenty-year-old Mia was out that evening, visiting friends, and came back home about eleven o'clock. The lights and the TV were left turned on but, as she entered the house, her father was nowhere to be seen. Stepping into the kitchen, she found the remains of her father's Chinese dinner, still in their white take-out cartons, standing on the counter. How could he leave such a mess, she thought. She wondered where her father could be as she moved on through the house. Finally, she reached the bathroom off of the living-room foyer.[37]

Nat lay on the floor, motionless. "I remember touching him, the way I'd seen on TV when people look for a pulse," Mia said. "He was still warm to the touch but I couldn't feel a pulse." As shock set in, her mind refused to take in the significance of what she was seeing. She only knew that she should get some help. She went to their neighbors' home, but no one was there, then she hurried back inside and called Coby Ruskin. "Dad's fallen asleep in the bath-room and I can't get him up," she told him, still unable to confront the truth. Surmising that something was terribly wrong, Coby got into his car and drove to the Hiken house. After taking a look at his friend, he told Mia, "Your dad's gone." He hugged her when she started to cry.[38]

Ambur and Lucy Ruskin had gone to dinner at a restaurant on Melrose Avenue before the opera and, because of the heavy fog that night, arrived late for the performance. They had been obliged to watch the first scene on the video monitor in the lobby before finally being admitted. When the opera ended, Ambur dropped Lucy off first, then arrived home fifteen minutes later. There, parked in the driveway, was the ambulance. She rushed to the front door, where Coby Ruskin intercepted her. "Is it Nate or Mia?" she said. Ruskin told her Nat was dead, and in another moment she was inside, finding the paramedics attending to Nat's body. They tried to keep her away from the bathroom, but she brushed past them to get to her husband's side.[39]

Hiken had died of a heart attack, like Billy Friedberg and Fred Allen before him. He was fifty-four. As Ambur and Mia struggled to absorb his sudden exit from their lives, they faced the grim task of spreading the news and making the final arrangements. In accordance with Jewish tradition, the funeral would be held within a few days. Dana got the call from her mother at two in the morning at her school in Indiana and boarded a plane just four hours later. Coby Ruskin made the call to the Rubens. Nat's mother, Minnie, was still alive and still living in New York City; the job of escorting her to Los Angeles fell to Peter Levin, living in nearby Connecticut. Minnie had been failing in recent years and was showing signs of senility, but her deterioration failed to spare her the awareness of her loss.[40]

Ambur did not want a showy Hollywood funeral, which certainly would have appalled Nat, and instead made an effort to personalize the service. She requested that his cousins, Peter Levin and Gerald Hiken, deliver eulogies, as well as Nat's cousin by marriage, Aaron Ruben. She also asked Edward Montagne to offer a remembrance. He had to decline. He could not bring himself to speak. The funeral was held three days after Nat's death, on Tuesday afternoon, December 10, 1968. Along with the family, the many mourners at Mount Sinai Memorial Cemetery included Carol Burnett, Al Lewis, Greg Garrison, and Phil Silvers.[41]

Aaron Ruben paid tribute to Nat's generous character and sharpness of mind and spoke about the Yiddish roots of his humor, based on the folktales he had heard at an early age and his exposure to the stories of Sholom Aleichem. When the time came for Gerald Hiken to speak, the funeral parlor director committed a glaring gaffe. In his introduction, he mispronounced Gerald's name, giving "Hiken" a short rather than long "i." This was especially unfortunate, to say the least, because Gerald shared the surname of the deceased. "Nobody made a sound," Gerald recalled. "I felt very uncomfortable as I went up to speak. I figured everybody was sitting there quite embarrassed. So I said, 'Well, if anyone would have laughed at what just happened, it would have been Nat.' "[42]

Levin devoted much of his eulogy to Nat's life apart from writing and show business, stressing his love of family and cultural traditions. But he also spoke about Nat's talent, apparent both in his work and at home, ultimately characterizing his cousin as "the man with the magic." He explained that this phrase referred to "what Nat could do in terms of transforming the world around him into good feeling and to humor and into the pleasures of simplicity." He closed his remarks with a reading of the epilogue from Shakespeare's *The Tempest*: The sorcerer, Prospero, now shorn of his powers, speaks about setting sail on a voyage that will return him to his rightful home.[43]

For all his ability to summon good feeling and humor, Hiken's last story had, nonetheless, eluded his narrative powers and slipped away from him. Months after his death, *The Love God?* inconveniently appeared, and, worse still, Ambur, Mia, and Dana were subjected to a premiere of the film. Billy Sands escorted them to the screening in a Westwood theater, where the experience of watching the movie proved to be as dreary as the Hiken women had anticipated. The movie was alarmingly unfunny. Except for an occasional glimmer of the writer-director's oblique perspective, it was difficult even to recognize the film as the work of Nat Hiken. Mia remembered thinking at the time, This is not possible, this is horrible. In retrospect, Dana had an even more severe assessment: "I think that film might have hastened my father's end."[44]

Hiken would have been mortified at the idea of being remembered for this failure. Mercifully, *The Love God?* passed through the theaters so quietly in the summer of 1969 that it was almost immediately forgotten. It also was spared the disgrace of a pan in the *New York Times*, for the simple reason that it did not even rate a review.

In 1954, Fred Allen had predicted that all of television's top comedians would be off the air within twenty years.[45] By the time of Hiken's death, only fourteen years later, this prophecy had already proved largely correct. Among those no longer appearing in their own series were such video comedy pioneers as Milton Berle, Jack Benny, Groucho Marx, Danny Thomas, Jimmy

Durante, Martha Raye, Wally Cox and Phil Silvers. Sadly, in Hiken's case, the prediction also had held true for writer-directors.

But, indirectly, Hiken's comedic legacy would soon resurface. Two years after his death, a comedy revival began to infiltrate the airwaves. The 1970–71 season marked the premiere of both *The Mary Tyler Moore Show* and *All in the Family*, followed in succeeding seasons by such programs as *The Bob Newhart Show*, *Sanford and Son*, and *Barney Miller*. After years of fatuous, assembly line comedies, a new wave of shows brought back sharply etched characters, fresh situations, and genuine hilarity.

The three-camera method, originally popularized by *I Love Lucy* and *The Phil Silvers Show*, now came back into vogue. Once again, actors performed theater-style in front of audiences. They worked for real, immediate laughs, instead of banking on deferred, machine-made responses. Receding from the airwaves were the antiseptic, chintz-curtain settings. In their place came the frayed decor of Archie Bunker's narrow, two-story house in Queens and the dingy ambience of Barney Miller's lower Manhattan squad room—places where Martha Raye and Officer Toody would certainly have felt at ease. Even middle-class protagonists played by Newhart and Moore led lives far removed from idealized, manicured suburbia. Their stomping grounds were citified, populated by characters always somewhere off center, from bitter group therapy patients to bubble-brained news anchormen, none of them likely to be found mowing the lawn alongside the Cleaver family property. Further invigorating the new sitcom scene was a heightened ethnicity. *All in the Family* led the way with its continuing dustups between Archie Bunker and anyone who happened to be non-Anglo, non-Protestant, or non-white. Less combative, and more in the Hiken manner, was *Barney Miller*'s easygoing, melting-pot mix.

To a great extent, this new era was masterminded by a new generation of talent, but it was also guided by old hands from New York's Golden Age, people such as Norman Lear, who had once succeeded Hiken on both the Carson and Raye shows; Mel Tolkin, a former member of *Your Show of Shows'* writing crew; and Nat's collaborator, Aaron Ruben. Another participant was Roland Kibbee, Hiken's old radio partner. They all played a key role in updating the best sitcom practices that had first been cultivated in their early broadcast years. Revitalized comedy returned to television without Nat Hiken, but not without the standards he had helped define years earlier.

His influence remained unsung through the years. Eventually, though, his work—or the shell of his work—returned to the spotlight. In 1994, Columbia

Tri-Star released a movie version of *Car 54, Where Are You?*. Two years later, Universal produced *Sgt. Bilko*, saddling Steve Martin with the hopeless task of re-creating a role specially tailored for Phil Silvers. If nothing else, the titles of Hiken's two most popular shows were back in circulation. Not much more, unfortunately, could be said for either remake.

The witless *Car 54* film lasted only a short time in theaters before moving on to home video. Few critics or viewers even noticed. *Sgt. Bilko*, at least, received wide theatrical release and attracted a great deal of media attention. Still, it did nothing to make a new generation understand the appeal of the original show. Like the programs that followed in the wake of TV's Golden Age, the Bilko movie settled for being slick and formulaic, aspiring only to the easiest gags. The makers of the film treated their source material as if it were little more than a product to be repackaged for a new era. There was no evidence of the original's idiosyncratic imagination, nurtured in a dilapidated West 48th Street office during a period when television sometimes allowed inspiration to command the video stage. The original series was, in fact, a product, but a product of another time, when Hiken could focus on conjuring up vibrant comic visions, when he could master, as his friend Alan King put it, the perfect twenty-four minutes.

Appendixes

Notes

Bibliography

Index

APPENDIX A

The Nat Hiken Shows

RADIO

The Grouch Club. 1937–39, KFWB. 1938–39, California Radio System. 1939–40, NBC. 1937–38—2 hours. 1938–40—30 minutes.
Creators: Nat Hiken and Jack Lescoulie. *Writers:* Nat Hiken and Roland Kibbee. *Cast:* Jack Lescoulie, Arthur Q. Bryan, Ned Sparks, Mary Milford, Phil Kramer, Jack Albertson, Don Brody.

The Fred Allen Show. 1940–44, CBS. 1945–47, NBC. 1940–42—60 minutes. 1942–47—30 minutes.
Writers: Fred Allen, Nat Hiken, Roland Kibbee, Terry Ryan, Aaron Ruben, Harry Bailey, Bob Weiskopf. *Cast:* Fred Allen, Portland Hoffa, Kenny Delmar, Minerva Pious, Parker Fennelly, Peter Donald, Alan Reed, Charlie Cantor, John Brown, Jack Smart, Shirley Booth.

The Milton Berle Show. 1947–48, NBC/**The Texaco Star Theater.** 1948–49, ABC. 30 minutes.
Creator, head writer, and director: Nat Hiken. *Writing collaborator:* Aaron Ruben. *Cast:* Milton Berle, Arnold Stang, Frank Gallop, Pert Kelton, Jack Albertson, John Gibson, Arthur Q. Bryan, Al Kelly, Mary Shipp.

The Magnificent Montague. 1950–51, NBC. 30 minutes.
Creator, producer, head writer, and director: Nat Hiken. *Writing collaborator:* Billy Friedberg. *Cast:* Monty Woolley (Edwin Montague), Anne Seymour (Lily Boheme Montague), Pert Kelton (Agnes), John Gibson (Zinzer), Art Carney (Cyril Montague and various featured supporting characters).

BROADWAY REVUES

Along Fifth Avenue. Opening: January 13, 1949. Broadhurst Theatre. Produced by Arthur Lesser.

Lyrics for "The Fugitive from Fifth Avenue," performed by Jackie Gleason, Lee Krieger, Ted Allison, Dick Bernie, George S. Irving. Music by Richard Stutz. Lyrics for "Chant D'Amour," sung by Nancy Walker. Music by Gordon Jenkins. "Sweet Surrender," a sketch, cowritten with Charles Sherman, performed by Nancy Walker, George S. Irving, Dick Bernie.

Two on the Aisle. Opening: July 19, 1951. Mark Hellinger Theatre. Produced by Arthur Lesser. Staged by Abe Burrows.

"Schneider's Miracle," a sketch, cowritten with Billy Friedberg, performed by Bert Lahr, Stanley Prager.

Two's Company. Opening: December 15, 1952. Alvin Theatre. Produced by James Russo and Michael Ellis. Directed by Jules Dassin.

"Jealousy," a sketch cowritten with Billy Friedberg, performed by Bette Davis and David Burns.

The Littlest Revue. Opening: May 22, 1956. Phoenix Theatre. Produced by T. Edward Hambleton and Norris Houghton by arrangement with Ben Bagley. Staged by Paul Lammers.

"East Is East," a sketch cowritten with Billy Friedberg, performed by Charlotte Rae, Tammy Grimes, Larry Storch, Dorothy Jarnac, Mary Harmon, Joel Grey.

TELEVISION

Four Star Revue: The Jack Carson Show. 1950–51, NBC. 60 minutes. *Producers:* Norman Zeno, Coby Ruskin. *Director:* Coby Ruskin. *Television Directors:* Gary Simpson, Grey Lockwood. *Head writer:* Nat Hiken. *Writing staff:* Billy Friedberg and Al Singer.

Cast: Jack Carson, Betty Kean, Hal March, the Honey Brothers, Jack Norton, Billy Sands, Jimmy Little, Jane Dulo, Jane Kean.

All Star Revue: The Martha Raye Show. 1951–54, NBC. 1951–52 and 1952–53 seasons: 60 minutes. 1953–54 season: 90 minutes (under title *The Martha Raye Show*).

Producers: Leo Morgan, Karl Hoffenberg. *Directors:* Ezra Stone (1951–52), Nat Hiken (1952–53 and 1953–54). *Television Director:* Grey Lockwood. *Choreographer:* Herbert

Ross. Head Writer: Nat Hiken. *Writing Staff:* Billy Friedberg, Al Singer, Hal Kemp. *Cast:* Martha Raye, Rocky Graziano, Sara Seegar, Nathaniel Frey, Herbie Faye, Jack Healy, Jimmy Little, John Gibson. *Recurring Guests:* Ezio Pinza, Cesar Romero.

You'll Never Get Rich/The Phil Silvers Show. 1955–59, CBS. 30 minutes.
Creator, Producer, and Head Writer: Nat Hiken (1955–56 and 1956–57). Staged by Nat Hiken (1955–56 and 1956–57). *Production Supervisor:* Edward J. Montagne (credited as producer 1957–58 and 1958–59). *Head Writer:* Billy Friedberg (1957–58 and 1958–59). Staged by Aaron Ruben (1957–58 and 1958–59). *Director:* Al DeCaprio. *Writing Staff* (partial list): Tony Webster, Coleman Jacoby, Arnie Rosen, Terry Ryan, Billy Blitzer, Arnold Auerbach, Leonard Stern, Neil Simon, Aaron Ruben, Phil Sharp, Sidney Zelinka. *Cast:* Phil Silvers (Sgt. Ernie Bilko), Paul Ford (Colonel Hall), Maurice Gosfield (Private Duane Doberman), Allen Melvin (Corporal Henshaw), Harvey Lembeck (Corporal Barbella), Joe E. Ross (Sgt. Rupert Ritzik), Beatrice Pons (Emma Ritzik), Harry Clark (Sgt. Sowici), Billy Sands (Private Paparelli), Herbie Faye (Private Fender), Mickey Freeman (Private Zimmerman), Jack Healy (Private Mullen), Walter Cartier (Private Dillingham), P.J. Sidney (Private Palmer), Terry Carter (Private Sugarman), Karl Lukas (Private Kadowski), Elizabeth Fraser (Sgt. Hogan), Hope Sansberry (Nell Hall), Jimmy Little (Sgt. Grover), Ned Glass (Sgt. Pendleton), Frederick O'Neill (Sgt. Birch), John Gibson (the chaplain), Maurice Brenner (Private Fleishman), Tige Andrews (Private Gander), Bernie Fein (Private Gomez).

Friars Club Man of the Hour. November 10, 1958, CBS. 60 minutes.
Producer: Nat Hiken. *Roastee:* Ed Sullivan. *Roasters:* Jack E. Leonard, Jack Carter, Joe E. Louis, Morey Amsterdam, Joey Bishop, Rocky Graziano, Wayne and Shuster.

The Ballad of Louie the Louse. October 17, 1959, CBS. 60 minutes.
Producer and Writer: Nat Hiken. *Director:* Greg Garrison. *Music:* Gordon Jenkins. *Lyrics:* Nat Hiken. *Cast:* Phil Silvers (Louie "The Louse" Cramfield), Eddie Albert (Paul Barton), Betsy Palmer (Tina Adams), Pert Kelton (Concrete Mary), Gerald Hiken (Leo Drayer).

The Slowest Gun in the West. May 7, 1960, CBS. 60 minutes.
Producer and Writer: Nat Hiken. *Executive Producer:* William Frye. *Director:* Herschel Daugherty. *Cast:* Phil Silvers (Fletcher Bissell III, aka The Silver Dollar Kid), Jack Benny (Chicken Finsterwald), Bruce Cabot (Nick Nolan), Ted de Corsia (Black Bart), Jack Elam (Ike Dalton), Jean Wiles (Kathy McQueen), Karl Lukas (Jack Dalton), Robert J. Wilke (Butcher Blake), John Dierkes (Wild Bill), Lee Van Cleef (Sam Bass), Marion Ross (Elsie May), Jack Albertson (Carl Dexter).

Summer in New York. June 30, 1960, CBS. 60 minutes.
Producer: Nat Hiken. *Director:* Greg Garrison. *Written by* Nat Hiken, Billy Friedberg and Charles Sherman. *Cast:* Phil Silvers, Jules Munshin, Carol Haney, Carol Lawrence, Heywood Hale Broun. *Cameos by* Maurice Gosfield, Joe E. Ross, Billy Sands, Herbie Faye.

Just Polly and Me. October 8, 1960, CBS. 60 minutes.
Producer: Nick Vanoff. *Writer:* Nat Hiken. *Director:* Coby Ruskin. *Cast:* Phil Silvers, Polly Bergen.

Car 54, Where Are You? 1961–63, NBC. 30 minutes.
Creator, Producer, Head Writer: Nat Hiken. *Coproducer and Writing Supervisor:* Billy Friedberg (1962–63). *Writing Staff* (partial list): Tony Webster, Terry Ryan, Gary Belkin, Ben Joelson, Art Baer. *Directors:* Nat Hiken, Al DeCaprio, Mickey Deems, Stanley Prager. *Cast:* Joe E. Ross (Officer Gunther Toody), Fred Gwynne (Officer Francis Muldoon), Al Lewis (Officer Leo Schnauser), Charlotte Rae (Sylvia Schnauser), Beatrice Pons (Lucille Toody), Paul Reed (Captain Block), Hank Garrett (Officer Nicholson), Nipsey Russell (Officer Anderson), Mickey Deems (Officer Fleisher), Bruce Kirby (Officer Kissell), Frederick O'Neil (Officer Wallace), Al Henderson (Officer O'Hara), Jack Healy (Officer Rodriguez), Nathaniel Frey (Sergeant Abrams), Gerald Hiken (Sam Katz), Molly Picon (Mrs. Bronson), Larry Storch (Charley the Drunk), Gene Baylos (Backdoor Bennie/Bennie the Bookie), Carl Ballantine (Al), Martha Greenhouse (Rose), Bernie West (Haberdashery Harry).

Carol + 2. March 22, 1966, CBS. 60 minutes.
Producer and Head Writer: Nat Hiken. *Executive Producer:* Bob Banner. *Writing collaborator:* Charles Sherman. *Director:* Marc Breaux. *Cast:* Carol Burnett, Lucille Ball, Zero Mostel.

Emmy Awards Won by Nat Hiken

1955

Best Comedy Series: *The Phil Silvers Show*.
Best Director—Film Series: Nat Hiken, *The Phil Silvers Show*.
Best Comedy Writing: Nat Hiken, Barry Blitzer, Arnold Auerbach, Harvey Orkin, Vincent Bogert, Arnie Rosen, Coleman Jacoby, Tony Webster, Terry Ryan, *The Phil Silvers Show*.

1956

Best Series—Half-Hour or Less: *The Phil Silvers Show*.
Best Comedy Writing—Variety or Situation Comedy: Nat Hiken, Billy Friedberg, Tony Webster, Leonard Stern, Arnie Rosen, Coleman Jacoby, *The Phil Silvers Show*.

1957

Best Comedy Series: *The Phil Silvers Show*.
Best Comedy Writing: Nat Hiken, Billy Friedberg, Phil Sharp, Terry Ryan, Coleman Jacoby, Arnie Rosen, Sidney Zelinka, A. J. Russell, Tony Webster, *The Phil Silvers Show*.

1962

Outstanding Directorial Achievement in Comedy: Nat Hiken, *Car 54, Where Are You?*

Notes

INTRODUCTION

1. Fred Gwynne, telephone interview by author, tape recording, Aug. 1989. This anecdote appears in somewhat different form in my article "Kingmaker of Comedy," *Television Quarterly* 24, no. 3, 1990, 21.

2. Milton Berle with Haskell Frankell, *An Autobiography* (New York: Delacorte Press, 1974), 267; Phil Silvers with Robert Saffron, *This Laugh Is on Me* (Englewood Cliffs, N.J.: Prentice Hall, 1973), 202; "Comedy Writers," *Time*, July 16, 1956, 60.

3. James Burrows, telephone interview by author, tape recording, May 1998.

1 . MILWAUKEE BOY

1. Vivian Hiken Gill, telephone interview by author, tape recording, July 10, 1997; Gerald Hiken, telephone interview by author, tape recording, July 8, 1997.

2. Gill, interview; Gerald Hiken, interview, 1997.

3. Sally Borotz, telephone interview by author, tape recording, Mar. 4, 1998; Gill, interview.

4. Gill, interview; Gerald Hiken, interview, 1977.

5. Gill, interview; Sid Kozak, telephone interview by author, tape recording, Aug. 5, 1997.

6. Dana Hiken Buscaglia, personal interview by author, tape recording, Oct. 7, 1997, New York, N.Y.; Nat Hiken, letter of agreement to Max Hiken, Nov. 3, 1951, Nat Hiken Collection, State Historical Society of Wisconsin.

7. Buscaglia, interview; Peter Levin, personal interview by author, tape recording, Mar. 7, 1998, Wilton, Conn.

8. Levin, interview.

9. Ibid.; Sandy Ruben, personal interview by author, tape recording, Sept. 1997, New York, N.Y.; Ben Barkin, telephone interview, tape recording, Aug. 29, 1997.

10. Kozak, interview; Gill, interview; Sandy Ruben, interview; Mia Hiken, telephone interview by author, tape recording, Oct. 20, 1997.

11. Sandy Ruben, interview.

12. Al Lewis, telephone interview by author, tape recording, Mar. 31, 1996.

13. Levin, interview; Sandy Ruben, interview; Buscaglia, interview.

14. Levin, interview.

15. Ibid.

16. Gill, interview; Levin, interview; Louis J. Swichkow, "A Dual Heritage: The Jewish Community of Milwaukee 1900–1970" (Ph.D. diss., Marquette Univ., 1973), 166.

17. Gill, interview; Levin, interview.

18. Kozak, interview.

19. Ibid.; Sandy Ruben, interview; Levin, interview.

20. Ibid.

21. Levin, interview.

22. Ibid.; Sandy Ruben, interview.

23. Levin, interview; Kozak, interview; Barkin, interview.

24. Aaron Ruben, telephone interview by author, tape recording, Aug. 1989; Sandy Ruben, interview; Levin, interview.

25. Charlotte Rae, telephone interview by author, tape recording, Sept. 5, 1997; Gill, interview; Barkin, interview.

26. Barkin, interview; Gerald Hiken, interview, 1997.

27. Mia Hiken, interview.

28. Gill, interview; Levin, interview.

29. Kozak, interview; Barkin, interview.

30. Levin, interview; Kozak, interview.

2. THE GROUCHMASTER

1. Sandy Ruben, interview.

2. Author's observations; Writers' Program, *Wisconsin: A Guide to the Badger State* (New York: Hastings House, 1954), 222–23, 230–33.

3. Nat Hiken, "Gripers' Club," *Daily Cardinal*, Sept. 26, 1935 (from the collection of Ambur Hiken Starobin).

4. Nat Hiken, "Gripers' Club," Sept. 27, 1935.

5. Gill, interview.

6. Sandy Ruben, interview.

7. Ibid.

8. Levin, interview; Sandy Ruben, interview.

9. Sandy Ruben, interview.

10. Ibid.

11. Ibid.

12. Ibid.

13. Lewis W. Gillenson, "Lescoulie—TV's First Second Man," *Family Circle*, Mar. 1955, 128–29; Larry Cronin, "Lescoulie of TV Got Big Break in a Saloon," *New York Inquirer*, May 21, 1958.

14. Sandy Ruben, interview.

15. Ibid.

16. Roland Lindbloom, "Hiken Steers Car 54," *Newark Evening News*, Aug. 19, 1962; *Family Circle*, Mar. 1955, 130; Sidney Fields, "Only Human," *New York Mirror*, June 15, 1956.

17. Ambur Hiken Starobin, personal interview by author, tape recording, New York, N.Y., Jan. 1998; *Family Circle*, Mar. 1955, 129; Sandy Ruben, interview.

18. Sandy Ruben, interview.

19. Ibid.

20. Ibid.

21. *The Grouch Club* radio script, Jan. 7, 1940, Nat Hiken Collection, State Historical Society of Wisconsin.

22. Review of *The Grouch Club*, *Variety*, May 25, 1938.

23. Sandy Ruben, interview.

24. Review of *The Grouch Club*, *Variety*, Apr. 19, 1939.

25. Sandy Ruben, interview.

3. FRED ALLEN WRITES HIS OWN MATERIAL

1. Robert Taylor, *Fred Allen: His Life and Wit* (Boston: Little Brown, 1989), 34, 142, 188.

2. Orrin E. Dunlap Jr., "A Comedian's Endurance Test," *New York Times*, Jan. 28, 1940, sec. 9; Fred Allen, *Treadmill to Oblivion* (Boston: Little Brown, 1954), 27.

3. Leonard Maltin, *The Great American Broadcast* (New York: Dutton, 1997), 21–23; *Current Biography Yearbook 1941* (New York: H. W. Wilson Co., 1941), 20.

4. Taylor, 259.

5. Ambur Hiken Starobin, personal interview by author, tape recording, Montauk, N.Y., Sept. 1989.

6. Sandy Ruben, interview; Arnold Auerbach, *Funny Men Don't Laugh* (Garden City, N.Y.: Doubleday, 1965), 124–25.

7. Sandy Ruben, interview.

8. Taylor, 96; Anthony Slide, *The Encyclopedia of Vaudeville* (Westport, Conn: Greenwood Press, 1994).

9. Taylor, 225.

10. Edward Montagne, telephone interview by author, tape recording, Sept. 8, 1997; Terry Ryan, telephone interview by author, tape recording, Mar. 1998.

11. Ryan, interview.

12. Starobin, interview, 1998.

13. Ibid.

14. Sandy Ruben, interview.

15. Ibid.

16. Starobin, interview, 1998; Sandy Ruben, interview.

17. Starobin, interview, 1998.

18. Ibid.

19. Ibid.

20. Lewis Nichols, review of *Winged Victory*, *New York Times*, Nov. 22, 1943.

21. Starobin, interview, 1998; Levin, interview; Sandy Ruben, interview.

22. Arthur Frank Wertheim, *Radio Comedy* (New York: Oxford Univ. Press, 1979), 336–37; Thomas M. Pryor, "F. Allen, Movie Salesman," *New York Times*, Dec. 3, 1944, sec. 2.

23. Grey Lockwood, telephone interview by author, tape recording, May 29, 1998.

24. Ryan, interview; Aaron Ruben, interview, 1989.

25. Ryan, interview; Aaron Ruben, telephone interview by author, Jan. 7, 1998.

26. Aaron Ruben, interview, 1998.

27. Fred Allen and Tallulah Bankhead, performers, *The Golden Age of Comedy, Volume One*, Evolution long-playing record, 1972.

28. *The Fred Allen Show*, NBC Radio, New York, Feb. 10, 1946.

29. Ibid., Dec. 30, 1945.

30. Ibid., Nov. 25, 1945.

31. Ryan, interview; Coleman Jacoby, personal interview by author, tape recording, Apr. 1998, New York, N.Y.

32. Aaron Ruben, interview, 1998; Sandy Ruben, interview.

33. Jacoby, interview; Ryan, interview; Aaron Ruben, interview, 1998.

34. Aaron Ruben, interview, 1998.

35. Sandy Ruben, interview; Ryan, interview.

36. Heywood Hale Broun, telephone interview by author, tape recording, Apr. 12, 1998; Ron Fried, *Corner Men* (New York: Four Walls Eight Windows, 1991), 31–53.

37. Ken Bloom, *Broadway* (New York: Facts on File, 1991), 196, 336.

38. Sandy Ruben, interview.

39. Eddie Jaffe, personal interview by author, tape recording, May 1998; Jacoby, interview; Leonard Stern, telephone interview by author, tape recording, Sept. 1989 and Dec. 1998.

40. Neal Gabler, *Walter Winchell* (New York: Knopf, 1994), 245.

41. Jacoby, interview.

42. Ibid.

43. Ibid.

44. Ibid.

45. Sandy Ruben, interview.

46. Aaron Ruben, interview, 1998.

47. Ibid.

48. Auerbach, 160–61; Starobin, interview, 1998.

49. Aaron Ruben, interview, 1998.

50. Auerbach, 166.

51. Aaron Ruben, interview, 1998.

4. NOT QUITE MR. TELEVISION

1. Cobbett Steinberg, *TV Facts* (New York: Facts on File, 1985), 398.

2. "Gag Machine," *Time*, Mar. 31, 1947, 94, 96; Jack Gould, "Programs in Review," *New York Times*, Mar. 23, 1947, sec. 2.

3. John Dunning, *On the Air* (New York: Oxford Univ. Press, 1998), 174, 461; Berle, *Autobiography*, 236.

4. "Gag Machine," 96.

5. Arnold Stang, telephone interview by author, tape recording, Dec. 1997; Aaron Ruben, interview, 1998.

6. Aaron Ruben, interview, 1998.

7. Ibid.

8. *The Milton Berle Show*, NBC Radio, New York, Sept. 30, 1947; *Berle Show*, Jan. 12, 1949.

9. *Berle Show*, Sept. 30, 1947; *Berle Show*, Sept. 16, 1947.

10. Aaron Ruben, interview, 1998; Stang, interview.

11. Aaron Ruben, interview, 1998.

12. "Gag Machine," 96; Berle, *Autobiography*, 267.

13. *Berle Show*, Oct. 28, 1947; *Berle Show*, Sept. 30, 1947.

14. Gould, "Programs in Review," Mar. 23, 1947; review of *Texaco Star Theater*, *Variety*, Sept. 29, 1948.

15. Stang, interview.

16. Douglas Watt, "Small World," *Daily News*, Sept. 28, 1958.

17. David Halberstam, *The Fifties* (New York: Villard, 1993), 185–86.

18. Starobin, interview, Sept. 1989; Alan King, telephone interview by author, tape recording, Sept. 1989.

19. Robert Sylvester, *Notes of a Guilty Bystander* (Englewood Cliffs, N.J., 1970), 64–65; Jaffe, interview.

20. "Funny Men Aren't Always So Funny—says the man who made so many into stars," article from unknown newspaper, from collection of Eddie Jaffe; Nancy Shulins, "Timing Trouble Plagues Agent," Associated Press, date unknown, from the collection of Eddie Jaffe.

21. Jaffe, interview; Jacoby, interview.

22. Allan Melvin, telephone interview by author, tape recording, Sept. 1989; Rocky Graziano with Ralph Corsel, *Somebody Down Here Likes Me, Too* (New York: Stein and Day, 1981), 77–82; Sylvester, 66–71; "Funny Men Aren't So Funny."

23. Jacoby, interview.

24. Sylvester, 76, 80; Jaffe, interview.

25. Al Lewis, telephone interview by author, tape recording, Sept. 1989; Sylvester, 66–67.

26. Lyrics to "Chant D'Amour" transcribed from performance of the song by Alice Ghostley on "Christmas at the 53rd," *Car 54, Where Are You?*, NBC-TV, New York, Dec. 24, 1961.

27. Aaron Ruben, interview, 1998; Sandy Ruben, interview.

28. Rae, interview; Aaron Ruben, interview, 1998.

29. Aaron Ruben, interview, 1998.

30. Starobin, interview, 1998; Mia Hiken, interview; Aaron Ruben, interview, 1998.

31. Levin, interview; Buscaglia, interview.

32. *The Magnificent Montague* radio script, Nov. 10, 1950, Nat Hiken Collection, State Historical Society of Wisconsin.

33. Ibid.

34. Richard Severo, "Monty Woolley, the Man Who Came to Dinner, Dies," *New York Herald Tribune*, May 7, 1963.

35. Review of *The Magnificent Montague*, *Variety*, Nov. 15, 1950; Val Adams, "Radio and TV in Review," *New York Times*, Nov. 11, 1950.

36. Robert Lewis Shayon, "Magnificent Monty," *Christian Science Monitor*, June 19, 1951.

37. *The Magnificent Montague*, NBC Radio, New York, Aug. 18, 1951.

38. John Strauss, telephone interview by author, tape recording, Apr. 14, 1998.

5. BOOK SHOWS

1. Pat Weaver, *The Best Seat in the House* (New York: Knopf, 1994), 172.

2. Ibid., 164–67.

3. Jeff Kisseloff, *The Box* (New York: Viking Penguin, 1995), 503–4; Weaver, 164–67.

4. Weaver, 183–84.

5. Gary Simpson, telephone interview by author, tape recording, Dec. 1997.

6. Edmund Leamy, "Jack Carson Likes Quiet Comedy, Scorns Comics' Gags and Antics, Calls for Story Line," *New York World*, Nov. 17, 1951.

7. John Crosby, "Radio and Television: A New Idea," *New York Herald Tribune*, Jan. 24, 1951.

8. Jaffe, interview; Lockwood, interview.

9. Nicholas van Hoogstraten, *Lost Broadway Theatres* (New York: Princeton Architectural Press, 1997), 247–48; Val Adams, "Television Deluxe," *New York Times*, Oct. 1, 1950, sec. 2.

10. Adams, "Television Deluxe"; Simpson, interview.

11. Ibid.

12. Robert Campbell, *The Golden Years of Broadcasting* (New York: Scribner's, 1976), 224; Kisseloff, 207,212.

13. Jack Gould, "Jack Carson Has TV Debut on N.B.C.," *New York Times*, Oct. 26, 1950.

14. *Four Star Revue*, NBC-TV, New York, Nov. 22, 1950, Shokus Video; review of *Four Star Revue*, *Variety*, Oct. 3, 1951.

15. Lockwood, interview.

16. Ronald L. Smith, *Who's Who in Comedy* (New York: Facts on File, 1992), 390–91.

17. David Robinson, *Chaplin* (New York: McGraw-Hill, 1985), 538, 549.

18. Herbert Ross, personal interview by author, tape recording, Oct. 1, 1997.

19. *All Star Revue*, NBC-TV, New York, Oct. 20, 1951, Museum of Television and Radio archives.

20. *All Star Revue*, Oct. 20, 1951.

21. Reviews of *All Star Revue*, *Variety*, Oct. 24, 1951, and Jan. 9, 1952.

22. Taylor, 281.

23. "Radio and Television," *New York Times*, Wednesday, June 28, 1950.

24. Jack Gould, "Mr. Allen on Video," *New York Times*, Oct. 1, 1950, sec. 2.

25. Taylor, 283.

26. Weaver, 215–16; Taylor, 283, 290.

27. Stern, interview, 1998.

28. Ibid.

29. Ibid.

30. Ibid.

31. Ibid.

32. Ibid.

33. Erik Barnouw, *Tube of Plenty* (New York: Oxford Univ. Press, 1975), 109–10; Stefan Kanfer, *A Journal of the Plague Years* (New York: Atheneum, 1973), 104–5.

34. *Red Channels* (New York: American Business Consultants, 1950), 9.

35. Ibid., 77; "Sponsors of the World Peace Conference," *New York Times*, Mar. 24, 1949; Richard H. Parke, "Our Way Defended to 2,000 Opening 'Culture' Meeting," *New York Times*, Mar. 26, 1949; William L. O'Neill, *A Better World* (New York: Simon and Schuster, 1982), 163–68.

36. Aaron Ruben, interview, 1998; Levin, interview; Sandy Ruben, interview.

37. Merle Miller, *The Judges and the Judged* (Garden City, NY: Doubleday, 1952), 48.

38. "Lee Cobb Admits He Is Former Red," *New York Times*, Sept. 30, 1953; William A. Henry III, *The Great One: The Life and Legend of Jackie Gleason* (New York: Doubleday, 1992), 123; Kisseloff, 416.

39. Lucy Ruskin, telephone interview by author, tape recording, Apr. 16, 1998; Jack O'Brian, "TView," *New York Journal-American*, Aug. 21, 1957.

40. Levin, interview.

41. Kanfer, 147–48, 163–71.

42. Kanfer, 163–71.

43. Karen Sue Foley, *The Political Blacklist in the Broadcast Industry* (New York: Arno, 1979), 196–97, 200–1.

44. Victor Navasky, *Naming Names* (New York: Viking, 1980), 274.

45. Foley, 198–99, 237–44.

46. Levin, interview; *Current Biography Yearbook 1941*, 805–7; Foley, 219; "Sokolsky Blasts 'Hatriots'," *Variety*, Nov. 11, 1953, 1.

47. Levin, interview; Aaron Ruben, interview, 1998; Starobin, interview, 1998.

48. Sandy Ruben, interview.

49. Levin, interview.

50. Starobin, interview, 1998.

6. CLOWN QUEEN

1. Graziano and Corsel, 80.

2. Ibid., 77–80.

3. James B. Roberts, *The Boxing Register* (Ithaca, N.Y.: McBooks Press, 1997), 256–59.

4. Graziano and Corsel, 80; Val Adams, "Rocky Graziano: TV Actor and Ex-Fighter," *New York Times*, Nov. 29, 1953, sec. 2.

5. Graziano and Corsel, 88.

6. Roberts, 257–59; Graziano and Corsel, 82.

7. Graziano and Corsel, 89.

8. Ibid.

9. Ibid., 92, 96.

10. *All Star Revue*, NBC-TV, New York, Sept. 27, 1952, Nat Hiken Collection, State Historical Society of Wisconsin; Jack Gould, "Television in Review: Martha Raye," *New York Times*, Nov. 18, 1953.

11. Review of *All Star Revue*, *Variety*, Oct. 1, 1952.

12. Graziano and Corsel, 97–98.

13. Bernie Seligman, telephone interview by author, tape recording, Oct. 1997.

14. Graziano and Corsel, 102.

15. Ibid., 103.

16. "Makeup Sketch," from the collection of Ambur Hiken Starobin.

17. Graziano and Corsel, 109; Greg Garrison, telephone interview with author, tape recording, Nov. 7, 1997; Starobin, interview, 1998.

18. "TV Actor and Ex-Fighter"; Graziano and Corsel, 105, 110; Garrison, interview.

19. Graziano and Corsel, 125.

20. Buscaglia, interview; Mia Hiken, interview.

21. Ibid.

22. Buscaglia, interview.

23. Mia Hiken, interview.

24. Stern, interview, 1989; Lewis, interview, 1996.

25. Review of *All Star Revue*, *Variety*, Oct. 7, 1953.

26. *The Martha Raye Show*, NBC-TV, New York, Dec. 26, 1953, Museum of Television and Radio archive; review of *All Star Revue*, *Variety*, Nov. 5, 1952; review of *The Martha Raye Show*, *Variety*, Nov. 4, 1953.

27. Review of *The Martha Raye Show*, *Variety*, Oct. 7, 1953, Gould, "Television in Review: Martha Raye."

28. "Saga of Schneider," *New York Times Magazine*, Aug. 5, 1951, 14.

29. "Jealousy Sketch," from the collection of Ambur Hiken Starobin; Carol Burnett, telephone interview by author, tape recording, Jan. 10, 1998.

30. Ross, interview; Lee Pockriss, telephone interview by author, tape recording, Dec. 1997.

31. Garrison, interview.

32. Pockriss, interview; Ross, interview.

33. Lockwood, interview.

34. Ross, interview.

35. "A Day's Work," *Time*, Mar. 1, 1954, 70; Ross, interview.

36. Seligman, interview; Starobin, interview, Jan. 1998.

37. Starobin, interview, 1998.

38. Lockwood, interview.

39. Ibid.

40. Starobin, interview, Sept. 1989; Lockwood, interview.

41. "Martha Raye Seeks Separation," *New York Times*, May 9, 1953; "Muggs and Cupid Put the Bite on Martha in a Busy Week," *Life*, May 3, 1954, 133.

42. Lockwood, interview.

43. Ibid.

44. Sidney Fields, "Only Human."

45. Jack Gould, "TV: Martha Raye Show," *New York Times*, Oct. 12, 1955.

46. Jean Maddern Pitrone, *Take It from the Big Mouth: The Life of Martha Raye* (Lexington, Ky.: Univ. Press of Kentucky, 1999), 100; Smith, 392.

7. YOU'LL NEVER GET RICH

1. Stern, interview, 1989.

2. Silvers, 117; *Phil Silvers: Top Banana, A&E Biography*, Arts & Entertainment Network, Sept. 3, 1997.

3. Irving Mansfield with Jean Libman Block, *Life with Jackie* (New York: Bantam, 1983),102–3.

4. Mansfield, 103; Silvers, 136.

5. Mansfield, 103.

6. Silvers, 202.

7. Mina Wetzig, "Bilko's Moving," *Daily News*, Sunday, July 6, 1958; Silvers, 202.

8. Silvers, 201–2.

9. Fields, "Only Human"; Silvers, 204.

10. Ryan, interview.

11. Silvers, 202, 204.

12. John Crosby, "What's with PR Now?," *San Francisco Examiner & Chronicle*, undated clipping.

13. Sylvester, 75–76, Gabler, 244.

14. Silvers, 205; Montagne, interview; Melvin, interview, 1989.

15. Mickey Freeman and Sholom Rubinstein, "But Sarge. . . ," *Television Quarterly* 22, no. 2, 10.

16. Garrison, interview; Freeman and Rubinstein, 11.

17. Freddie Fields, telephone interview by author, tape recording, Oct. 15, 1997.

18. Silvers, 206–7; Freeman and Rubinstein, 12.

19. Montagne, interview.

20. Mickey Freeman, personal interview by author, tape recording, New York, N.Y., Mar. 1998; Freeman and Rubinstein, 11.

21. Silvers, 207.

22. Ibid., 208; Freeman and Rubinstein, 12–13.

23. John Crosby, "Very Funny Show," *New York Herald Tribune*, Sept. 26, 1955; Jack Gould, "A Nice Guy," *New York Times*, Mar. 4, 1956.

24. J. P. Shanley, "Long Road to Fame," *New York Times*, May 27, 1956, sec. 2.

25. Philip Minoff, "Boffolas in the Barracks," *Cue*, Oct. 29, 1955, 12.

26. Billy Blitzer, telephone interview by author, tape recording, Aug. 1989.

27. Minoff, "Boffolas in the Barracks"; Mickey Deems, telephone interview by author, tape recording, Dec. 1997.

28. Blitzer, interview.

29. Ibid.; Ryan, interview; Stern, interview, 1989.

30. Blitzer, interview; Ryan, interview; Aaron Ruben, interview, 1989.

31. Ryan, interview; Blitzer, interview, Aaron Ruben, interview, 1989; Stern, interview, 1989.

32. Jacoby, interview.

33. Burrows, interview.

34. Melvin, interview, 1989.

35. King, interview; Stern, interview, 1989.

36. Gerald Hiken, telephone interview by author, tape recording, Sept. 1989.

37. Silvers, 189.

38. Broun, interview.

39. King, interview; Freeman, interview; Freeman and Rubinstein, 12.

40. Silvers, 221; "The Court-Martial," *The Phil Silvers Show*, CBS-TV, New York, Mar. 6, 1956, Museum of Television and Radio archive.

41. Allan Melvin, telephone interview by author, tape recording, May 6, 1998; Montagne, interview.

42. Strauss, interview; Montagne, interview; Silvers, 218; Freeman, interview.

43. Silvers, 217; Starobin, interview, 1989.

44. Aaron Ruben, interview, 1998; Thomas O'Neil, *The Emmys* (New York: Penguin, 1992), 66.

45. Blitzer, interview; Montagne, interview; Silvers, 217; Stern, interview, 1989.

46. Aaron Ruben, interview, 1998.

47. Melvin, interview.

48. Montagne, interview.

49. Freeman and Rubinstein, 10.

50. O'Neil, 47–49; King, interview; Joe Cohen, "Nat Hiken, 54, Dies of Coronary," *Variety*, Dec. 11, 1968.

51. Montagne, interview.

52. Silvers, 224.

53. "Coax," *New Yorker*, Sept. 1, 1951, 16–17; "Cantor Faces the East as First LA-to-NY Comm'l TV Show Bows," *Variety*, Oct. 3, 1951.

54. Montagne, interview.

55. Weaver, 200, 261.

56. Barnouw, 193–94.

57. Weaver, 259–270; Barnouw, 191–92.

58. Stern, interview, 1989; Buscaglia, interview.

59. Buscaglia, interview.

60. Mia Hiken, interview; Buscaglia, interview.

61. Starobin, interview, 1998; Buscaglia, interview.

62. Mia Hiken, interview; Buscaglia, interview.

63. Gill, interview.

64. Starobin, interview, 1989.

65. Aaron Ruben, interview, 1989; "Nat Hiken, TV Writer, Is Dead," *New York Times*, Dec. 9, 1968.

66. Montagne, interview.

67. Silvers, 230.

68. Montagne, interview.

69. Starobin, interview, 1998.

70. "Fred Allen Dies While on Stroll," *New York Times*, Mar. 18, 1956.

71. Allen, 240.

8. BURNOUT

1. Stern, interview, 1989.

2. Ibid.

3. Ibid.

4. Ibid.

5. Ibid.

6. Ibid.

7. Starobin, interview, 1989.

8. Roland Lindbloom, "Car 54 Is Right There," *Newark Evening News*, Aug. 12, 1962, sec. E; Hank Garrett, telephone interview by author, tape recording, Apr. 17, 1998.

9. Montagne, interview.

10. Starobin, interview, 1989; Freeman, interview.

11. Montagne, interview; Erskine Johnson, "TV Cop Finds Ingrid Arresting," *New York World Telegraph*, Oct. 27, 1962.

12. "A Mess Sergeant Can't Win," *The Phil Silvers Show*, CBS-TV, New York, Nov. 13, 1956, CBS Video.

13. Montagne, interview; Silvers, 218.

14. O'Neil, 53–55.

15. Broun, interview; Freeman, interview.

16. Milton Berle, *B.S. I Love You* (New York: McGraw-Hill, 1988), 98–99.

17. Broun, interview.

18. Garrison, interview; Fields, interview.

19. Montagne, interview.

20. Silvers, 222; Freeman and Rubinstein, 14.

21. Silvers, 222; Montagne, interview.

22. Montagne, interview; Freeman, interview; Silvers, 222.

23. Freeman, interview.

24. Freeman and Rubinstein, 10; Montagne, interview.

25. Val Adams, "Nat Hiken Takes Leave of Absence," *New York Times*, May 30, 1957.

26. "Comedy Writers," *Time*.

27. Hal Humphrey, "Gag Writers Also Flee TV," *New York World Telegram*, July 29, 1957; Starobin, interview, 1989.

28. Montagne, interview.

29. Aaron Ruben, interview, 1989.

30. Ryan, interview; Jacoby, interview.

31. Jacoby, interview; Ryan, interview; Neil Simon, *Rewrites* (New York: Simon & Schuster, 1996), 43–44.

32. Silvers, 226.

33. Montagne, interview.

34. Silvers, 230; Fields, interview.

35. Val Adams, "Sgt. Bilko May Get His Discharge Next Season," *New York Times*, Mar. 15, 1959, sec. 2.

9. BETWEEN ENGAGEMENTS

1. "Kent & Revlon in 'Montague' Dicker," *Variety*, Mar. 26, 1958; "Where Are the Laughs Coming From?" *TV Guide*, Mar. 23, 1958, 22–23.

2. Kisseloff, 246.

3. Pilot episode, *The Magnificent Montague*, Eupolis Productions, CBS-TV, New York, 1958, Nat Hiken Collection, State Historical Society of Wisconsin.

4. Ibid.

5. " 'Montague' Out in 64G Shift," *Variety*, May 21, 1958.

6. Penny Bigelow, telephone interview by author, tape recording, Oct. 8, 1997.

7. "A Child in the House," *The Magnificent Montague*, Eupolis Productions, CBS-TV, 1958, Nat Hiken Collection, State Historical Society of Wisconsin.

8. Buscaglia, interview.

9. Hubbell Robinson, "The Producer's the Villain," *Saturday Review*, Dec. 27, 1958, 23; Rod Serling, "TV in the Can vs. TV in the Flesh," *New York Times Magazine*, Nov. 24, 1957, 49–50, 54, 56–57.

10. Montagne, interview.

11. Jack Gould, "TV under Assault," *New York Times*, Sunday, June 22, 1958, sec. 2.

12. "Where Are the Laughs Coming From?" *TV Guide*.

13. Les Brown, *Les Brown's Encyclopedia of Television* (Detroit: Gale Research, 1992), 445–46; Barnouw, 243–46.

14. Kisseloff, 497.

15. *Phil Silvers Special: Summer in New York*, CBS-TV, New York, June 30, 1960, Museum of Television and Radio.

16. *The Ballad of Louie the Louse* television script, Oct. 17, 1959, Nat Hiken Collection, State Historical Society of Wisconsin.

17. Gerald Hiken, interview, 1989.

18. Ibid.

19. Garrison, interview.

20. *The Slowest Gun in the West* television script, May 7, 1960, Nat Hiken Collection, State Historical Society of Wisconsin.

21. Review of *The Slowest Gun in the West*, *Variety*, May 11, 1960.

22. Ibid.

23. Garrison, interview.

24. Ibid.

25. Kay Gardella, "Nat Has High Hopes for 'Louie the Louse'," *New York Daily News*, Oct. 11, 1959.

26. Garrison, interview.

27. *The Friars Club Man of the Hour*, CBS-TV, New York, Nov. 10, 1958; Garrison, interview.

28. *Madhouse 60* television script, 1960, Nat Hiken Collection, State Historical Society of Wisconsin; King, interview.

29. Nat Hiken, "The Thrill Is Gone," *New York Herald Tribune*, July 20, 1960; Starobin, interview, 1998.

30. Levin, interview.

31. Ibid.

10. THE LAST STAND

1. Lindbloom, "Hiken Steers Car 54"; Harold Mehling, "The Man Who Pushes Car 54," *Pageant*, Oct. 1962, 48.

2. "Bronx Background: New Series in Works by Hiken," *New York Morning Telegraph*, June 26, 1961; Lindbloom, "Hiken Steers Car 54"; Mehling, "The Man Who Pushes," 48.

3. "Bronx Background."

4. Levin, interview; Montagne, interview.

5. Deems, interview.

6. Gwynne, interview; Deems, interview.

7. Lindbloom, "Car 54 Is Right There"; Gwynne, interview.

8. "Bronx Background"; Garrett, interview.

9. Kay Gardella, "Fasten Your Laugh Belts: Hiken's 'Car 54' Is Due," *New York Daily News*, Sept. 7, 1961; Margaret McManus, "More TV Fun," *Newark Evening News*, Aug. 8, 1961.

10. Art Woodstone, "Hiken's Lament: Nothing Exciting Happens Anymore," *Variety*, Sept. 13, 1961; "Comedy Cops," *New Yorker*, Aug. 19, 1961, 20–21.

11. Ruskin, interview; Aaron Ruben, interview, 1989; Montagne, interview.

12. Deems, interview.

13. RKD, review of *Car 54*, *New York Herald Tribune*, Sept. 18, 1961; John P. Shanley, review of *Car 54*, *New York Times*, Sept. 18, 1961; review of *Car 54*, *Variety*, Sept. 20, 1961.

14. "Something Nice for Sol," *Car 54, Where Are You?*, Eupolis Productions, NBC-TV, New York, Sept. 17, 1961, Republic Pictures Home Video.

15. Gilbert Seldes, review of *Car 54*, *TV Guide*, Dec. 23, 1961, 20.

16. "Hiken's Lament."

17. Roger Director, "Life's No Joke for the Court Jester of the Friar's Club," *New York Daily News*, Mar. 20, 1981; Garrett, interview; Jaffe, interview.

18. Irving Hoffman, "Tales of Hoffman," undated column from the collection of Eddie Jaffe; Jaffe, interview; Garrett, interview.

19. Jaffe, interview; Ward Morehouse, "Broadway after Dark: Yes, Big Mr. Pully Is in the Legit Now," undated column from the collection of Eddie Jaffe.

20. Lewis, interview, 1989; Deems, interview.

21. Rae, interview.

22. Ibid.; Deems, interview.

23. Rae, interview.

24. Deems, interview.

25. Gwynne, interview; Garrett, interview; Deems, interview.

26. Deems, interview.

27. Ibid.

28. Broun, interview; Edith Hamlin, telephone interview by author, tape recording, Jan. 1998; Lewis, interview, 1989; Rae, interview; Gwynne, interview.

29. Garrett, interview.

30. Howard Epstein, letter to David Grossberg, Jan. 27, 1962, Nat Hiken Collection, State Historical Society of Wisconsin.

31. Howard Epstein, letter to Writers Guild of America, Dec. 1, 1961, Nat Hiken Collection, State Historical Society of Wisconsin.

32. Deems, interview.

33. Ibid.

34. 1962 Emmy Awards broadcast, New York-Washington, D.C.-Hollywood, Museum of Television and Radio.

35. Hamlin, interview.

36. Ibid.

37. Ibid.

38. Ibid.

39. Broun, interview.

40. Hamlin, interview.

41. Ibid.; Garrett, interview.

42. Hamlin, interview.

43. Ibid.

44. Garrett, interview; Lewis, interview, 1989.

45. Hamlin, interview.

46. Deems, interview.

47. Arthur Hershkowitz, letter to NBC, Dec. 15, 1961, Nat Hiken Collection, State Historical Society of Wisconsin; Garrett, interview; Strauss, interview; Lewis, interview, 1989.

48. Strauss, interview.

49. Lewis, interview, 1989; Hamlin, interview.

50. Strauss, interview.

51. Deems, interview.

52. Lewis, interview, 1989.

53. Gwynne, interview.

54. Strauss, interview.

55. Starobin, interview, 1989.

56. "Something Nice for Sol," *Car 54*.

57. "How Smart Can You Get?" *Car 54, Where Are You?*, Eupolis Productions, NBC-TV, New York, Feb. 25, 1962.

58. Gary Belkin, telephone interview by author, tape recording, Apr. 18, 1998; "I Won't Go!," *Car 54, Where Are You?*, Eupolis Productions, NBC-TV, New York, Oct. 15, 1961.

59. "Occupancy, August First," *Car 54, Where Are You?*, Eupolis Productions, NBC-TV, New York, Oct. 21, 1962.

60. Broun, interview.

61. "Joan Crawford Didn't Say No," *Car 54, Where Are You?*, Eupolis Productions, NBC-TV, New York, Mar. 17, 1963.

62. Belkin, interview; Terry Ryan, letter to Writers Guild of America, Nat Hiken Collection, State Historical Society of Wisconsin.

63. Strauss, interview.

64. Ryan, interview; Starobin, interview, 1989.

65. Ryan, interview.

66. Hamlin, interview.

67. Tim Brooks and Earle Marsh, *Complete Directory to Prime Time Network TV Shows* (New York: Ballantine, 1979), 925; Donald Mainwaring, "Car 54, Where Do You Go from Here?" *Christian Science Monitor*, Jan. 12, 1963.

68. Lewis, interview, 1996; Garrett, interview; Belkin, interview.

69. Grant Tinker, telephone interview by author, tape recording, June 1998; Herb Schlosser, telephone interview by author, tape recording, Aug. 1998.

70. Rae, interview; Deems, interview.

71. Hamlin, interview.

72. Levin, interview.

73. Buscaglia, interview.

74. Hamlin, interview; Montagne, interview.

75. Montagne, interview.

76. Starobin, interview, 1989.

77. Gwynne, interview.

11. CONTENT IS OUT

1. Stern, interview.

2. *The Magnificent Montagues*, Sunshine Productions, CBS-TV, New York, 1963, Nat Hiken Collection, State Historical Society of Wisconsin.

3. Deems, interview.

4. John David Griffin, "I See by TV," *New York Mirror*, Oct. 1, 1963; review of *The Magnificent Montagues*, *New York Herald Tribune*, Aug. 17, 1964.

5. Lewis, interview.

6. *The Alan King Show*, a "Speak Out" production, CBS-TV, New York, Jan. 25, 1964; King, interview.

7. Sally Bedell Smith, *In All His Glory: The Life of William S. Paley* (New York: Simon and Schuster, 1990), 423; Louis J. Paper, *Empire: William S. Paley and the Making of CBS* (New York: St. Martin's Press, 1987), 215–16, 234.

8. Bedell Smith, 423; Brooks and Marsh, 806.

9. Gordon F. Sander, *Serling* (New York: Dutton, 1992), 160, 162; Bedell Smith, 428; Grant Tinker, *Tinker in Television* (New York: Simon and Schuster, 1994), 59–61.

10. Hamlin, interview.

11. Montagne, interview.

12. Paper, 234; Sander, 161.

13. King, interview; Bedell Smith, 424.

14. Bedell Smith, 425–27; Paper, 235–37.

15. Stern, interview, 1989.

16. Lewis, interview, 1996.

17. Dick Kleiner, "Hollywood Gossip . . . Al Lewis Likes Nat Hiken—and Says So," undated clipping, Nat Hiken Collection, State Historical Society of Wisconsin; Gerald Hiken, interview, 1989.

18. King, interview.

19. Starobin, interview, 1989.

20. *Phil Silvers: Top Banana*.

21. Obituary for Maurice Gosfield, *New York Daily News*, Oct. 20, 1964.

22. Montagne, interview.

23. "Maurice Gosfield, Pvt. Doberman of 'Bilko' TV Series, Dies at 51," *New York Times*, Oct. 20, 1964.

24. Hamlin, interview; obituary for Billy Friedberg, *New York Times*, Apr. 8, 1965; Jacoby, interview.

25. King, interview.

26. Starobin, interview, 1989.

27. King, interview.

28. Starobin, interview, 1989; Lewis, interview, 1989.

29. *Hail to the Chief* treatment, collection of Ambur Hiken Starobin.

30. Starobin, interview, 1989.

31. Ibid.; King, interview; Sandy Ruben, interview.

32. Burnett, interview; Bob Banner, telephone interview by author, tape recording, Jan. 14, 1999.

33. Burnett, interview; Banner, interview.

34. *Carol + 2*, CBS-TV, Hollywood, Mar. 22, 1966, collection of Carol Burnett.

35. Burnett, interview.

12. HOLLYWOOD BOUND

1. Starobin, interview, 1998.

2. Ibid.; Buscaglia, interview.

3. Ibid.; Cohen, "Nat Hiken, 54, Dies," *Variety*; King, interview.

4. Montagne, interview.

5. Ibid.

6. Garrison, interview; Buscaglia, interview; Jacoby, interview.

7. Burrows, interview.

8. Aaron Ruben, interview, 1989.

9. Lockwood, interview; Montagne, interview; Garrison, interview.

10. Garrison, interview.

11. Ibid.

12. Aaron Ruben, interview, 1989; King, interview; Mia Hiken, interview.

13. Sandy Ruben, interview; Fields, interview.

14. Buscaglia, interview; Levin, interview.

15. Starobin, interview, 1989.

16. Ibid.

17. Don Knotts, telephone interview, tape recording, July 18, 1997; Montagne, interview.

18. Knotts, interview; Montagne, interview.

19. Starobin, interview, 1998; *The Love God?*, Universal, 1969, MCA Universal Home Video.

20. Knotts, interview; Montagne, interview.

21. Montagne, interview.

22. Montagne, interview.

23. Montagne, interview.

24. Montagne, interview.

25. Buscaglia, interview.

26. Gerald Hiken, interview.

27. Montagne, interview.

28. Starobin, interview, 1989.

29. Mia Hiken, interview; Montagne, interview.

30. Montagne, interview.

31. Knotts, interview; Mia Hiken, interview; Buscaglia, interview; Cohen, "Nat Hiken, 54, Dies," *Variety*.

32. Montagne, interview; Sandy Ruben, interview; Aaron Ruben, interview, 1989.

33. Montagne, interview.

34. Sandy Ruben, interview.

35. Ibid.

36. Starobin, interview, 1998; Ruskin, interview.

37. Mia Hiken, interview.

38. Ibid.

39. Starobin, interview, 1998; Mia Hiken, interview.

40. Buscaglia, interview; Sandy Ruben, interview; Levin, interview.

41. Starobin, interview, 1998; Montagne, interview; "Nat Hiken, TV Writer, Is Dead," *New York Times*; Sandy Ruben, interview; Garrison, interview.

42. Aaron Ruben, interview, 1989; Gerald Hiken, interview, 1989.

43. Levin, interview.

44. Mia Hiken, interview; Buscaglia, interview.

45. Allen, 239.

Bibliography

BOOKS

Allen, Fred. *Treadmill to Oblivion*. Boston: Little Brown, 1954.

Auerbach, Arnold. *Funny Men Don't Laugh*. Garden City, N.Y.: Doubleday, 1965.

Barnouw, Erik. *Tube of Plenty*. New York: OxfordUniv. Press, 1975.

Berle, Milton, with Haskell Frankel. *An Autobiography*. New York: Delacorte Press, 1974.

Berle, Milton. *B.S. I Love You*. New York: McGraw-Hill, 1988.

Bernstein, Walter. *Inside Out: A Memoir of the Blacklist*. New York: Knopf, 1996.

Brooks, Tim, and Earle Marsh. *The Complete Directory to Prime Time Network TV Shows*. New York: Ballantine Books, 1979.

Brown, Les. *Les Brown's Encyclopedia of Television*. Detroit: Gale Research, 1992.

Dunning, John. *On the Air: The Encyclopedia of Old-Time Radio*. New York: Oxford Univ. Press, 1998.

Eisner, Joel, and David Kinsky. *Television Comedy Series*. Jefferson, N.C.: McFarland and Company.

Foley, Karen Sue. *The Political Blacklist in the Broadcast Industry*. New York: Arno Press, 1979.

Fried, Ron. *Corner Men*. New York: Four Walls Eight Windows, 1991.

Gabler, Neal. *Walter Winchell*. New York: Knopf, 1994.

Gavin, James. *Intimate Nights: The Golden Age of New York Cabaret*. New York: Grove Weidenfeld, 1991.

Graziano, Rocky, and Ralph Corsel. *Somebody Down Here Likes Me, Too*. New York: Stein and Day, 1981.

Halberstam, David. *The Fifties*. New York: Villard, 1993.

Henry, William A. *The Great One: The Life and Legend of Jackie Gleason*. New York: Doubleday, 1992.

Howe, Irving, with Kenneth Libo. *World of Our Fathers*. New York: Harcourt, Brace, Jovanovich, 1976.

Kanfer, Stefan. *Journal of the Plague Years*. New York: Atheneum, 1973.

Kisseloff, Jeff. *The Box*. New York: Penguin Books, 1995.

Lackman, Ron. *Same Time . . . Same Station*. New York: Facts on File, 1996.

Landscape Research. *Built in Milwaukee*. Madison, Wis.: Univ. of Wisconsin Press, 1983.

Maltin, Leonard. *The Great American Broadcast*. New York: Dutton, 1997.

Mansfield, Irving, with Jean Libman Block. *Life with Jackie*. New York: Bantam Books, 1983.

McDougal, Dennis. *The Last Mogul: Lew Wasserman, MCA, and the Hidden History of Hollywood*. New York: Crown, 1998.

McNeil, Alex. *Total Television*. New York: Penguin Books, 1980.

Miller, Merle. *The Judges and the Judged*. Garden City, N.Y.: Doubleday, 1952.

Navasky, Victor. *Naming Names*. New York: Viking Press, 1980.

Newcomb, Horace, ed. *Encyclopedia of Television*. Chicago: Fitzroy Dearborn, 1997.

Nizer, Louis. *The Jury Returns*. Garden City, N.Y.: Doubleday, 1966.

Oppenheimer, Jess. *Laughs, Luck—and Lucy*. Syracuse, N.Y.: Syracuse Univ. Press, 1996.

Paper, Lewis J. *Empire: William S. Paley and the Making of CBS*. New York: St. Martin's Press, 1987.

Pitrone, Jean Maddern. *Take It from the Big Mouth: The Life of Martha Raye*. Lexington, Ky.: Univ. Press of Kentucky, 1999.

Red Channels. New York: American Business Consultants, 1950.

Rico, Diana. *Kovacsland: A Biography of Ernie Kovacs*. San Diego: Harcourt, Brace, Jovanovich, 1990.

Roberts, James B. *The Boxing Register*. Ithaca, N.Y.: McBooks Press, 1987.

Sander, Gordon F. *Serling*. New York: Dutton, 1992.

Silvers, Phil, with Robert Saffron. *This Laugh Is on Me*. Englewood Cliffs, N.J.: Prentice Hall, 1973.

Simon, Neil. *Rewrites*. New York: Simon and Schuster, 1996.

Slide, Anthony. *The Encyclopedia of Vaudeville*. Wesport, Conn.: Greenwood Press, 1994.

Smith, Ronald L. *Who's Who in Comedy*. New York: Facts on File, 1992.

Smith, Sally Bedell. *In All His Glory: The Life of William S. Paley*. New York: Simon and Schuster, 1990.

Steinberg, Cobbett. *TV Facts*. New York: Facts on File, 1985.

Sylvester, Robert. *Notes of a Guilty Bystander*. Englewood Cliffs, N.J.: Prentice Hall, 1970.

Taylor, Robert. *Fred Allen: His Life and Wit*. Boston: Little Brown, 1989.

Tinker, Grant, and Bud Rukeyser. *Tinker in Television*. New York: Simon and Schuster, 1994.

Van Hoogstraten, Nicholas. *Lost Broadway Theatres*. New York: Princeton Architectural Press, 1997.

Variety and Daily Variety Television Reviews. New York: Garland Press, 1992.

Weaver, Pat. *The Best Seat in the House*. New York: Knopf, 1994.

Wertheim, Arthur Frank. *Radio Comedy*. New York: Oxford Univ. Press, 1979.

Writers' Program, *Wisconsin: A Guide to the Badger State*. New York: Hastings House, 1954.

ARTICLES

"Bluecoat Blues." *TV Guide*. Jan. 19, 1963: 6.

"Bronx Background: New Series in Works by Hiken." *New York Morning Telegraph*. June 26, 1961.

"Comedy Cops." *New Yorker*. Aug. 19, 1961: 20.

Crosby, John. "Radio and Television: A New Idea." *New York Herald Tribune*. Jan. 24, 1951.

"Day's Work, A." *Time*. Mar. 1, 1954: 70.

Dunlap, Orrin E. "A Comedian's Endurance Test." *New York Times*. Jan. 28, 1940: sec. 9.

Fields, Sidney. "Only Human." *New York Mirror*. June 15, 1956.

Freeman, Mickey, and Sholom Rubinstein. "But Sarge . . ." *Television Quarterly*. 22, no. 2 (1986): 7.

"Gag Machine." *Time*. Mar. 31, 1947: 94.

Gardella, Kay. "Fasten Your Laugh Belts; Hiken's 'Car 54' Is Due." *New York Daily News*. Sept. 7, 1961.

Gillenson, Lewis W. "Lescoulie—TV's First Second Man." *Family Circle*. Mar. 1955: 34.

Hiken, Nat. "The Thrill Is Gone." *New York Herald Tribune*. July 20, 1960.

Hirschfeld, Al. "Fred Allen: A Grim Success Story." *New York Times Magazine*. July 2, 1944: 18.

Leamy, Edmund. "Jack Carson Likes Quiet Comedy, Scorns Comics' Gags and Antics, Calls for Story Line." *New York World*. Nov. 17, 1951.

Lindbloom, Roland. "Car 54 Is Right There." *Newark Evening News*. Aug. 12, 1962: Sec. E.

Lindbloom, Roland. "Hiken Steers Car 54." *Newark Evening News*. Aug. 19, 1962.

Minoff, Philip. "Boffola in the Barracks." *Cue*. Nov. 29, 1955: 12.

"Muggs and Cupid Put the Bite on Martha in a Busy Week." *Life*. May 3, 1954: 133.

Robinson, Hubbell. "The Producer's the Villain." *Saturday Review*. Dec. 28, 1958: 23.

Seldes, Gilbert. Review of *Car 54, Where Are You?* Dec. 23, 1961: 20.

Serling, Rod. "TV in the Can vs. TV in the Flesh." *New York Times Magazine*. Nov. 24, 1957: 49.

Shayon, Robert Lewis. "Magnificent Monty." *Christian Science Monitor*. June 19, 1951.

"Where Are the Laughs Coming From?" *TV Guide*. Mar. 23, 1958: 22.

Woodstone, Art. "Hiken's Lament: Nothing Exciting Happens Anymore; Defends Paar." *Variety*. Sept. 13, 1961.

INTERVIEWS BY AUTHOR

Banner, Bob. Jan. 14, 1999.

Barkin, Ben. Aug. 29, 1997.

Belkin, Gary. Apr. 18, 1998.

Bigelow, Penny. Oct. 8, 1997.

Blitzer, Billy, Aug. 1989.

Borotz, Sally. Mar. 4, 1998.

Broun, Heywood Hale. Apr. 12, 1998.

Burnett, Carol. Jan. 10, 1998.

Burrows, James. May 1998.

Buscaglia, Dana Hiken. Oct. 7, 1997.

Deems, Mickey. Dec. 1997.

Fields, Freddie. Oct. 15, 1997.

Freeman, Mickey. Mar. 1998.

Garrett, Hank. Apr. 17, 1998.

Garrison, Greg. Nov. 7, 1997.

Gill, Vivian. July 10, 1997.

Gwynne, Fred. Aug. 1989.

Hamlin, Edith. Jan. 1998.

Hiken, Gerald. Sept. 1989, July 8, 1997.

Hiken, Mia. Oct. 20, 1997.

Jacoby, Coleman. Apr. 1998.

Jaffe, Eddie. May 1998.

Kean, Jane. Feb. 17, 1998.

King, Alan. Sept. 1989.

Kozak, Sid. Aug. 5, 1997.

Knotts, Don. July 18, 1997.

Levin, Peter. Mar. 7, 1998.

Lewis, Al. Sept. 1989, Mar. 31, 1996.

Lockwood, Grey. May 29, 1998.

Melvin, Allan. Sept. 1989, May 6, 1998.

Montagne, Edward. Sept. 8, 1997.

Pockriss, Lee. Dec. 1997.

Rae, Charlotte. Sept. 5, 1997.

Ross, Herbert. Sept. 1997.

Ruben, Aaron. Oct. 1, 1989, Jan. 7, 1998.

Ruben, Sandy. Sept. 20, 1997.

Ruskin, Lucy. Apr. 16, 1998.

Ryan, Terry. Mar. 1998.

Schlosser, Herb. Aug. 1998.

Scoppa, Peter. Apr. 6, 1998.

Seligman, Bernie. Oct. 1997.

Simpson, Gary. Dec. 1997.

Stang, Arnold. Dec. 1997.

Starobin, Ambur Hiken. Sept. 1989, Jan. 1998.

Stern, Leonard. Sept. 1989. Dec. 1998.

Strauss, John. Apr. 14, 1998.

Tinker, Grant. June 1998.

Index